# THE EXAMINED LIFE

# DENNIS HELMING

# THE EXAMINED LIFE

The Art of Knowing, Owning,

and Giving Yourself

Spence Publishing Company • Dallas
1997

Published in the United States by
Spence Publishing Company
501 Elm Street, Suite 450
Dallas, Texas  75202

*Library of Congress Cataloging-in-Publication Data*

Helming, Dennis M.
    The examined life : the art of knowing, owning, and giving
    yourself / Dennis Helming
        p.  cm.
    Includes bibliographical references and index.
    ISBN  0-9653208-1-2
    1.  Conduct of life    I.  Title.
BJ1581.2.H444   1997
158—dc21                                                97-33588

Printed in the United States of America

*Vacate et videte.*

("Be still and see.")

— King David 972(?)B.C.

# CONTENTS

## PART III: SELF-GIVING

## EPILOGUE: NOW WHAT?

# PREFACE

THIS ISN'T YOUR USUAL ETHICS TEXT, with rule upon rule. Nor your usual how-to guide for modifying behavioral externals that promises a richer, more fulfilling life, almost for nothing. Nor your usual vicarious moral prescription to instill values and virtues, lest the underclass dismantle what remains of our republic. Nor even your usual conservative jeremiad that, implausibly, seeks to turn the clock to a glorified rural simplicity.

Rather, isn't it about time for a coherent program that grounds theories about how to behave on the reality of how we're built— with the aim of pursuing happiness effectively? An added bonus would be if the quest could take place amid the thick of everyday life, without premature and often counterproductive appeals to authority, tradition, or religion. Another desirable quality would be for this ethic to recognize our social, mutually dependent condition: the fact we spend most of our days reacting to others' good and bad points, while their contributions (and withholdings) are critical to our completeness and fulfillment. Finally, we could all use a moral guide that meets us where we slackers tend to congregate. Thus it must explain how easily we trip ourselves up and what developmental steps would allow us to leave our self-inflicted misery behind and to become reflective, free, love-capable persons. In other words, the traditional definition of humans as reasonable animals may be a point of arrival, rather than one of departure—though perhaps not our ultimate destination.

My goal has been to come up with a comprehensive ethical map valid for everyone, wherein we prospectors answer only to ourselves and to the primal hunger for happiness that underlies all we do. Readers will soon realize that my contribution to this work has been to supply some updated and finishing touches to the cumulative moral corpus of Socrates, Plato, and Aristotle. They were the heirs of the Delphic oracle, whose self-knowing injunction marks the first moral stage. To this they added the four cardinal virtues, whose acquisition makes up the second moral stage.

However modest, my additions might just represent the "missing link," whose absence explains the skepticism long surrounding the ancient sages' ethical project. Why stop at enlightened self-interest where they—at least theoretically—left off? In trying to go beyond them, we'll also see why emotion-dependent love without strengthening virtue proves to be illusory, while virtue, accompanied by natural gifts without being motivated by disinterested love, turns proudly rancid. Perhaps the two qualities need to be joined for us to develop into complete human beings?

At its highest reaches, very enlightened self-love—our third and final moral stage?—may just turn, paradoxically, into the most generous of other-loves. We fickle weaklings simply can't continue to put forth the unconditional love others so desperately need, unless our self-forgetting efforts in others' behalf satisfactorily answer the gnawing, existential question, "What's in it for me?" Now to use others to fulfill myself is manifestly base and crass;

moreover, such manipulation and folly cannot long be sustained. Quite another thing is striving to fulfill others *in order to* fulfill myself; even better: *while* fulfilling myself; best of all: forgetting about fulfilling myself. Authentically working toward others' fulfillment requires such full-time enterprise that little, if any, attention is left to fret over personal deficits. The question is best clarified from within the context of the basic human desire to love others.

This desire becomes more and more effectual, the more we conquer and possess ourselves through virtue. We can only bestow on others what in fact we have come to own. When I have succeeded in integrating into a single whole what was once a far-flung civil war in my psyche, then, and only then, am I truly free to love completely, with all my belatedly domesticated being. And when I do so, when I finally package myself into a gratuitous gift to someone, can others object if this giving also fulfills and rewards the no-strings-attached giver?

Only to the uninitiated might this seem base or even impossible. Just let scoffers reflect that they're never happier than when consistently making others happy. The reason why invitations to virtue and ethical systems have fallen short is that they too often focus on the moral "what," right and wrong, to the exclusion of the "why," our ultimate intention, in following a given path.

THIS WORK REVEALS ITS ORIGINS. Some ten years ago I decided to dust off my philosophy degree and to offer seminars largely in ethics to bright, young adults, who gave every sign of being disoriented and increasingly the worse for wear. In 1989 this was brought home to me, tragically and dramatically, when a close student committed suicide in a fit of rage. If they failed to get their own moral and spiritual house in order, they ran the risk of not bringing an open mind to their exploration of the macrocosm of ideas, traditions, culture, and even religion.

These seminars met once or twice a month usually for two hours, with no institutional support or auspices. If I received no money, neither did the participants lay out any. I wanted all parties to be spurred only by a questing love for wisdom, as when philosophy came into the world over 2,500 years ago. Neither was there any organized, certainly no costly, promotion. Of course no academic credits were available. As intended, interest—such as it was—spread almost exclusively by word of mouth. The process evoked how universities were born in the twelfth and thirteenth centuries, when students coalesced around competing professors.

What to read? what questions to study and discuss? what slant or approach? what goals to pursue? Rather than wait for definitive answers to such unknowns, I experimentally plowed ahead, trying to learn from hits and misses, mainly the latter. I soon ran up against a dearth of philosophical works aimed at a general, non-technical public (except for the likes of neo-Aristotelian Mortimer Adler, who perhaps shares the incompleteness of his mentor). Other authors insisted on mixing morals with religion (which confusion largely explains in practice the usual sterility of both). In the strictly ethical field more authors abounded, but most of them, with their obsession for defining *what* to do as opposed to *why*, duly generate as much interest as a computer manual. Increasingly I confronted the need to come up with some tailor-made readings.

The seminar's constituency, as mentioned, was largely young adults. In the absence of finding themselves, they just might be open to other discoveries. Among which, I was keen on their discovering that there simply is no self, except that which forms around commitments made and kept.

In keeping with the age-old maxim that "man knows more, but woman knows better," how could the two sexes help each other: how could head best complement heart, and vice versa? Now to such matters as certain virtues, relationships, commitments, and love, women seem predisposed (though to those who shun that inclination the venerable adage applies: *corruptio optimi pessima*: the "corruption of the best is the worst"). Meanwhile their male counterparts are more inclined by nature (and maybe nurture) to conquer truth, amass power and wealth, analyze and solve problems, build, domesticate the physical world, and the like. Since over the past five hundred years masculine science and technology have held sway (with, at best, mixed results), isn't it about time that this imbalance was righted? This preoccupation with external conveniences and benefits psychoanalyst Karl Stern has dubbed *The Flight from Woman.*

Now, women by reactively shirking their feminine role may have indirectly abetted this rationalization (and even contributed to it by aping heart-arrested men in the workplace). But men stand in more manifest need of ethical reform and reinforcement. Their "sexual inferiority" to women (their procreative function is over and done with in a few seconds) carries over into other moral areas, making of them "naked nomads," in two felicitous phrases of George Gilder.

Thus, the seminar (and this work) came to have a somewhat male slant, not out of any chauvinism, but rather out of an overdue desire to help men to catch up. Probably sooner than later, readers will note this due blame and bias. But also they'll see what effects a new morality tailored to include men will have on women, as the two helpmates ratchet their way to ever higher personhood. That's also why, as reflected in the acknowledgments to follow, I sought advice and comments largely from men who are likewise struggling to overcome the traditional moral poverty of their sex.

Readers will note as well a certain amount of repetition in the text. Most of it is deliberate. Here's why: Many readers, maybe most, will read the book as it's laid out: first, five theoretical chapters intended to show how we humans are constituted, then, fifteen practical ones that cover almost every facet of our ordinary lives. Far from hindering our moral growth, everyday tasks and chores, executed well and for the right reasons, can become giant steps in our moral enrichment. On the other hand, some readers, less speculatively inclined, may choose to begin with chapter 6, continue to the end and then go back to read the first five. Still other readers may be concerned about only a particular moral front (sagging motivation, say, on the job) and will turn to the relevant chapter. Since work, family, and friendship are here presented mainly as an excellent venues or means for growing in self-knowledge, self-ownership, and self-giving, each practical chapter was conceived and written as, in large part, a stand-alone case, mixing the theoretical and practical.

Moral improvement in one specific area can easily elicit interest in the rest of the ethical project. "All roads lead to Rome," it was said of those stone-paved imperial arteries. May something similar happen here. Wherever one starts, let's discover, both theoretically and practically, at the core of our human make-up something objective and inalterable: our so far unsatisfied appetite for bliss.

*Bon voyage!*

# ACKNOWLEDGMENTS

FIRST, I MUST THANK all those seminar participants through the years who somehow believed in me, when I had nearly stopped. Wittingly or less so, they proved helpful in some three ways. There's nothing like a deadline (not unlike an execution) to concentrate one's mind (especially my spasmodic specimen) and to marshal the energy to produce copy that isn't a waste of time for all parties. Secondly, attendants served as patient and responsive "guinea pigs" for whatever ideas were aborning, at least in me. Finally, how rewarding it was to perceive, in both their gaze and little character pluses, how the ethical program was taking root and making a difference in their lives.

Four seminar veterans, wherever they may find themselves, keep egging me on; namely, John Hellmuth, Tom Hirsch, Scott Millard, and Frank Russo. Of more recent vintage are others, who brought not only themselves but others as well to our ethical workouts. They are Brian Burke, Peter Lynch, Joe Mancias, Dominik Nogic, David Stainback, David Wannen, and Greg Wierzynski.

Then there are others, too numerous to mention them all, who kindly helped in various ways. For the hospitality they extended me at crucial moments of the work's gestation, I must thank Paul and Dianne Check, Cathy Hickey, Mike McDonald, and Brenda O'Reilly. The latter's husband, Sean, has long been my ethical sparring partner, when not fathering children and books himself. Friend and philosopher David Gallagher was a perceptive guide through some trying moral straits (speculative—not just personal). Psychiatrists James Egan and Richard Gallagher graciously served as sounding boards and loyal "enablers." Early on Carl Schmitt helped me delimit the book's scope. To both Jeff Langan and David Alvis I'm grateful for invitations to speak at their respective colleges—learning experiences that helped me over several hurdles. Let me also thank Chris Check, Pat Fagan, Rob Greving, Sim Johnston, Phil Lawler, and Russ Shaw for having read chunks of the book and offered their comments and advice.

I'm grateful to Ann Landers (and Creators Syndicate) for granting me permission to reprint letters that originally appeared in her column, one of my windows on the world. My thanks also to John Powers at Scepter Publishers for permission to reprint and adapt the text of a booklet I wrote several years ago.

Finally, deserving thanks go to my editor at Spence, Mitch Muncy, for his neither few nor slight suggestions to strengthen not only the work's substance but the style as well. Having him in my corner made it easier to shed any premature complacency and to meet a series of deadlines. I am both happy and lucky to have landed in the clutches of my ever buoyant publisher, Tom Spence. He surely topped all his other risks in launching a new publishing house by betting on me as one of his maiden authors. Since, as most experts agree, my namesake Dionysius Exiguus ("Denis the Small") was off by three or four years in his computations for the Gregorian calendar, 1997 is probably the year 2000. For the debut and duration, then, of the new millennium, I wish Tom and all at Spence a big, fat jackpot.

# PART I

# THE
# EXAMINED
# LIFE

# 1

# MADE FOR BLISS?

We have immortal longings in us.
—William Shakespeare, *Antony and Cleopatra*, 1606-07

Nothing ever becomes real till it is experienced
— even a proverb is no proverb to you
till your life has illustrated it.
— John Keats, *Letters*, 1814-21

T HE MASS OF MEN lead lives of quiet desperation." So wrote Henry David Thoreau in *Walden*. A century and a half later, America's collective psyche is surely not in better shape. The only novelty may be that ours is, if anything, a less quiet hopelessness.

But, we might ask, what if matters had turned out otherwise? What if we had gone from early hopes to dreams fulfilled, if not exceeded? Our "pursuit of happiness" may have gone awry largely because of scant patience and reflection. Maybe also we let embittered but pandering cynics talk us out of the quest soon after we began to see uncomfortable personal truths and the

3

toilsome need for self-improvement. But what might happen—it may not be too late—if we were to examine our lives? Might they not finally prove worth living?

Even etymologically, despair implies initial hope later abandoned (or "dis-hope"). That our native human condition is a hopeful, confident, expectant one can be read in the eager faces of unsullied children, if somewhat less in those of casino and lottery patrons. The Brothers Grimm, Hans Christian Andersen, J.R.R. Tolkien, bards, minstrels, and poets of all times, the assorted, anonymous spinners of fairy and nursery tales—these and many others have set us dreaming. Their accounts of grounded, conditional optimism have always enthralled the young with exciting adventures and trials that lead, so long as not abandoned, to living "happily ever after." In our day William Bennett, with his best-selling *Book of Virtues*, has made no little cottage industry out of repackaging these morality tales and hope-whetting stories. Rare is the youth that, in a more callow past, has not read (or had read to him or her) at least one volume of C.S. Lewis's spell-binding *Chronicles of Narnia*.

But is the hope of bliss unbounded something we must all outgrow, a propitiatory victim sacrificed to the stern gods of adult demands, frustrations, and skepticism called "the real world"?

Between early hopes and weary adult disillusionment lies an intermediate phase that's often overlooked as an opportunity to escape the depressing jungle. Before reluctantly settling down to emptiness and anxiety, we actually do explore various bliss-promising avenues. Alas, in all too many cases they turn out to be dead ends. As if those missteps aren't bad enough, most of us go on to blame the hopeful *end* pursued, rather than the failed *means* we employed to achieve it. But that's about as logical as to give up on all medical science because of one doctor who's a thorough quack. Aren't we guilty of chucking the baby along with the proverbial dirty bath water? It may make more sense (and maybe eventually lead to more happiness) to stoke our hopes, while more keenly prospecting for better means to realize them.

To head off any possible misunderstandings, let's turn to the dictionary (in this case, the *American Heritage Dictionary*, third edition) for some terminological precision. It defines "bliss" as "extreme happiness; ecstasy; spiritual joy;" it derives from the Old English *blithe*. "Ecstasy" in turn is defined as "intense joy or delight," though originally the word denoted a trance-like condition, making it synonymous with rapture, transport, elation, and exaltation. "Euphoria: a feeling of great happiness or well-being" is largely equivalent. "Happiness" stems from the Middle English "hap" or luck. Its first meaning therefore is a condition of "good luck, fortune;" secondarily, "pleasure, satisfaction or joy." It easily slips down into "contentment": an unruffled state of "satisfied desires." When happiness is used here, the reference is usually to a higher happiness, quite independent of propitious circumstances.

For our purposes, bliss, ecstasy, and euphoria, used comparably, mean extreme, intense happiness. In common parlance today "bliss" is sometimes limited to the high, strong pleasure brought on by either orgasm or illegal mind-altering drugs. Unfortunately those seem to be the only occasions of bliss in the experience of many. That psychic poverty is a challenge this book addresses directly.

Late in the tenth century the Muslim leader Abd-er-Rahman III, then ruler of most of the Iberian peninsula, spoke of his precious moments of intense joy: "I have now reigned about fifty years in victory or peace, beloved by my subjects, dreaded by my enemies and respected by my allies. Riches and honors, power and pleasure have waited on my call, nor does any earthly blessing appear to have been wanting to my felicity. In this situation I have diligently num-bered the days of pure and genuine happiness that have fallen to my lot: they amount to fourteen."

Readers should know from the outset that I am an inveterate "eudemonist": a proponent of "a system of ethics that evaluates actions in terms of their capacity to produce happiness." Why should we settle for just fourteen days?

## THE RIGHT GOAL, WRONGLY PURSUED

The whole problem dogging humans seems to be that we usually seek the right thing in the wrong places (or the wrong ways). And what is the right thing we wrongly seek? That, too, is self-evident. Aristotle was the first to point out that we cannot *not* seek happiness, bliss, fufillment, euphoria. We do so, either directly or indirectly, all day and night long, however consciously. We always desire for ourselves what is, at least apparently, best for us. Pursuing our self-interest is not something optional.

In itself this appetite for supreme happiness might serve as a compass leading us to what, ultimately, may satisfy our vital cravings. When it is not properly or adequately fed, however, that very appetite can lead us to short-circuit and to work at cross-purposes with ourselves. No problem would arise if what could deeply pacify this hunger for bliss were some manifest object. But such is not the case. Meanwhile, to our chagrin, we get so impatient and even desperate for what promises bliss that we hastily pounce upon whatever apparent benefit comes within reach. We tend to leap before we look—and almost never to look back after we jump.

How to seek the right thing in the right places is our only challenge. It is not a question of deflating our desires, but rather of fueling them properly. If we are to find ineffable and unending bliss, we would be well advised to be hot-blooded, in passionate pursuit of ecstatic joy. If we are made for sirloin steak, let's stop trying to convince ourselves that soy-bean burgers are the real thing. We are driven by a craving for happiness. When deprived, it can turn traitor, making us fall for fool's gold. Take the three escape mechanisms of alcohol, drugs, and sex. What we are really looking for when we indulge in these is deliverance from our ego-cage, from our quiet desperation, *into* the bliss we seem to be made for. The morning after, we must acknowledge that their attendant emotions could not come across with what they teasingly promised.

Yet, the whole purpose of these teases may be to whet our appetite for real happiness.

Another thing worth noticing is that, with each of those gratifying escapes, there comes a point when we forfeit self-dominion. So strong becomes our captivation to pleasure that, even when we realize there is to be no deliverance, we either cannot stop or just toss in the towel. Moreover, peaks of pleasure soon turn into valleys of sadness, loneliness, and disgust. That is how our tendency to seek the right thing in wrong ways plays itself out. We tend to blame the shortfall on circumstances (among others, not enough quality or quantity). But the real culprit may be ourselves. Might we not have to engage our mind much more, if we are effectively to seek bigger, better, more lasting sources of bliss?

If Diogenes were still around, he would doubtless be on the lookout for a few honest folk willing to hold out for real happiness and pay the price of undeceiving themselves and disavowing assorted infatuations. We may not yet be the "reasonable animals" we thought we were. The invitation is to go on a diet of truthfulness, to think things through, exercising both foresight and hindsight. We are called to become realists: neither to scorn nor idolize what is very finite and impermanent indeed. We're summoned to rectify, to "verify" ourselves. But to rise above what is at the moment unenlightened self-interest, we have to unmask and renounce it, if we're to achieve enlightened self-interest—and possibly even more.

## PERMISSIVE OR OPPRESSIVE?

Countless dwellers in today's existential desert are dying of thirst—not to mention society itself. Many people today are preoccupied with this problem, to put it mildly, and are seeking solutions. "Just say No." Values clarification. "Tough love." Forming character via good literature. Ratings for movies, TV, and music. Packaging into ethics courses the qualities all Americans presumably subscribe

to. The "True Love Waits" and "Promise Keepers" boomlets.
Outward Bound. Sex and "Safe Sex" education. Campaigns against
underage drinking and smoking. Home schooling. "Kill your television" bumper stickers. The war on drugs. These are but a few of
the initiatives—from the right, center, or left—aimed at recovering
at least some behavioral bounds and standards.

But let's face it: any uptick on the ethical radar screen has
been ever so slight. Such measures are but stop-gaps. They address
symptoms as observed and interpreted by worried, older adults
much more than the anxieties ravaging young and not-so-young
victims. Too often such programs seek to modify (or, if not, at
least to defer) unenlightened behavior with a generous serving of
fear, but without encouraging a radical change of heart or presenting
a persuasive case for the mind. Clearly more sweeping reforms are
called for. But by "sweeping," we don't mean implanting the V-
chip, soon to be in television sets, in the brain. With so many of
such crusades, the underlying and condescending assumption seems
to be that, since most people, unfortunately, cannot improve or at
least change, the best we can do is to spare them, or at least
minimize, the negative fallout from their foolish choices.

Part of the blame for superficial and technical solutions, as
some of those same worried adults lament, lies with our increasingly
multicultural and pluralistic society. Our nation is no longer held
together by a moral consensus, a public orthodoxy subscribed to
by most everybody. Given, moreover, the constitutional restraints
imposed by the courts, introducing all but the most toothless ethics
in schools will surely be dubbed some sort of generic religion that
breaches the hallowed "separation of church and state." The
alternatives seem limited to helping kids define their own values
or pushing values that will not provoke objections: honesty, fairness,
compassion, and the like.

We have here a variation on the freedom-versus-authority
question. Do all of us, on our subjective own, in full use of our
wits and freedom, determine what is right or wrong, at least for us

and ours, with some conventional compromises thrown in as part of the "social contract"? Or must we knuckle under to long-standing norms of right or wrong as laid down by various authority figures, even when we do not or cannot understand their origin or binding character, but especially when they seem to clash with our personal search for happiness? Behold a seemingly irresolvable dilemma.

Is there no moral road map to authentic character and happiness except for quick-fading religion and tradition? Besides a sprinkling of innocuous voluntarism and do-goodism, the remaining choices seem limited to the extremes of anything-goes relativism or question-us-not authority. Yet the former easily turns opportunistic, arbitrary, self-serving, and self-defeating. Meanwhile, the latter often comes across as oppressive, mindless, manipulative, fear-riddled, and fear-driven. In any case, neither works very well or for very long. Is there no way out?

## Untangling the Personal Knot

Personal experience suggests there may be. Couldn't we voluntarily and sincerely try to discover in our own subjective world what has objective, permanent, perhaps even universal value? Don't we recognize in ourselves something like a partially developed structure leading us in certain directions, a hazy constitution we did not make and cannot alter at will?

Granted, we are so busy trying to remake reality in our own image and likeness, to bend the objective world to our subjective wishes and whims, that we may never discover whether we have something like a human nature. We approach infinity in no dimension more than in our capacity for self-deception. How we exaggerate both pleasures and pains, while cheating others no less than ourselves! Nevertheless, since both things and other people resist becoming putty in our hands, by exploiting them we manage to create most of the troubles haunting us. And so long as we don't see the futility and frustration of trying to get the world to do our bidding, we will quite naturally resist with all our might any outside (or even inside) attempts to influence our behavior. But once we acknowledge that what we are doing not only doesn't work but is counterproductive, might that painful admission not point to how things might be set right? If, in sum, our frustration and lack of fulfillment stem from the distorting "rape" of reason and reality, won't some overdue intellectual "chastity" and humility be at least part of the solution?

When we do peer into our mind and heart, not all is black and bleak. Even the worst possible deed contains some good dimension, however small, which we unthinkingly inflate to justify our choice. For example: the decision to murder someone is reached by concluding, however mistakenly and perversely, that here and now eliminating this person will remove at least an irritant and thus serve our interests. On the other hand, even the objectively best option involves trade-offs or drawbacks. A student, for instance, who elects to attend Princeton necessarily excludes the greater skiing opportunities offered by Dartmouth. Were we to take the trouble to weigh conscientiously all their respective pros and cons, moral options would seem to run the gamut from 1 to 99 percent good. Though the moral spectrum largely offers all shades of gray, still we occasionally do author deeds and decisions that actually contribute more obviously or directly to our welfare. These "hits" we must also recognize for the clues they are. Further reflection may disclose whether it was *what* we did that left us less miserable, or  the *how* or *why* of our doings.  In any case, we certainly generate enough vital evidence to be able to contrast good deeds with bad, and good motives with those that are less so. This probing should guide us somehow to accentuate the positive, shrink the negative, and thus stumble on toward greater fulfillment.

Yet our deeds and misdeeds are not all that simple to analyze. As we just saw, every deed in itself contains both positive and negative aspects, or at least seems to. Moreover, we can do the best of virtuous deeds for the foulest of mean motives—and vice versa. No wonder, then, that the most self-denying of mothers might find no ultimate fulfillment in her self-denial, since as it turns out she is driven by her need to be needed. In a converse example, a research scientist may slightly fudge an experiment's results, angling for a better position all in the name of alleged love for his family. We rarely seem to align our deeds with the reasons for doing them. It is the combined mixture of both good and bad in the deed itself *and* in the motive behind it that makes reflectively sorting out the objective from the subjective quite a challenge. So much so, that many pessimistically think the attempt is doomed to sink in the quicksand of wishful thinking.

Yet, especially for those who "question authority," is there any other way to right their lives than to study, as honestly as possible, their experiences, good, bad, or neutral? Given our piecemeal thoughts and tentative will, none of our choices or decisions is, fortunately, definitive or irrevocable. Whether progressing or regressing ethically, we seem to be built for trial-and-error experimentation, for proceeding by elimination. Even bad experiences can be turned to good effect, if we eventually do a double-take and learn what wrong turns, mixed motives, and even dangerous circumstances to avoid in future. Recognizing our propensity to err and thereby thwart our drive for happiness should lead us to weigh consequences both before and after the fact. If we desire to be genuinely fulfilled (and who does not?), shouldn't we consider carefully whatever options lie ahead, and for purposes of review, whatever choices we've made and their results? Not for nothing did IBM's founder, Thomas Watson, affix a sign reading "Think" over every employee's work station. So, the first rung in scaling the heights of a better life would seem to be to look before you leap—and after.

## NO MORE THE OSTRICH

If pondering both future and past steps can be so valuable and rewarding, why is it done so rarely? Frankly, we don't seem ready or able to take in very much reality all at once. Self-knowledge can be very painful. Not only do we usually rack up many more misses than hits, but we also repeat the same missteps, even when their inability to make us happy is obvious. How short-sighted we are to fall for mirages again and again! Then, of course, there is our tendency to explain away why particular actions or even more long-term commitments don't measure up to expectations.

Who, moreover, wants to assume the often exclusive blame and shame for his own misfortune? It's so much easier to pass the buck to adverse circumstances or uncooperative others, especially when, as now, perceived victimhood has been raised to artful heights. Equally artful are our mental machinations for avoiding the truth: spinning out excuses a mile a minute, sweeping the dirt under the proverbial rug. Yet even harder to accept than the consequent lack of fulfillment is the fact that we created the whole mess, that we duped ourselves. Paradoxically, it is when we most desire to rid ourselves of the blues that we barricade ourselves most thoroughly therein by ignoring, impatiently, even desperately, any warnings of impending failure.

Now, since we ourselves distort reality, we alone can overcome our exaggeration or underestimation of reality, as a necessary, if still insufficient, condition for living aright. There's no getting around it: if we put the blinders on, we must take them off. If we're to conform ourselves to reality, we must stop dictating to it. So long as we mistakenly think that we're our best friend (instead of our worst enemy), there can be little right reading of others or the rest of reality and certainly no growth in personal fulfillment.

What really needs doing is for each of us to conduct a scientific experiment with the requisite commitment and rigor. Granted, this experiment is somewhat unusual and risky, inasmuch as the object of investigation is the very subject of the research. Consequently, without utmost self-honesty, the quest for the key to the human condition won't get very far. But woe to us if we don't act, for only by testing such intuitions can we possibly formulate the hypotheses that call for exploring each variable one by one. Does all-out pleasure work? Or, conversely, utmost dedication?

We'll never find out unless our experiment excludes for a considerable length of time our usual moral ambiguity: oscillating between stabs at goodness and at unenlightenedness. The story of Penelope in Homer's *Odyssey* is very relevant. An evil fate awaited this woman at the hand of her captors, when she finished weaving a tapestry. So, during the day, under close super-vision, she would complete half of the job. Then at night, alone, she would unravel what she had done earlier. Morally, we too do and undo. For instance, though we manage to advance five miles into the territory of goodness, we can erase that distance and may even go backwards by unwitting moral inconsistencies. Whether virtue contributes to happiness can only be determined unambiguously by eliminating anything but virtue for a month or two.

Yet any answer, even the objectively right answer, can't be shared automatically with others, at least not the non-transferable subjective conviction. We can't do others' experiments for them, nor can they do ours. We might be impressed with their results and even envy them, but won't we have to duplicate for ourselves the steps that led them to those results? In this quest for fulfillment, each person is pretty much on his or her own.

## CAN EXPERIENCE TEACH?

A tall order, you say? Few will carry out the experiment? Maybe so, but is there any alternative? Moreover, don't many young people already invoke a principle that could, if adroitly handled, light the way? They often claim that "experience is the best teacher." Now, granted, that incantation usually serves as a battering ram against generally accepted (especially parentally enforced) codes of behavior. "Don't tell us how to behave; we want to find out for ourselves; let us find ourselves first" is what the saying usually means. Oftentimes "finding out" is the last thing these youths really seek, as actual or imagined wave after wave of new experiences and delights wash over them. Nevertheless, a small change in that "experience principle," along with whatever change of heart is required of those who appeal to it, could turn it inside out, perhaps fully validating it. Experience *can* be the best teacher—on the condition that there is a good pupil to study under that best of teachers. Let's try to justify this important claim.

In order for experience to teach anything, as opposed to its being a senseless blur of random phenomena, there must be a touch-stone. In this case it's our appetite for happiness. Does this particular deed or motive add to, or subtract from, our well-being? When we don't bother to inquire honestly, what's left are only chaos and absurdity, the stuff of existential nausea. But for the person who recognizes being driven by this longing for bliss, the experience-teaching principle could work, when and if coupled to truthfulness.

Now, we might not seem to have an instruction manual for the human machine. Then again, we are usually too passive to sift through vicarious experiences for clues as to how to live. But we still have our own experiences, our vital explorations of, and experiments with, this instinct for happiness. Without this truly "inside information" of what works and what doesn't, all the many suggested answers to Life add up to a free-for-all shouting match, where the only winners are confusion and skepticism.

## Rising above Ambiguity

Whether there is such a thing as human nature, its structure, contents and purpose are obviously not self-evident. If they were as overwhelmingly plain, as necessary, and compelling as, say, 2+2=4, life would offer little risk and even less excitement. If you had but to open your eyes to see how to live, there would be no problem, no need for a map. Determinism would reign. Excluded would be any quest, adventure, romance, or responsibility. If the truth of the human condition were glaringly self-evident, we would feel compelled to live in accord with it, whether we wanted to or not. But that doesn't mean that we are given an utterly blank slate on which to write whatever we wish. It just means that the question of human nature is somewhat ambiguous and open-ended. How else could people exercise their freedom to live in ways contrary to authentic human fulfillment? If the slightest misdeed were greeted with an electric jolt, wouldn't we be cowed overnight into becoming a goody two-shoes? Similarly, if our weakest virtuous deed were rewarded with ecstasy, misbehavior would disappear, but then so would freedom.

Only in a scenario that includes a non-evident destiny do our deeds or choices matter. Otherwise, all is play-acting, with our every move dictated or manipulated by forces offstage, just as circumstances call the shots, so to speak, for animal behavior. But that doesn't seem to be our case. Psychologically, we're not conscious of being mere corks bobbing on waves. We seem to be free, more or less, though how free seems to vary according to times and settings. We seem at least in part to possess ourselves, to be real, if not yet full, persons.

In such a state and in such vital matters we can't expect more proof than is available. That is why so much of this introductory chapter has been merely suggestive. You may ask, "Why doesn't the author come right out and tell us what's what?" What good would it do to trot out any conclusions (positive, to be sure), when most readers are just starting to find their legs?　Since in this question the best evidence can only be internal and subjective, all we can do for now is to whet appetites, while avoiding the impression that ironclad arguments are even possible. While logic does play a role, much more crucial and convincing will be brutal honesty.

Moreover, how could any evidence, especially early on, be other than partial, though perhaps eventually cumulative? What you're being invited to do is to shore up, by consistent and increasingly thoughtful deeds over a period of time, a personality that is now very subtle, embryonic, potential, not to mention flabby. If you're shooting ultimately for moral and psychological fitness, you're just going to have to face the unavoidable need to develop, through not a few workouts, sorely underdeveloped ethical muscles. Yes, even you! As with acquiring any physical or technical skill, there's no getting around the commitment of time, persistence, perspective, patience, reflection, and many failures, which all must play their indispens-able sifting, sedimentary, and strengthening roles.

So, it looks as if the only way to escape from the uncertainty or ambiguity surrounding the human condition is to go prospecting within for an objective base of operations, what common sense has long dubbed "human nature."　If indeed we are built in a certain fashion, then (in theory at least) living accordingly should prove more or less rewarding.　But it takes a long time for us to mature. Unlike physical growth, which just happens, moral maturity does not come with age.　The world, especially swinging singles bars, is full of people who have outgrown only acne, if that. Meanwhile, our actions and decisions are often so tentative and makeshift that any subjective rewards or punishments are barely perceptible, especially in the short run.　Is it any wonder, then, given such scanty evidence, that we tend to lack both perspective and patience to read aright what leads to our fulfillment?

## HONESTY BEGINS AT HOME

The problem is not with the experiential teacher but with the all too fallible, lazy, and dishonest student. In matters of happiness we have been known to deceive ourselves not infrequently, whether we come from the rose-colored glasses school or from the one that paints everything black. But this self-assessment and scrutiny not only can be done, they must be done, especially by those who have rejected any authoritative guidance from without. If we don't want to answer to others, must we not, consequently, answer to ourselves? What we can't afford to do in this vital matter is to plow ahead in an unthinking, slap-dash fashion. If we do, then we rarely act, but rather react, gorging ourselves at the smorgasbord of experiences, only to collapse eventually into a heap of burnt-out cynicism and skepticism.

Instead of starving or denying our personality, might we not try to heed and husband it at least as much as those brave men of the classical world who, at the dawn of reason, clear-sightedly saw that we come with a built-in structure? If we try to follow in their footsteps, we too may thrill to the prospect of coming up with a science of how we are to conduct ourselves, with the promise of bliss no less. If we're possibly to go beyond them (for they may have stumbled, only partly fulfilled, at the half-way mark), must we not humbly accom-pany them at least as far as they got? Before doing so, let's air a preliminary question that could be, if not addressed, at least a pesky distraction. How much do we, or can we, resemble our animal cousins?

# 2

# HOW ANIMAL ARE WE?

I stand and look at [animals] long and long.
They do not sweat and whine about their condition. . . .
Not one is dissatisfied, not one is demented
with the mania of owning things. . . .
Not one is respectable or unhappy over the whole earth.
— Walt Whitman, *Leaves of Grass*, 1867

HOW VIABLE IS THE ANIMAL MODEL that most of us tend to follow more or less consciously? In comparing and contrasting humans with animals, some light may also be shed on whether any human difference is merely one of degree, something evolutionists seem determined to maintain, or is one of kind.

"It's a dog's life," we enviously mutter. There lies Fido, curled up on the throw rug, dozing by the warming fireplace, digesting his supper, with nary a care in the world, on the receiving end of lots of pampering. What an uncomplicated, faultless existence! Predators and other natural enemies rarely cross his path. Fido needn't scramble for food, water, shelter, or comfort.

Working on the pleasure-pain principle, the various appetites stemming from the canine's instinct of self-preservation find satisfaction in consuming objects needed by his body. Unless overly domesticated and spoiled, the dog doesn't normally eat or drink more than he needs or take in harmful substances. (Or if he does, he has enough instinctive "sense" to munch however much grass is required to induce vomiting.) His various appetites seem to kick in or out automatically, according to some built-in objective "governor." The golden mean of neither too much nor too little but "just enough" comes naturally to the dog (among other fauna). Apparently he is spared on-the-job training.

As far as we know, in animals the workings of this drive to survive just happen, without deliberation or choice. Willy-nilly, Fido is attracted to what truly benefits him, while steered away from what might prove harmful. Circumstances "benevolently" manipulate the attraction-repulsion mechanism for the animal's seemingly unconscious welfare. Thus does the canine machine work infallibly, yet with uncanny simplicity. Not for Fido any scrupulosity or binges, no diets, nor, for that matter, even a tad of insomnia. Neither in general do animals usually divorce the pleasure inherent in eating (or in other actions favoring the body) from its biological purpose. While animals are spared the exaggerations of idolized gratifications or, conversely, of scorning them, so too are their instinctive aversions to dangers largely proportionate to the objective dangers. Not for Fido any analysis paralysis or phobias or neuroses or other inflated fears. Everything remains straightforward in his reflexive, apparently unreflective, hold on life. "Doing what comes naturally" is the dog's successful formula for an unruffled, fulfilled existence.

So much for Fido's truly enlightened, though instinctive, self-interest, but what about his companion drive to perpetuate the species? Is there here also cause for humans to envy their tail-wagging best friends? Left to their own devices (that is, neither spayed nor castrated), dogs have a very simple, programmed sex life with but the single aim of bringing forth puppies. Fido quite literally has no sex life until his female counterpart sends forth a scent signaling the release of eggs awaiting fertilization. Finding the source of this olfactory invitation, he soon discharges his duty. Throughout the animal kingdom no sexual concourse takes place except in response to recently released and beckoning ova.

In the dynamics of this second instinct, it's possible that for the male the goad of sexual pleasure is so huge that he's driven to risk limb and even life to unite with the more passive female. Nature contains few moments more dramatic than the self-endangering feats of a stud horse imperiously summoned to his siring role. How much of this carries over into a human context? While the sex drive in men can be strong, most men have some say over its progressive intensity, especially early on. That's not to say, however, that some men don't disingenuously appeal to animal instinct to justify their lack of sexual control. Whether or not the female animal experiences any copulatory pleasure, she thereby contributes nothing more to reproduction, since ovulation has already taken place. Researchers tell us that most women are more inclined to engage in sexual intercourse when conception can take place, an apparent carryover.

## MODELS OF CHASTITY?

Is there a rank among the instincts? While not manifestly a matter of choice, the good of the species clearly supersedes the individual's welfare. The possible death of the aroused male is apparently a small price to pay for the near certainty of many more births. So too does the mother of newborn animals risk her life to protect her progeny. The drive to propagate brooks no opposition from the more selfish inclination to survive. Animals seemingly husband their own existence only to bring forth new and more populous generations.

Let's dwell a bit on the sex drive's dormancy except with the immediate prospect of conception. The male animal hardly ever indulges in the activity that leads to conception—highly gratifying though it may be—except in response to the vehement biological drive to reproduce. Among beasts, sexual activity aims only at propagation. What happens to humans when they suppress the reproductive orientation of the sexual act and largely treat it as recreation? All the consequences from which animals are exempt: contraception, pornography, prostitution, sodomy, homosexuality, masturbation, impotence, frigidity, abortion, orgies, sadomasochism, bestiality.

In effect, if chastity can be defined as keeping sexual activity within proper bounds and respecting its reproductive orientation, animals are amazingly, though effortlessly, chaste, at least when contrasted with humans. While fauna cannot refuse to gratify the imperious demand of the activated instinct, they do not divorce it from its reproductive aim.

Neither for that matter do our carefree animal cousins indulge themselves with artificial stimulants or pleasures, chemical or otherwise. No hangovers, no addictions, no highs or lows infest animal haunts. The only escaping they seem to need takes the form of defensive and protective reflexes mandated by their survival instinct, and any camouflaging coloration allowing them to blend with their surroundings.

## ANIMALS DON'T THINK

Yet for all the mistake-free life that Fido leads, there's no evidence that the dog gloats over his master with respect to fulfillment and satisfaction. For all we know, the nuzzling, tail-swaying canine, as well as the contentedly purring feline, isn't consciously aware of his physiological well-being or of any toil that brings it about. At periodic intervals made possible by duly fed appetites and the absence of threats, animals are freed from the tugs of their instincts. It is this temporary truce in the struggle to survive and reproduce that sparks envious longings in humans.

We seldom stop to consider that to Fido it apparently makes no difference (other than the ensuing corporeal benefits, all unconscious) whether he is in tension or at rest. In both states the dog responds to circumstantial stimuli, present or absent. This necessary stimulus-response mechanism holds even when, through human agency, automatic reflexes have been conditioned, as Pavlov originally discovered. (Long before the Russian scientist, interestingly enough, gypsies came up with their own conditioned reflex, which gave the world dancing bears. They would place a young bear on a metal surface with a fire beneath; meanwhile a fiddler would sound his instrument. Thereafter, whenever a fiddle sounded, the bear would begin to prance.)

In various settings Fido's response is invariable and predictable. Consequently, there is no evidence of self-awareness, consciousness, deliberation, choice or freedom in dogs or other species. As the telling tombstone in a New York pet cemetery claimed: "Here lies Hildegaard: she did not even know she was a rabbit." Neither, apparently does Fido *know* that he is fulfilled and at peace with himself. He just *is* relieved or tense, with no apparent ability to step outside of, and reflect on, his vital experiences. Fido is as unaware of our sorry straits as he is of any superior fortune that has come his way.

Were we mere animals, our lives would unfold with comparable ease and equally satisfying, if unconscious, results. But we aren't, and they don't. This is not to say that we don't share with beasts the instincts of self-preservation and reproduction. Clearly we do. If not, we might never have been conceived or, once born, have survived long enough to be reading this. Our nature, therefore, is at least part animal with corresponding inclinations and aversions.

Though humans seem more (and often less) than mere animals, we have no reason to disdain and slight our bodily constitution, with its specific requirements and rewards. It's hard enough to keep a sane mind in a healthy body, let alone in one that's been abused. It's to our advantage to ply within proper limits corporeal pleasures—sleep, rest, good food and wine, play, the outdoors, marital relations, exercise—lest an overly strained and tense body seduce us into binges. There's a relevant Italian aphorism: "When the body's fit, the soul dances." Not coinciden-tally, the Italian moralist Silvano Borruso has come up with six helpful indications of physiological health:

- Sound sleep that is both timely and deep;

- Healthy appetite trained by reasonable, balanced, spaced meals (false hunger can be dispelled by water, which dilutes the stomach's contents, lest it overproduce gastric juices, which, in turn, prematurely call for more food);

- Healthy elimination of waste;

- Cardiovascular and respiratory fitness through regular, pro-tracted physical exercise;

- Healthy, clean skin (moist, neither dry nor wet; odorless; wounds heal quickly); and

- Resistance to infection: a healthy body can destroy all but the largest concentrations of microbes.

## "Improving" on Instincts

There has to be something in our makeup that at least accounts for how we can, for good or ill, interfere with the spontaneous and necessary workings of self-preservation and reproduction. For clearly we do butt in. In anticipation don't we, for instance, tend to exaggerate, on the one hand, how enjoyable an upcoming vacation will be? Though to relatives, neighbors, and friends we apologetically put on the best of faces, vacations never seem to live up to their advance billing. On the other hand, don't we exaggerate how cold and unappealing is the sixty-nine-degree sea-water our big toe has just encountered. Only we humans misread or distort reality, and only actual, honest experience can disabuse us. From what we can piece together, animals always seem to be objective, however oblivious to the process or result. For our present purposes, it doesn't matter where this human interfering mechanism comes from or what ultimately may be inferred from it. For now it's enough to establish that we do interfere with our own well-being, which distinguishes brutes from women and men, however brutish.

There are some of us who do little but tinker with this internal gyroscope. Cleverness prompts us to try to improve on the instinctive system. In order to reap pleasures with a minimum of both effort and consequences, we can and therefore often do abstract from, and thereby hinder, an instinct's function. When that does not prove fully satisfying, rather than blame the interference, we tend to redouble the search for stronger stimuli in the hope of getting bigger kicks from a gratifying response. And then, when under the sway of the law of diminishing returns even that tactic turns perverse, we may resort to chemical agents (alcohol or drugs) to escape from all the interference. Gullibly, we may hope thus to escape *into* an artificial, transient state of mega-pleasure that promises to fill fully our vital screen, welcoming us to oblivion. Might the desire to achieve this sub-human, pre-rational, pre-voluntary life, with its promise of superior tranquillity, lie behind much of the contemporary attraction to Eastern religions? Since, in their view, both desiring and thinking are what lead us astray, undermining our fulfillment, we would be better off if the activity of our will and mind were repressed.

If with our meddling we try to maximize pleasure, we likewise seek to minimize, if not abolish, all pain, suffering, effort. We sometimes follow this line of least resistance even when, ironically, this may clash with an overall campaign to exploit pleasures as much as possible. But the more usual way we seek to banish hardship (and thus "dis-ease") is to arrange our lives so as to be able to feed on an expansive diet of gratifications and conveniences, which in and of themselves may be wholly or relatively harmless. The danger is that in our softness we may falsely conclude that we can't do without them. Of such minor stuff are hatched petty addictions, which can predispose us to get hooked on the more serious, corrosive practices that make up compulsive vice.

## WHENCE BACKFIRING?

Human efforts to interfere with our animality and improve upon its instinctive structure usually, if not always, backfire, at least psychologically. How does this "shorting" come about? Humans seem to depart from and transcend the merely animal condition, because we know ourselves and the outside world reflectively. This peculiar ability is revealed and implied by the tendency to envy and imitate subhuman carefreeness. For now, let's consider a paradox: our desire and determination to imitate our animal cousins' supposedly nirvana-like state manifestly arise from what sets us apart from them. Humans come uniquely equipped to ponder, compare, ruminate, think, reason, however little we may actually do so.

That's not to say, though, that Fido doesn't somehow *know*. The combined reports from eyes, nose and ears certainly alert him to the existence of this succulent bone, or that even more succulent burglar. But animal knowledge, a compound of what the five senses pick up, never seems to get beyond particular facts, even when Fido notes that to this bone cling more shreds of meat than to the other—and therefore apparently *chooses* the fleshier. The instinct to preserve itself automatically activates both the appetite for food and, thanks to sensory perception, the stronger attraction to what offers more needed nourishment. That no real deliberation or choice is involved can be inferred from the canine's invariable pattern of always consuming first the meatier morsel.

Human knowledge, however, is not limited to particular facts or truths obvious only to the senses. Somehow we get beyond ourselves when we reflect on self no less than others, thereby learning enough to function on something more than instinct. Our various abstract notions and generalizations do in fact surpass what we're told by our senses, individually or jointly. We surpass merely sensory knowledge when we envy our animal counterparts. Thus we long to return to the womb, or to a pristine state of blissful innocence, or even to live the contented life of a dog, our appetites satisfied and at rest. Try as we might to match Fido, it never seems to work—at least not enough to satisfy us. Yet the attempt reveals two powers unique to humans: knowledge of and hunger for more than particular goods.

Just as we know more than mere animals, so too do our various appetites play themselves out differently. Our instinctive cravings don't operate as necessarily and mechanically as those of other fauna. While we often do obey the call of appetite, experience shows that we're not coerced into doing so. Somehow or other we can (and sometimes do) resist and thus counter the attraction exerted by an object on one or another of our appetites. Unlike mere animals, we can override these instinctive pulls and tugs. Neither need we settle for the particular physical goods our senses disclose and our strictly animal appetites covet. We can search for and appropriate more subtle, less obvious, broader and, let us hope, better goods, a quest made possible by the mind's independence from knowing only particular facts. Above and beyond the hungers shared with the rest of the animal kingdom, there seems to be in us something like a broader appetite that is never fully satisfied with the particular objects that satisfy more limited corporeal appetites.

## A NON-ANIMAL APPETITE?

These added powers of knowing and willing beyond quite limited facts and goods evidently distinguish human beings from mere animals. But don't our powers also open the door to such human exclusives as agony and ecstasy, extremes of degradation or exaltation utterly foreign to beasts? We see evidence around us every day that they do. There would thus appear to be only two radical alternatives. Either we're made for some object specifically human (a difference in kind) or for maximum corporeal pleasures (more of the same). But hasn't the latter option, however seemingly promising, been tried literally millions of times and still been found wanting?

If, indeed, we are possessed of powers not limited to material things, the human condition would thus seem to point to and call for a vital quest in search of non-manifest objects that could put to rest, by genuinely satisfying, our capacity for ultimate truth and goodness—or at least higher embodiments of both qualities. The failure to recognize and heed these hungers for objects unknown is what lands us in trouble. When our transcendent capacities to know and desire are not directed toward what may actually fulfill them, they tend to interfere with each other and, as if that weren't bad enough, with our lower appetites as well. We might try to tell ourselves we're only sentient beings, with but a more sophisticated neurological setup. Then in our attempt to play the mere animal, we paradoxically deny ourselves whatever fulfillment, both animal and human, we might otherwise attain.

There are three ways of trying to imitate animals. Try as we might to act spontaneously, we don't seem to be able to make ourselves into merely instinctive beings that can sidestep thinking and choosing. At best we blithely reap only short-lived pleasures, enjoyable only so long as we repress our reason-dependent appetite. This is one unsuccessful way to copy animals. Second, even granting our superior capacities for knowing and desiring, we do not succeed for long in harnessing those powers to improve craftily upon animal instinct by manipulating the pleasure-pain principle. Both scenarios, the unwitting and the shrewd, lead to the dead end of trying to maximize pleasures and minimize pains. But how can a broader—better? superior?—appetite be satisfied by overfeeding a merely animal one? There's no such confusion in the way animals live. Theirs is an instinctively perfect match between bodily need and available object.

The only good way of imitating animals would seem to be to do humanly, that is, deliberately and willingly, what we see our mute cousins doing instinctively, automatically. One consequence would probably be to accept gratification, largely, if not exclusively, as an incentive or reward for addressing authentic bodily requirements. That also would entail truthfully figuring out what our animality's objective needs are, lest we give our body too much or too little.

This virtuous submission to how our body best functions may not deliver complete fulfillment and utter peace, but it is an indispensable start. At least such a course can keep us from wasting time and energy exploring dead-ends and fend off the false hopes of harvesting a bumper crop of bliss from hedonism's quite limited plot. The only time that the golden mean of "just enough" escapes animals is when the goods required by their body (or species) escape them. This also takes place when contradictory reflexes are triggered at once, rendering the animal vulnerably paralyzed, at least momentarily. In being true to their animal half, humans can practice, at least in part, their specific brand of enlightened self-interest. Such self-dominion may also be requisite for the quest for whatever can satisfy our distinctively human appetites being carried out with a reasonable hope of success.

Might it not be our misguided, unwarranted tendency to *infinitize* quite limited bodily pleasures that occasions most of our troubles? The problem does not apparently lie with the body's animal drives, but with the distortions and exaggerations wrought by an overactive and undomesticated imagination. Is there any alternative to failure when we foolishly persist in trying to squeeze blood from the proverbial turnip? What then seems to be happening is that our bodily appetites, in connivance with our imagination, somehow bully the mind and will, which, in turn, fight among themselves to the detriment of both, not to mention their owner. We're all too gullible in face of "the sweet poison of the false infinite," to quote C.S. Lewis.

An overdue project, therefore, suggests itself. First, to admit that this meddling is happening all too stealthily and often. And then, to take whatever remedial steps are required, so that each power or appetite may return, and limit itself, to its proper turf. Isn't it time, in other words, to go prospecting for whatever ground of self-knowledge and self-discipline we can discover?

# 3

# Know Yourself

This above all—to thine own self be true.
— William Shakespeare, *Hamlet*, 1600-01

For the great majority of mankind are satisfied
with appearances, as though they were realities,
and are often more influenced by things that seem
than by those that are.
— Niccolò Machiavelli, *The Prince*, 1513

T
HE CITY OF DELPHI, seat of the most important ancient Greek temple and oracle, dates back at least to the fourteenth century B.C. The oracle was consulted on private matters, to be sure, but also on affairs of state, war, and colonization. So often was the same brief message—"Know thyself" —given to inquirers that it was soon carved in stone on one of the temple walls. "Know thyself" is in the imperative mood. That is to say, the gods weren't suggesting this as a bit of helpful advice, take it or leave it; they were commanding it. Much as we might say, "Know yourself—or else."

Most Greeks believed that the god Apollo had spoken and thus must be heeded. "Know thyself" was most frequently interpreted to mean, "Beware of *hubris*; don't overstep your bounds; you're not godly." In any event, the earliest sages and even later philo-sophers adopted it as a (when not *the*) guiding principle at the very dawn of reason. It implies at least two directives, one negative, the other positive. First, we aren't well acquainted with ourselves, which ignorance probably occasions most of our vital mishaps. Second, to those willing to submit to a diet of personal truth, fulfillment beckons.

Note that Delphi distinctively comes down uncompromisingly on the spartan side of "thyself": personal responsibility or accountability. It necessarily implies, while inviting, as much personal freedom, autonomy, and self-dominion as possible. Each of its adepts is to look *within*—not without. We customarily elude responsibility, thinking that our happiness (or lack thereof) is tied up with external circumstances or other people or even the dispensations of some mysterious gods or "fate."

It's truly amazing how many and varied are the contemporary causes *out there* with which we agitate and distract ourselves. The compelling but unspoken goal seems to be for each to discover a favorite enemy or conspiracy, but always conveniently in the remote third person, to be reviled for all the world's ills. Many militants seem to be acting on the psychological need to believe in something —anything—sufficiently evil on which to vent a big head of moral steam, and thus to justify their existence. They often inhabit, as G.K. Chesterton put it, "the clean well-lit prison of one idea."

It's as if the oracular voice were telling us: "Stop this childish finger-pointing; better yet, point it at yourself. The only thing standing between you and utmost bliss is you, thoughtless you, lying you, self-destructive you."

## TRUTH THERAPY

Note also that the oracle calls directly for knowledge, not greater unselfishness, virtue, love, or other commendable qualities. Bent human beings are to be straightened out, if at all, by a more assiduous and penetrating use of their reason. Apparently only a healthy dose of reality and truth will liberate them from their self-made prison of untruths. But the truths to be discovered aren't some arcane, ethereally subtle truths accessible only to some initiated gnostics, gurus, or geniuses. There's no talk of rarefied metaphysics or ascetical austerity or theosophy or revelations or mysticism whose secrets can be disclosed only to a privileged elite, who in turn mediate the access of all others.

No, something much more common and democratic and non-institutional and personal is afoot, something independent of rare, limited, external opportunities or chance encounters or temporal and geographical vicissitudes, something likewise unrelated to age or sex or IQ or skills or state in life. It's something that every man, woman, and child can conceivably do, at any time, where privilege and advantage need no longer count, with no wiggle room for rationalizations. That's not to say, however, that this intro-spection comes easily. It may just be the most demanding toil we'll ever undergo. But without it there is no touchstone, no sympathetic vibration, for recognizing truth. As Julius Caesar once observed, "Men willingly believe what they wish."

Self-knowledge is simply a matter of turning one's mental gaze on oneself: to sit down and belatedly make one's own acquaintance. Much as we might want, how are we to befriend someone who amounts to a total stranger? But that's it; that's all. In no more (and no fewer) than two words may be the whole solution to all of life's problems and conundrums.

The oracle also seems to imply that self-knowing is a game where there are only relative winners. Apparently, to seek is to find, and to seek more is to find more. We need only to move from sterile *je m'excuse* to *je m'accuse*. Note besides that the oracle does *not* say that this self-probing is popular or makes for popularity. Reflecting on self will doubtless deflate illusions about ourselves and disclose damning evidence of sloth, willfulness, and shallowness, not to mention hypocrisy and vindictiveness. It's never easy to turn on oneself as the sole culprit for one's misery. But that way alone lie truth and emancipation.

Those unwilling simply to admit, "I'm to blame," will surely scorn and scoff at Delphi. With their privileged intellects overflowing with superior knowledge and worldly wisdom, some raise up complicated, esoteric systems of philosophical and theological speculation to disprove the long-silent oracle and justify themselves. Others claim there's nothing wrong with man that improved circumstances and the inexorable march of progress can't cure. Or, a variant, still others preach the gospel of self-acceptance, wherein all human problems originate in our futile efforts to strive for impossible objectives; we'll all be content if we but reject taboos and reduce any remaining principles to the level of our undistinguished practice. These rationalizations seem little more than adult variations on the childish alibi: "I didn't do it!" Perhaps the oracle's pithy message provides us with a yardstick wherewith to measure any and all programs for happiness and fulfillment. Highly suspect are all those not grounded in the rock-bottom confession: "I wronged myself, but I too can right myself, starting with my reason, while gladly welcoming any outside assistance there may be."

## TRUE AND FALSE SELFISHNESS

Yet even subscribers to common-sense realism tend to think that most, if not all, of our benighted failings stem from selfishness. Their prescription, then, is to escape the ego-trap by suppressing our self-love or otherwise converting it into other-love. Selfless dedication is, for them, the adequate answer. But is this what the oracular voice is really saying? It may be faulting not so much self-interest or self-love itself, as the unenlightened unwise, unreasonable self-interest that falsifies reality because it refuses to conform to it. We may love ourselves not too much, but unwisely, in a less than truthful fashion, in ways departing from, or even contrary to, genuine fulfillment. Shakespeare's Othello seems to agree, when just before dying he says, "Remember me as one who loved, not wisely, but too well."

Might we be called by our very being to graduate from unenlightened to ever more enlightened degrees of self-interest? This would seem to square with Delphi's betting everything on ever better knowing one's personal truth. We may be thereby summoned to love ourselves more—instead of less. This may even lead to the paradoxical conclusion that the highest self-loving is the fullest self-giving. While this conclusion may exceed the oracle's terms, it certainly dovetails with its prime insistence. Only progressive self-knowing makes possible ever more enlightened self-loving. This personal knowledge may not be a sufficient condition for fully ratifying human nature, but it is an indispensable prerequisite.

Most schemes for happiness, especially the do-it-yourself varieties, collapse in their failure to analyze what has gone wrong in our behavior. Our job is to dig for the double truth of the human condition. We need to admit we wrong ourselves by not living in accord with the way we're constructed. Only then can we begin to right ourselves by developing and nourishing our personality. And that's a requirement for getting anything else right. It's that simple, yet profound. Truth—not wishful thinking—is the only possible formula for the happiness that is part of our human heritage. Without such a map, life is pure accident, mere helter-skelter. How otherwise can we know our destination or how to get there or even what pitfalls to avoid? We could even bypass what alone may deliver bliss—and not even realize it.

Now this self-knowledge comes with labor pains. We all wince and can barely believe our senses whenever we hear our recorded voice or see ourselves in photos or videos. Likewise, we all hate tests, because they expose our ignorance, laziness, and fuzzy-headedness. We're experts at bending the truth around to what only seems to be our advantage. We tend to kid ourselves, without ever stopping to realize that in the process we may be defrauding ourselves. That's why, as if obeying a reflex, we almost automatically flee people or things or situations that threaten to expose us, to make us look bad. That's also why we tend to surround ourselves with acquaintances or ideas which are non-threatening crutches for our unexamined selves. We all tend to play the ostrich, which, since it can't fly away, reputedly reacts to danger by sticking its head in the sand.

On the other hand, let's not exaggerate the trouble of trying to see ourselves objectively, the way others more readily tend to see us. Exaggerating hardships out of all proportion is another universal failing. This automatic, immature, pain-avoiding mechanism can slow us down and even leave us in knots, perhaps permanently. If you're suffering from a deadly disease, isn't the worst thing to stay away from the discerning physician, lest the prescription be painful surgery or other onerous remedies? Here too—maybe above all here—the maxim "no pain, no gain" is true.

Chastening experiences invite us to admit progressively some uncomfortable personal truths and some underlying defects. Prospectors must be patient and open-minded; we're to concentrate, use our noggin, listen. This is hard work. As someone once wrote: "Thinking is the hardest work in the world, and the most repugnant to our [undisciplined] nature." Also let's distance ourselves from those who would reduce us to our glands, who view us only as recent émigrés from the jungle. We may stand to lose only our misery.

Now there's at least one area of human endeavor where we all acknowledge that "no one is a good judge in his own cause," and so we seek and submit ourselves to outside help, in order to improve. Any athletic coach worth his salt must get his players to see themselves as they truly are, so that they can take the steps to get to be as good as they mistakenly think they already are. But why is it that players heed their coach's advice? If they put it into practice over time, they see that it works, gives good results—that's one source of motivation. But the main reason why people obey their coaches (and seek ever better and more demanding coaches) is that they're sick and tired of being mediocre also-rans. They refuse to settle for second- or third-best; they're committed to being the very best they can possibly be. Can we afford to do less when our fulfillment is at stake?

## THREE ATTITUDES

Who are likely to get the most out of this ethical program? The least defensive, the most prone to take risks, who have the guts to admit in their heart of hearts they're not really happy, despite all their efforts. Nor are any of their cock-eyed schemes likely to make them so, certainly not leave them so. So, if you haven't found joy, either personally or vicariously, in a bottle, can, joint, bed, romance, bank account, commitment, or even in glowing achievements, you've come to the right place. Especially if you can admit you may be mostly to blame for all your hollowness and frustration.

This program will make no sense to any who think that the only thing standing between them and all the happiness they need is just a set of more favorable external circumstances: better luck, more money and freedom, a little more of this and a little less of that, a blonde instead of a brunette. . . . Such people are too busy dreaming about the future and betting everything on it: "Next time, for sure." They've yet to realize that a vacation or trip or new job or new husband or new car never measures up to our bloated expectations. Such perpetual adolescents have never learned to curb their exorbitant desires for what can never slake their thirst for bliss. They blow totally out of proportion what are actually quite minor and relative goods. These forty- and fifty-year-old teens are reluctant to learn from their misery-generating mistakes. They deceive themselves, shelling out big bucks for breast enlargement, hair transplants, cosmetic surgery (not to mention the zillion-dollar cosmetics market), fashions, jewelry, diet fads, and related pills and potions.

There's still a third type: those who are relatively good and content with things as they are. These achievers are well-rounded and busy; they usually stay out of mischief. They're not likely to be nabbed for speeding; they keep their lawns mown. They steer clear of most compulsions and addictions; their act so far sticks together. So, they ask, "Where's the beef? What's all the fury about? I have my friends, good ones too. I get on well with my family; parents and spouse give me lots of support. I've got enough engrossing interests and hobbies and sports to keep me occupied and thriving. My job (or studies) is under control, certainly good enough to get ahead. Sure, like everybody else, I have my share of foibles and weaknesses that will probably shrink, if not disappear, with time and a little more effort. . . . So, why all the huffing and puffing?"

Well, to any who see themselves in the preceding paragraph, the suggestion is this: Be patient with the program and a little impatient with yourself. It may take some digging, but if you really confront yourself, you'll sooner or later discover you're built for more, much more, than Brownie points or merit badges. Don't settle for the trappings of achievement, which, in some workaholics, can become almost as addictive as a narcotic. You may be content, or think you are, at least for now. Anything else may seem just "too good to be true." But what if the invitation may be for something "too good *not* to be true?" In any case, let's get down to this business of getting better acquainted with ourselves.

## MORALITY'S TEN PRINCIPLES

Without, perhaps, your having noticed it, we've already covered quite a bit of ground. What follows are ten observations or principles, most of them alluded to earlier, which sum up what our efforts at knowing ourselves should uncover. We're seeking clues to how our behavior backfires and how we might right it. Those who ignore their past, wrote George Santayana, "are condemned to repeat it."

1.  We noted that we easily go wrong and mess ourselves up. Why? Because we act thoughtlessly, with neither malice nor goodness aforethought. Until I admit that I fool myself regularly, I'll never be able to discover the steps I need to right and fulfill myself.

2.  One of the ways we go wrong is the tendency to foresee, exaggerate, and therefore cunningly sidestep such negatives as pain, suffering, annoyance, and effort, which never prove in fact to be so bad as we had feared.

3.  We similarly distort reality when we habitually inflate and thus excessively desire an upcoming pleasure or good. Again, when we actually experience these longed-for prizes, we discover that they're not all we naively made them out to be.

    In sum, we unconsciously deprive ourselves whenever in anticipation we exaggerate the truth about things, both good and bad. If we're to be true to ourselves and to see the broader world for what it really is, we must exercise realism by using our mind better.

4.  We need, therefore, something like a "reality check" to set ourselves right. Experience can be "the best teacher," if we honestly want to learn from it and not merely to embellish it.

The counterproductive behavior we cannot foresee will have to be discovered after the fact by candidly sifting through our not-so-fulfilling experiences with a fine-tooth comb.

5. Active within us are various appetites or drives, instincts or passions, whatever you want to call them, that tug and pull on us and may explain, at least in part, how we distort reality. Most of our vital mistakes—painting things in false colors, either better or worse—arises when these drives start interfering with one another, each refusing to confine itself to its own bailiwick. Note that of these appetites only some are shared with animals.

6. Whatever else we may come endowed with, we definitely share with other animals a corporeal nature, with its built-in, definite needs, appetites, tendencies, and aversions. We can, however, control our instincts, at least theoretically. Even when we apparently resist or transcend our instincts, we must, however, be on our honest guard.

Our instincts are quite adroit at camouflaging themselves. It may seem to us that we control them, when in fact they may still determine our behavior. Yet where we come closest to falling under the imperious command of instinct is the case of raging sexual passion. Its near-irresistibility, however, suggests that we may be made for real, lasting bliss. While too fleeting, orgasm at least may whet the appetite for whatever can definitively satisfy us, if anything can. This sets us up to understand better what our higher appetite may be, one that is specifically and exclusively human.

7. What leads us to short-circuit, to deceive ourselves and fall for all kinds of inadequate "puppy loves" is our restless, meddling, roving will, especially in complicity with an unfettered imagination. This apparently bottomless hunger has no immediately identifiable object whose possession will tranquilize the will (or heart) and call at least a temporary halt to its floundering quest for happiness.

The slightest reflection shows that whatever humans do (or omit), we always do it because we at least *think* it will make us happy, either directly or indirectly. We cannot *not* want happiness, our strongest drive, identical with our self-interest. Yet this craving for happiness, if we're not careful, can land us, paradoxically, in deepest despair.

It's absurd to think we can do evil to ourselves (though that may well be the upshot of our actions). Even suicides think their self-willed death (and in their eyes whatever, if anything, follows therefrom) is better than their present hellish condition. Yet, as experience abundantly and sadly documents, what we think will fulfill us usually doesn't work or at least last. Thus we tend mistakenly to identify happiness with maximizing sensual pleasures and minimizing sources of bodily discomfort or pain. In effect we try to satisfy a non-corporeal appetite by satisfying merely physical appetites. This mistake points to a misjudgment: the conclusion (in which the imagination always has a hand) that this or that good will make us happy. For this mistake, the will is ultimately to blame, because it alone can force the mind to seek the deepest causes. The mind can only do what the will commands it to do.

8. We cannot choose or love what we don't know. In other words, the will in itself is not only restless and dissatisfied but blind as well.

The knowledge reported by our mind need not be fully true to reality. The mind might offer the will only apparent goods, exaggerated or minimized to the point of falsehood. Does this distortion mean that the mind has erred? Yes, but only indirectly. It does mean that the mind functions well, truthfully, only so long as it is allowed to do its natural probing, only so long as it is not deflected by some interfering outside agent, which leads to a ninth self-evident moral and psychological principle.

9.   To deliver truth, our reason must become wholly voluntary,
     will-directed and -defined, as distinguished from the half-
     thinking that is only partially voluntary.

Often our mind is filled with a seemingly incessant, internal
dialogue of sentence fragments, reflecting a welter of desires and
aversions  that are often contradictory because we have acknowledged no hierarchy among them. We don't bother to reason fully,
unless doing so somehow seems to promise more happiness than
not. Yet how much we reason, what we reason about, and when
we reason are all calls made by the often impatient and even
desperate will in its craving for bliss, often spurred on by pulsating
lower appetites.

The all too human reality is that hardly ever do men and women
sufficiently reason so as to minimize and even perhaps eliminate
wrong assessments—something the mind is fully capable of doing
if given its head and spared the haste that invariably makes waste.
Thus the usual scenario for all this intellectual and moral erring
born of our own interference is as follows: the lower instincts,
when left undomesticated by the will, tend to divorce sensual pleasure from biological need and, with their incessant clamor, to bully
the insufficiently independent will. The will in turn tends to bully
the truth-finding and -telling mind into malfunctioning. A rushed,
partial judgment sets us up for bad or wrong choices: we don't
stop, look, and listen enough before we leap. There, in summary,
is how humans go wrong. When the appetite of the will, through
its own faulty, blameworthy stewardship, is not fed an object that
at least comes close to satisfying its instinctive craving for happiness,
it tends to go haywire, to avenge itself, to cheat itself of what alone
can tranquilize it into fulfillment.

The problem is not selfishness by itself, or even the feverish
pursuit of pleasure, but the failure to heed the objective inadequacy
of quite limited goods to slake our seemingly endless appetite for
bliss. But does reinforcing the very neglected truth-finding mind

set us free? Will it rein in our blind appetite for bliss? After all, to know truth is not necessarily to will it, to do it automatically. And that leads us to at least a preliminary conclusion as to *how* we're to comport ourselves if we're to aspire effectively to the enlightened, satisfying life that ratifies our being.

10. Through a combination of both foresight (careful scrutiny of options) and hindsight (studying both positive and negative feedback), we are supposed to discover, via a certain amount of experimentation, what works and what doesn't, what steps lead to enriching our life and what missteps deprive us of the bliss we seem to be made for.

The mind must be allowed to do its job of reading reality; the will must submit itself to the mind's findings, while instructing it to find, again somewhat experientially, which are less and less inadequate objects to love. To do so, the will must stop exaggerating the pleasurable worth of the objects of our physical appetites. The will, instead, must exercise its native sovereignty by working toward the submission of mind, will, imagination, and corporeal appetites to objective reality. It must impose the tandem of reason and reality on our bodily needs and cravings; this imposition goes by the name of moral virtues, especially the so-called cardinal virtues.

These good moral habits give us, as it were, a "second nature" (or, perhaps better, develop and give firm shape to what was before only a very rudimentary nature). They steer us away from the two extremes of compulsive, unthinking excess (too much) or defect (too little) and towards just enough. Virtue represents a "golden mean," a pinnacle between undesirable valleys on either side. By thus domesticating our bodily drives, both the undeceived mind and the disinfatuated will are progressively freed to explore for their respective objects: truth and goodness. And as they do so, the joint quest proves successful in part and thus progressively more rewarding. It may not yet be euphoric bliss, but this growing happiness is certainly deeper and longer-lasting than any we were able to patch together or improvise during our pell-mell days of unenlightened self-interest.

# 4

# OWN YOURSELF

Nature, to be commanded, must be obeyed.
— Francis Bacon, *Novum organum*, 1620

Than self-restraint there is nothing better.
— Lao-Tzu, *The Simple Way*, *circa* 604-531 B.C.

W HAT DO YOU MEAN 'own yourself'? If I don't
own myself, who does?" Interestingly enough, the same
freedom-brandishing inquirer, in practically the next
breath can claim, and often does, "The devil [or genes, nurture,
whatever] made me do it." Behind this common inconsistency
may lie more than just self-serving convenience or the mistaken
confusion of political liberty with interior freedom or self-
possession.

The freedom from external restraints or coercion, a birthright
recognized and upheld by most legitimate civil governments, is
one thing. Quite another is the absence of internal or internalized
restraints—the topic that concerns us now. The former is freedom
*from*, the latter freedom *for*. By freedom we mean the greater or

44

less power of self-determination that rises above both corporeal tugs and psychological fears. Literally millions of people in this century alone have given their lives to keep tyranny and oppression at bay. Yet perhaps even more have busied themselves with the futile and ironic—but no less deadly—task of avoiding the onus of personal freedom and (especially) responsibility.

We all tend to dig in our heels when the time comes "to pay the price," to "sacrifice for your liberty," as a once-popular ballad put it. We seek refuge in the anonymous, amorphous, acephalous crowd. We exaggerate influences on our behavior, allowing them to turn into mandates or compulsions. Our body, the crowd, maxims, personal whims, and phobias bite into our behavioral choices. We somewhat knowingly and freely (though barely) consent to misdeeds that become, thanks to prior dalliance and foreplay, psychologically overpowering. "I can resist everything," as Oscar Wilde was wont to complain, "but temptation." Tired of choosing and having to answer for our choices, we can desperately want to be emotionally overwhelmed, say, by fervent rage or libido. We anxiously reassure ourselves that "we can't help ourselves"; so "let's stop berating ourselves." We gullibly fall for the apparent "deliverance" of determinism (and similar "-isms"). We recklessly or naively, sometimes even deliberately, welcome circumstances or companions that prey on our weaknesses, inflaming our passions into an immoral juggernaut.

## EKING OUT FREEDOM

Yet, for all those pressures, there remains at bottom a smidgen of freedom and choice—so our still-not-totally gagged conscience tells us. However habitual and even compulsive misdeeds become, there nevertheless is (or *was*, at the very least) a point when we could have abstained or, more positively, gone in a virtuous direction. There's usually just enough of us—foreknowledge and volition—in the various deeds we author to merit either censure or praise (though certainly not very much of either). Willy-nilly, all our deeds fall somewhere on the spectrum between freedom and compulsion. Naturally we're loathe to admit that we're often not our own master, that we seldom serve our own best interests. But, in a rare access of honesty and bravery, we are led to admit that we do own ourselves, though only partially. What would seem to be even more culpable is the willful reluctance to face and do something about this moral ambiguity. Isn't it a bit perverse—or just childish—to revel in remaining mini-men and mini-women? We're so busy mouthing exculpatory incantations ("we're only human" or "to err is human") that we fail to see we are barely human. It's our semi-conscious, semi-voluntary failure to mature into personhood that makes continued erring so easy and likely, and we have plenty of company. As hard as it might be today to bring people around to acknowledging that they're sick and therefore stand in need of some sort of cure, it's much more challenging to get them to accept the diagnosis of their maladies: the admission that their ills and crippled freedom are self-inflicted.

"Till we have faces," till we take virtuous charge of our lives, till we define who we are and are called to become (on the basis of what at root we know ourselves objectively to be), we'll keep on getting pushed around, but principally by our brain-dead, runted selves. We may be constitutionally forgetful or clumsy, but none of us can claim to be necessarily errant. Ours is usually a dwelling divided against itself, unless and until we commit ourselves to making of our lives something noble and beautiful. When we're not energized by an overarching, challenging purpose, our almost good will or our nearly good intentions so often get caught off-guard, side-tracked, pushed out of shape. Moral mediocrity reigns by default.

To understand better our episodic but major moral failures, we must understand what has subtly been happening to us. How has our character been developing; what habits of mind have taken root in us? This exploration should be carried out on two fronts. Let's scrutinize our ultimate motives, especially when our deeds tend toward being exemplary (and complacency, if not worse, can set in). Then let's track down any possible imbalances that have crept into our doing even good, right, necessary deeds. Often we fail to heed the due limits that ought to have circumscribed the doing of them. Being affectionate, making money, resting, eating, educating ourselves, enjoying beauty, and taking interest in cultural matters—these are all good things. But when we disregard measure and proportion in our enjoyment of them, we quite unknowingly arrest our moral growth and even begin to shrink. Yet we won't grow very far if we merely try to yank out the weeds. Negative habits, concur most moral guides, are best crowded out with an abundance of positive deeds.

At the very least, don't we all harbor inconsistencies between long-range objectives and immediate goals, between ends and means, between our deep-seated appetite for happiness and our craving for mere gratification? It is this split personality that healthy introspection is supposed to uncover in support of some overdue housecleaning and greater self-possession. Before we can successfully address our happiness deficit, we must firmly ensconce ourselves in the driver's seat by trying to free both mind and will from assorted untruths and puppy loves. Otherwise "the closing of the American mind" (the title of Allan Bloom's 1987 best-selling cultural critique) may become permanent.

A step-by-step program of liberating virtue would thus seem to be in order. First we're to muzzle and discipline our merely corporeal appetites and thus graduate from unenlightened self-interest. That goal, though perhaps intermediate, will necessarily entail an arduous program of acquiring key moral virtues. But, thanks to these virtuous exertions, we can hoist ourselves from the first moral stage (self-knowledge) to the second (self-possession). At its most basic, the project consists in at least deferring those gratifications that would otherwise hinder the pursuit of certain personal objectives. This self-discipline leads to integrity, to a more unified character. It points to dominion over a once splintered and contradictory moral landscape.

A self-owning person is (or at least can be) a self-directing one. A lack of moral virtue lies at the root of many contemporary identity crises and tortuous mental hells. Without it, each of us is a jumble of impulses, glands, platitudes, thoughtless reactions, and various fears, especially fear of rejection. Those who don't or won't define, affirm, and commit themselves are in fact bereft of a self to discover, however much they might probe themselves on Paris's left bank or amid the vales of Vail or Aspen. Let's start this inquiry into the need for self-conquest where it all began.

## ANCIENT GREECE:
## BIRTHPLACE OF ETHICS

Why did Western civilization dawn in Greece midway through the last millennium B.C.? A number of factors, many even physical, converged to make this cultural birth possible. A benign, largely temperate climate reigned over a number of relatively independent Hellenic port cities, many of them islands, involved in shipping and trade in the Aegean and eastern Mediterranean. Their maritime commerce, with ships transporting goods to and fro, exposed Greeks to various cultures. Along with growing afflu-ence, there also arose a division of labor among citizens that allowed these small cities to become largely self-sufficient city-states. Education could then take off and outgrow mere hand-me-downs within the family and its branches. Slaves provided their masters the leisure indispensable to cultural development.

Now this slowly accumulating freedom, wealth, and education also spelled the gradual obsolescence of the Greeks' old natural religion and their former ways of austere life. Moreover, as these Hellenes came to see how the world worked, they began to discover natural causes to replace gods and goddesses, thus giving rise to both science and philosophy. So long as theirs had been a hand-to-mouth existence, ancient Greeks disposed of little leisure. What good qualities they seemingly had were not so much virtues (habits freely chosen and interiorized) as circumstantial impositions (diminished opportunities to go wrong). But with the decline of the gods (and their threats of retribution hereafter, if not here) and the proliferation of gratifications, Greeks began to grow soft and to indulge themselves—why not? They thus forfeited their manliness, courage, and diligence in their shortsighted pursuits. (This decay occurred also in late-republican Rome and throughout the Western world in the second half of this century.)

Now, the more thoughtful, Greeks were not pleased with what they saw about them: social decay and personal lives unraveling. Augmenting pleasures and sparing themselves pains, though apparently the formula for fulfillment, were proving costly to justice and the common good, not to mention to individuals. Whetted appetites clamored for ever more entertainment, when not for genuine perversions. As reasonableness and virtue declined, an infantile paralysis of mind and will began to set in. The merely rationalist and rhetorical game of sophistry was taking over, displacing the search for and love of wisdom that defines philosophy.

Athenians in particular, of whom we know more, seemed to be heeding less and less the prescription "know thyself." Then, along about 2,500 years ago there came on the scene a man who stood out because of his claim to know nothing. With his cease-less questioning, of himself no less than of his interlocutors, he tried to get all parties to think, to reflect, to analyze, especially on moral matters. This self-dubbed "gadfly" was Socrates, Plato's mentor, who was later put to death on the trumped-up charge of undermining the gods and unsettling Athens's young men. But perhaps the most subversive utterance of Socrates was his immortal claim that "the unexamined life is not worth living."

For him self-scrutiny would disclose that various appetites were engaged in a civil war. Socrates could see that contemporaries were semi-consciously and semi-voluntarily surrendering to their whims and wants. Thus for him the classical definition of humans as "reasonable animals" was more a goal than a given, more a point of arrival than of departure.

## YOU CAN'T LIVE CROOKED AND THINK STRAIGHT

While both more mystical *and* systematic, Plato duly filled the shoes of his master. He saw that most humans were living in a shadow world of self-deceit, failing to reason their way to dominion over their unruly appetites and instincts. Despite vocal contrary claims, this uncritical commitment to self-indulgence was not working. Its practitioners found themselves duped again and again. How to get off the self-defeating treadmill? As laid down by Plato in his *Republic*, the benighted stand in need of both philosopher-kings and philosopher-rescuers.

In his memorable parable of the cave, humanity finds itself trapped in a huge cavern on the back wall of which are reflected shadows from the world outside. The imprisoned inmates cannot distinguish between the real objects and their shadows because they can't turn their heads around. They can only rid themselves of the deception if former inmates return to the cave. The latter, through both honesty and growth in virtue, have managed to escape singly and to saturate their minds and hearts with the real world. They are consequently eager to share their discoveries. Yet even then those habituated to the shadow world don't readily assent to second-hand truth. They can only take it on faith, until they, too, escape to the sun-drenched world outside.

Now there might never be a cavern if society were radically to restructure itself along the best educational lines and to adopt a wise philosopher-king. The parable is doubtless autobiographical. Plato was frustrated in his untiring efforts to get his peers to take charge of their lives by corrective habits of reflection, virtue, and meditation.

It fell to Aristotle, Plato's disciple, to develop and systematize ancient Greece's moral philosophy in his landmark *Nichomachean Ethics*. He managed to come forth with a map to, and rationale for, enlightened human behavior. Less successful were his tutorial efforts to raise up a philosopher-king in the person of Alexander, son and heir of King Philip of Macedonia. Let's attempt an overview of Aristotle's ethical system.

Where do we tend to go wrong? Aristotle pointed out four main areas: (1) we magnify pleasures; (2) we do likewise with pains and fears, especially when pursuing longer-range, harder challenges; (3) we tend to defraud others, not giving them their due; (4) we usually do not think well; not even afterwards, when faced with unforeseen negative consequences, do we sufficiently study our mistaken moves. "I count him braver," wrote Aristotle, "who overcomes his desires than him who conquers his enemies, for the hardest victory is the victory over self." By practicing self-discipline in these four areas through better reasoning, we free ourselves from the impositions of blind appetite, of compulsive, instinctive behavior. The resulting golden mean of virtue represents a peak between two contrary extremes: courage, for example, towers over both cowardice (irrational exaggeration of risk) and recklessness (irrational disregard of hazards). Thus was born the doctrine of the so-called four cardinal virtues, traditionally called temperance (or moderation), fortitude, justice, and prudence (or practical wisdom). They're so called, not because cardinals, be they men or birds, come already equipped with them. Rather, in Latin, *cardo* means hinge. Thus on these good, acquired habits rests and swings the whole moral enterprise. A synonym would be "pivotal."

For Aristotle virtue *is* truth: living according to reality, rectifying one's life. By living more reflectively and virtuously, humans' capacity to reason would disentangle and assert itself. Men and women could then engage in more specifically human pursuits, such as art, intellectual discourse, contemplation, friendship, family, governance. Seeing how shortsighted hedonism backfired, Aristotle taught any receptive fellow Greeks that a life of enlightened self-interest would solve the nagging human problem of how to attain character, fulfillment, and happiness. These good habits would form a second nature, heeding which would make people fully reasonable.

Aristotle also taught that to know the truth of how humans are best to behave was virtually to ensure that they do so. For him, perhaps because he always generously followed the lead of reason, there was no distinction between knowing and desiring the truth. Vice was simply ignorance. Thus it fell to later philosophers to discover the broader appetite of our will, its native indeterminacy or freedom and the consequent ability either to do ill to ourselves or to raise ourselves to unsuspected heights of generous self-giving.


## NOT ENLIGHTENED ENOUGH?

But this ethical program didn't work out quite as Aristotle and other assorted sages had thought and hoped. They had generalized from their own commendable but particular cases of identifying knowledge of the truth with loving and pursuing it. They thus had oversold their ethical program, promising more than it could deliver. They, or at least their disciples, were left confused and depressed by failures—personal or vicarious—to follow the moral map. Where did this erring come from, since the disciple had been shown what was clearly the best, maybe the only, way to live?

Had the Aristotle, however, analyzed how other humans err, they would have discovered both free will and with it the possibility for a third moral stage. He and his partners in virtue should have continued to heed Delphi. For their followers as for us, weakness and infidelities intervene between the theoretical ideal and practice. We tire of all this thinking and forethought and measuring. Even enlightened love of self doesn't necessarily eliminate inconsistencies and thoughtless impulses or reactions. The virtuous life, if indeed cultivated, helps prevent us from getting pushed around by embroidered attractions or aversions. It also can lessen our short-changing others. But is virtue its own reward?

To the extent one has struggled to own and domesticate oneself, to that degree one can decide what to do with the rest of one's life. For many ancient sages, excluding Socrates, Plato, and Aristotle, good habits didn't usher in definitive, lasting bliss. If anything, virtues tended to make their possessors priggish in their ivory-tower righteousness, smugly superior to the self-gratifying masses. Enlightened self-love alone proved an insufficient motive to be faithful to the program. In moments of weakness, the sirens of fake blisses could still cast their spell. As a result, the cardinal virtues didn't spread throughout society as hoped. Social decadence continued to take its ever broader toll. Gradually a cloud of pessimism and melancholy spread throughout the upper, learned classes, first in Greece and then in Imperial Rome.

The Renaissance and the Enlightenment were periods that represented rebirths of classical studies and ideals, of humanism and virtuous self-cultivation. But, truth to tell, they were probably more a tool of liberation from conventional, organized religion than an honest commitment to reason and virtue. Consequently, they failed to restore the ancients' map to human felicity. Ethics or morality as an objective instruction manual for the human machine fell on hard times, leaving many skeptical as to its viability. People also lost faith in the mind's ability to read reality aright. Skepticism, relativism, materialism soon occupied the vacuum. Today, how we are to live is, apparently, anybody's guess.

## ON THE SHOULDERS OF GIANTS

Nevertheless, the original challenge still stands. We need to rectify our behavior: to see things (both appetites and their due, adequate objects) as they objectively are and to manage them accordingly. To be ruled by reason, we need to exit the platonic cavern of our shadow world. If we know the best ways to live, but inconsistently depart from them, our impatient, desperate heart will overpower foot-dragging reason, leaving us confused and miserable. But even then a distinction drawn by Aristotle can point to the way out. People can abjure misdeeds born of weakness and lack of reflection and remedy them with a belated return to reason. But if we rape reason by claiming that behavior that frustrates our appetite for happiness is working fine, that in effect our misdeeds are fulfilling us, there's nothing to be done, until this lie is acknowledged.

The moral challenge, in sum, is twofold: to get both thought and desires, however slight, to conform to reality. Only then does experiential reward confirm theoretical persuasion. Classical ethics cannot be faulted for advancing only as far as it did. But it need not have stopped where it did. If a third moral stage, higher than enlightened self-interest, is to be reached, it must rest on that second moral stage.

When we don't earnestly cultivate the cardinal virtues (which is the same as saying husband ourselves), we run the risk of never finding out whether or not we are built in a definite way, to which structure we must answer. In the absence of that discovery, we can easily conclude we can live any which way with impunity, since ours, presumably, is an utterly clean slate. But if we reflectively act on our primal hunger for happiness, we can find out, if we're truthful to ourselves, which behaviors contribute to fulfillment and which detract from it. In this sorting process, we come to trust our unhampered mind's ability to know reality. How else could we possibly ascertain how we're built and how we're called to foster and more sharply delineate that constitution? Morality is nothing else than the largely practical science of determining which deeds satisfy and which thwart our appetite for authentic bliss.

But when ethics is not grounded in at least a subjectively verified notion of what it means to be human—inferring how humans are built and even, one hopes, for what—it has no foundation, no touchstone, no justifying theory. When that occurs, many people pattern their comportment on what everybody else is doing or thinking. But since when has the crowd proved all that infallible? Or, conversely, how one is to live can easily become a strictly private affair (valid only for its unique author). But what will stop that moral project from becoming an arbitrary, self-serving whim?

Here as elsewhere is confirmed Aristotle's observation that, while truth may be one, like a circle's center, there are many ways —360, for starters—to go wrong. When people begin to doubt common sense or the mind's ability to know reality (or, usually an accompanying movement, to distrust authority and tradition reflexively), the effect is blindness. And in the kingdom of the blind, as bitter experience shows, how persuasive is the one-eyed demagogue! So, when the ancients' commonsensical realism (or, a reflective step or two beyond, their philosophical realism) is jettisoned, morality cannot help but become a patchwork (and needless to add, the less demanding, the better). This moral groundlessness is visible in today's five most commonly held answers to the nagging question "What will make me happy?"

## TRUTH'S TOUCHSTONE

1. While religion, with its ostensible "good news," addresses the same craving for happiness, it does so obliquely, remotely and, if at all, paradoxically: not so much here as hereafter. Moreover, with its otherworldly emphasis on deferring and self-denial, religion, at least the Judeo-Christian amalgam, seems to go

contrary to the ways most people explore for whatever
happiness they can glean from this life. This perceived conflict
explains much of today's lukewarmness among, and attrition
from, the dwindling ranks of church, synagogue, and mosque.
God or his envoys do not seem to answer convincingly the all-
too-human challenge: "What's in it for me here and now?"
Religion seems to drain this life of meaning ("just avoid
pitfalls"). Proponents of religion or at least tradition tell us:
"You can't see or understand, at least for now. So, take it on
faith: trust those who have your best interests uppermost."
Authoritative religion or tradition is much better at saying
what not to do than what, positively, to do. Then it comes
across as an onerous, arbitrary, extrinsic, legalistic imposition
guided by its promoters' own interests.

2. If not the West's organized religion, what about Eastern
   mysticism in all its variants and "New Age" embodiments?
   Isn't transcendental meditation the key to unlock peace and
   contentment? Granted, humans generate precious little reflection and meditation. Granted also that our benighted desires
   often spell distress. But is the solution to strip ourselves of all
   personality, suppressing both mind and will, while letting
   ourselves be re-absorbed into the all-pervasive deity whence
   we came? Besides turning their backs on the "evil," encompas-
   sing body and an equally perverse society, pantheistic Eastern
   mystics, with their self-absorption and incantations, strike many
   as seeking something not unlike suspended animation.

3. So, if neither Western nor Eastern religion, what about the
   psychological healing arts, which for many today serve as a
   substitute religion? Under their tutelage many are able to disin-
   ter irrational phobias and thus more or less undo psychic
   abysses and compulsions. Who, moreover, does not appreciate
   the opportunity to unburden oneself to a sympathetic ear,
   even if a well-paid one? So far, so good. But in psychologists'

commitment to drain off guilt almost at any cost, might not these soul doctors consent to "anything goes"? When we don't elevate deeds to the level of ethical principles, we invariably lower those standards to the level of actual practice.

If we frustrate our happiness appetite by not feeding it what it really craves, ought not we to feel some reflex guilt or shame to warn us back to reality, similar to how the hint of a painful burn elicits an automatic withdrawal of the hand? Many psychiatric practitioners seem to imply that, since there's no way we can change or improve, the best thing is to accept and love ourselves the way we are—and get rid of all those nasty taboos and neurotically impossible goals. But can we really live any old way, scot-free, and still pretend to address our wearying hunger for happiness?

4. These three "technical" answers have attracted zealous ad-herents, but surely they account for less than a quarter of the American population. The vast majority of us are unreflec-tive, bungling moral amateurs most of the time. Positive emo-tions garnished with rose-colored dreams often conspire to dupe us into thinking we can morally soar at will, that we can change overnight, if we really want to, if for once we can sum-mon enough of that hitherto elusive will power. Actually there's everything right with these common dreams, with our homespun scenarios for fulfillment. When thoroughly sifted, our untried answers to the nagging happiness question probably boil down to "love," "commitment," "honesty," "authenticity," "unselfishness. . . ." Not a bad list, but all too often these desirable qualities remain a dreamy wish list, honored about as often and as long as New Year's resolutions. The goals are fine; it's the steps thereto that prove woefully unrealistic.

Most of us can see, both personally and vicariously, that selfishness backfires and generosity fulfills, but try as we might, unenlightened selfishness usually ends up ruling the roost. We see what would make ourselves and others happy, but we somehow lack the wherewithal to redeem those dreams. However many Hallmark cards or do-gooding *Reader's Digest* sermonettes we may ingest, moral and spiritual inconsistency and frustration reign in the humdrum, workaday world. So, at least, all those country-western ballads remind us with their tales of broken hearts and vows. It's almost enough to make happiness skeptics of us all.

5. As if that were not bad enough, we fickle humans also have to put up with the supercilious sneers and condescending cynicism of our intellectual, professional, financial, artistic, and even moral betters. Driven by ambition, pride, rivalry, plus uncommon mental dexterity and intellectual acuity, these "superior" men and women have usually mastered the stuff of deferred gratification, at least enough to get where they are. Theirs is a veneer of fragmented virtues, both intellectual and moral, wherewith these prigs or snobs or simply nabobs can look down upon the lowly, bungling, tippling, largely "illiterate" mob. Such titans on stilts may not be manifestly happy (if anything, it's probable they are interiorly contorted and bitter), but at least they are high enough to see through others' thoughtless schemes.

By way of summary: First, religion tends to favor the "narrow path" here, while promising bliss only hereafter: not exactly a formula for broad acceptance. Second, renouncing the moral struggle, Eastern religionists claim to have landed beyond good and evil—and maybe even beyond humanity. Third, psychiatry (and psychologized liberal religion) tries to get rid of guilt (or sin) by getting rid of any behavioral norms (or commandments); thus does it bequeath us, "I'm OK, you're OK, [and even] God's OK." Fourth, the vast crowd of frustrated, ordinary men and women see a succession of ineffectual dreams slip through their fingers, even with the best of intentions and the truest of aims. And, finally, the proud and powerful elite may avoid some of the pitfalls that swallow up others, but in the process they often grow embittered high up on their lofty perches. How easy it is to come up with inadequate, unsatisfactory answers to the elusive happiness question! All one has to do is to ignore that at our being's core there is an objective orientation to genuine happiness.

## REFUSAL TO GROW STILL MORE

It was the fifth, proud moral stance that infested classical moral theory, giving the whole ethical project a bad name. That's why Augustine referred to the ancient sages' virtues as "splendid vices." There's nothing wrong with the cardinal virtues, in theory or practice, that can't be cured by a combination of generosity and humility. The self-possession earned by virtue, you see, can go either way. It can be deployed as self-giving or, as readily, for self-getting. Thanks to virtuous striving, we can find ourselves, maybe for the first time, as part of an elite. Aren't practitioners of enlightened self-interest almost as rare as Lamborghinis?

Interestingly enough, the word "virtue" stems from the Latin *vis*, which means strength, power. Virtuous persons can do more and reach farther, thanks to heightened abilities to concentrate both their mind and efforts. Compared with more lowly peers, men and women strengthened by some virtues can be, if they wish, more immune to both padded pleasures or pains. Further, they can, if they so desire, more readily give others their due, while giving themselves the reflective fruits of the deliberation they owe themselves. All in all, thanks to the self-dominion that liberates both mind and will, they can be more thoughtful and deliberate, more dispassionate and free, certainly less hassled.

What actually happens, however, is that people tend to pick and choose among the cardinal virtues, cultivating only those required to achieve their ultimate goal. The most common scenario is to limit the intake of certain pleasures (moderation) and to steel oneself in face of hardship, tedium, and fears (fortitude). This is often done solely to succeed professionally, artistically, or athletically. By not cultivating simultaneously both counter-balancing fairness (justice) and practical wisdom (prudence), one easily ends up shortchanging, but now more shrewdly and powerfully, both others and oneself. The same selective imbalance, for example, lies behind obsequiousness (exaggerating one's debts to others) or paralyzing scrupulosity (prudence's inflated caricature in cahoots with cowardice).

When one does not strive to live *all* the cardinal virtues together, there is no true passage from unenlightened to enlightened self-interest. The former only becomes more cunning and artful in its unacknowledged self-deceptions and self-privations. Lesser, baser, commoner pleasures are scorned in the throes of a more sophisticated hedonism. Hardships are only borne to catapult one to a higher pedestal. In any case, such pretenders to moderation and fortitude can harness their humanity, less distractedly and fitfully, to long-term goals and often log no few accomplishments. Their superior acquisitions and attainments, forged amid uncommon self-discipline, set them apart from the more bungling mass of humanity.

## CHARACTER'S CANCER

Behold the worst of all vices, more subtle and deadly than the more conspicuous and therefore humbling vices or just occasional misdeeds born of an untamed nature. Conceit can cunningly hide behind a veneer of virtues; actually it is often the generating force behind them. Many are the proud, self-respecting persons who overcome lust, dishonesty, or a bad temper by thinking such failings are beneath their dignity. As C.S. Lewis wrote: "Pride is spiritual cancer: it eats up the very possibility of love, or contentment, or even common sense." When this second moral stage of enlightened behavior does not go beyond itself, it paradoxically turns rancid, transforming the proud, complacent possessor of something approximating virtue into a veritable misanthrope.

It is this proud, exaggerated sense of self-worth and its craving for recognition, repulsively obvious to all except the "worthy," that arrested the noble attempt to develop a moral science of how humans are to conduct themselves. The ancient sages stopped short in their self-knowing and self-owning and thus turned bad. Had classical ethics really delivered authentic happiness, its popularity would have known no bounds. As it was, we can imagine moral outsiders opining, "If that's the repulsive result of ethics, we want no part of it." Thus truncated, ethics was dismissed as a mere hobby or curio of ancient pagans.

Many would lay the blame for natural morality's derailment on such as Darwin, Freud, Nietzsche, their intellectual heirs, assorted existentialists, and sundry deconstructionists. Such savants certainly provide an intellectual justification for deriding and even abandoning the quest for ethics. But their corrosive effect would have been much less had there not been abroad a wholesale fulfillment deficit, which they artfully exploited. Had, instead, a complete ethical program been developed and spread, one that effectively feeds the deep-seated human longing for bliss, there simply would not have been much demand for contrary views.

But it is vice—not virtue—that has given ethics a bad name, even though it is virtue that makes vicious conceit possible. Pride precisely feeds on the competitive edges that deferred gratification sires. But what a different world ours would be if its self-knowers and self-owners were to occupy themselves in helpfully raising others to their superior level—and beyond. Then virtue and the generosity it makes possible would be seen for the liberating and fulfilling things that they truly are. Instead, instinctive aversion to priggish pride has spilled over onto the acquired moral qualities that alone feed human happiness and form character. But, now wary of termite-like pride and its confusions, let's press forward in our quest for a fully reliable moral program.

## A THIRD MORAL STAGE?

The two failures of counterproductive virtue without love and ineffectual love without virtue are very instructive for the whole ethical enterprise. They don't disprove the viability of a moral science. If anything, they show the need for a moral map by documenting the damage wrought by straying from the plan. They also reveal the danger of not living all the cardinal virtues. There's nothing wrong with these two failures except their incompleteness—something that can be cured by uniting one to the other. They imply the need to press on to yet a third moral stage. Ours, apparently, is to be a loving self-discipline, a toughened love. The cardinal virtues represent an indispensable condition—the wherewithal of self-ownership—for authentic love. Truly loving others is the only motive that can save moral virtues from degenerating into self-defeating conceit.

We're closer now to being able to answer the whole, hoary question of whether there can be an objective guide to happiness that may be universally valid for everybody. Upon observing which ways of behaving developed human nature and which did not, the ancient Greek and Roman sages thought they had discovered the successful formula for ethics—for happiness, finally—in their program of virtuous, enlightened self-interest. Yet in the end, the result was only an apparent (or temporary) fulfillment, though certainly a giant step beyond indiscriminate hedonism. In reality, it was insuficient because it did not adequately feed our specifically human appetite for bliss. The ancient sages ended up cynically superior or bewilderingly sad, eventually tossing in the ethical towel. For all practical purposes, their pessimism and skepticism have dogged all subsequent generations and ethical projects down to our day.

But even if those venerable thinkers abandoned the moral task half-finished, let's try to see how the classical Greeks and Romans arrested both their intellectual and ethical growth by mistaking a necessary, intermediate goal for the final end. In the next chapter we'll ask how these philosophers might have discovered, on their own, what may well be life's ultimate aim or purpose. We might be, after all, on the threshold of *the* virtue that is its own reward.

# 5

# GIVE YOURSELF

Love sought is good, but given unsought is better.
— William Shakespeare, *Twelfth Night*, 1601-02

LET'S INQUIRE as to whether humans find their highest fulfillment in disinterestedly loving and serving others. Before doing so, however, we do well to ask why our ancient Greek moralists did not take this step, at least theoretically, into the third moral stage.

Enlightened and virtuous self-interest represented a huge ethical step above and beyond rank hedonism, as we just saw. But it did not sustain itself, historically, as a viable philosophy of life, however much subsequent sages have tried to resurrect this noble experiment, at least for themselves individually, if not for others.

A century or so, however, after the city-state's golden age, Socrates, Plato, Aristotle, and other moralists did not apparently experience any inadequacy of the second moral stage. These original lovers of, and seekers after, wisdom did not, ostensibly, experience any vital dissatisfaction—at least there are no historical clues that they did. Consequently they saw no need to revise and complete their moral system. For them it was whole and viable, satisfying and fulfilling. Why hanker after anything more, if what you already have gives good results?

Note, however, that this trio of Athenians didn't revel alone in their moral discoveries, hoarding them for themselves. All three were teachers, thinkers, writers, tutors, gadflies, doubtless moved by the experience and conviction that their moral system had objective validity for one and all. Perhaps theirs were simply fortunate circumstances, to which were added honest personal effort, both moral and intellectual, and a greater willingness to heed the Delphic oracle and thus to know themselves truthfully. In any event the three sages did manage to escape from the shadow world of mere opinion and uncertainties (Plato's cave) into a solid, real world. Such a breakthrough was so rewarding and superior that they couldn't keep it to themselves, however resistant and scoffing their shadows-satisfied audiences might prove to be. Out of gratitude for this liberating enlightenment, they could not *not* teach.

## ENLIGHTENING OTHERS

In fact, they saw educating or illuminating their more or less benighted peers in the arguments for reality as the only way to help them. Many ancient thinkers, especially this threesome, basing themselves on their own experience, believed that to know the truth was to live it, abide by it, keep it (as they in fact did). Conversely, immorality was for them only ignorance of how to live. So, if they were to help others to live enlightened lives and to forsake self-defeating pleasure-grasping, their grateful task boiled down to teaching, discussing, and arguing with them. Once disciples *saw* what the enlightened life consisted of, they would necessarily adopt and heed it in their comportment.

Now, you might quickly object that our three philosophers were extraordinarily wrong (or inhabited quite an ivory tower, far removed from incessant calls to human weakness). How else could they claim that to know what ought to be done almost automatically ensures our doing it? "Why," you might add, "I spend most of my time *not* doing what I very well know I ought to be doing. So, what gives here, anyway?" That's not only a good question, but a telling one, too. All of us are generally so weak or unmotivated that our deeds often contradict the moral principles we at least pay lip service to. You see, neither Socrates nor Plato nor Aristotle had discovered the human will, our broader appetite for goodness, our innate power of self-determination (and self-frustration, one might add), our free will, in a word. You would be less surprised at this glaring omission and more forgiving of the overlooking trio if you tried harder to put yourselves in their shoes.

The three philosophers did not explicitly describe a moral stage beyond enlightened self-interest. Yet the reason can only be because they were already living it as part of their undifferentiated search and love for wisdom, without realizing that they had gone beyond enlightened self-interest. For them, to know the truth of the human condition was not only the same as living in accord with that truth, but also the same as wanting to share it as teachers with others. For them, existentially, the way they experi-enced the vital process, to know, to live, and to share were inseparable as-pects of the very same reality. It wasn't so much that they inhabited a temptationless ivory tower, so much as that they found them-selves generously acting out the answer to the question, "Now that I morally possess myself, what am I do about it?" They were so busily and joyfully dedicated to teaching others the liberating truth that they had already discovered through experience the ultimate goal of life, what we might call the third and final moral stage.

## THE TRIO'S MORAL PROGRESSION

Thanks to their honesty and generosity, Socrates and his disciple Plato, and the latter's disciple Aristotle, had courageously looked within themselves. There they discovered that much of their own behavior was inconsistent, unthinking, and plagued by questionable motives. They admitted to themselves in their growing self-acquaintance that they were short-changing themselves and consequently were their own worst enemies (though probably much less so than many of their peers). This acknowledgment moved them to renounce what remained of hedonistic attachments (equally mind-dulling and will-binding) and thus to move fairly early out of the first moral stage into the second.

You see, their increasing self-knowledge was not merely negative. They were also reflectively discovering the general contours of the human condition. In the light of these findings, they were coming to identify which deeds are humanly concordant, developing, fulfilling good deeds and which are the opposite. Thus was born the ethical theory of the moral virtues, especially those called "cardinal" (and their opposite vices). They were to cultivate these good habits by filtering their appetites through reason, lest in haste they unduly inflate or deflate the worth of the objects of those appetites. They imposed reality on their desires.

While the trio realized that building virtue and razing vices would require no little personal effort and self-discipline, it must have been a thrill to these pioneers to realize that they had midwifed an incalculable boon for all humanity. Heeding the oracle had disclosed to them—and whoever wanted to listen—the secret to human happiness in the form of an objective moral science valid for everyone. Living these virtues was also liberating their mind from the appetites' interference that led to intellectual erring. They were thus empowered not only to map how humans are to live (moral philosophy), but also to delineate the non-manifest causes of all reality (metaphysical philosophy). At their virtuous hands the mind was free to discover answers to the ultimate questions that had long gnawed at human consciousness. Much more than their own private pursuit of fulfillment, consequently, was at stake. They were to lead others to both practical and theoretical truth.

That social mission must have also reinforced their commitment to personal virtue.

## LIVING TRUTH LED TO SHARING IT

Since for these men knowing themselves was equivalent to owning themselves virtuously, their pursuit of virtue must have been relatively unwavering and uncommonly rewarding. They were probably spared the temporizing and backfiring that characterize the moral ambiguities and weaknesses afflicting most people's lives. This speculation is further borne out by the fact that their owning themselves and thus appropriating deep insights into reality led them almost automatically to the desire to share their insights with their contemporaries. Their progression from self-knowledge to self-discipline and thence to self-giving was a seamless escalation: moral stages two and three followed almost inexorably from their having taken the first step. Might not the same happen to us if we were less wavering and calculating?

Furthermore, their generous giving of themselves as disinterested and unflagging teachers of the Athenians (with Socrates's even assenting to being put to death by their authorities) must have so filled them with joy that their cup of happiness contained little room for anything more. They found their all-consuming and all-rewarding mission and vocation in spiritual paternity: fathering their peers in truth and virtue. Since they didn't abuse reality or their freedom by dalliances with lesser truths and goods, they had no reason or, better, occasion to discover the higher appetite for bliss that is the will. It is we—not they—who are to be faulted for failing to act on the truth once acquainted with it.

Would that all of us were to follow suit, to yield actively to the development from self-knowledge to self-ownership, and from self-ownership to self-giving, for it is in this development that human fulfillment apparently lies, especially the kind that seeks to help others to undeceive themselves, if we are to believe Socrates, Plato, and Aristotle. They may not have explicitly articulated) the fact that their enlightened self-interest had spilled over onto super-enlightened self-interest, but that it in fact did so is hard to deny. That is one clue that humans are called by their make-up to discover that the best, most fulfilling way to love oneself is freely, fully, lovingly to give oneself to others. This truth of the human condition highlights the contradiction between the centripetality of self-interest and the centrifugality of other-love. At first glance it doesn't make sense. Confronting us, therefore, may be a paradox that can be understood through only experience. Yet once experienced, one may not necessarily realize that the second moral stage, honestly and hotly pursued, has evolved into the third stage. For the motive of self-love underlies both, though an ever more enlightened, purified self-love.

## TWO LEAPS IN THE DARK

Oddly enough, the same transformation of self-interest had already taken place in the graduation from the first moral stage to the second, from unenlightened indulgence to an illuminated life of virtue. To the besotted and sated, surely, the second moral stage must also represent a contradiction, no small threat to their program of maximizing pleasure. Openness to this hypothesis usually takes the form of growing disbelief in one's failed schemes for happiness.

Genuine self-love had already led from instant gratification to deferred gratification, from thoughtlessness to self-liberating reflection. Why should not an even more enlightened self-interest set one up psychologically, given the shortcomings of the second moral stage, for a further but analogous happiness hypothesis? The same disbelief and distrust in self that led from the first to the second stage also seems to lead from the second to the third. Even though this second leap in the dark comes across as more obscure and demanding than the first, it seems likely that the mind is to lead from the second stage to the third, as it did from the first to the second.

Are there any other clues that humans are made for the gratuitous, disinterested service that flows from genuine love? Yes, but keep in mind that all further clues will largely fall on deaf ears until one personally admits to dissatisfaction with one's current style of life. Vital truths usually won't be adopted on the strength of vicarious evidence; they must be discovered through experience and confirmed personally.

By trying to leapfrog over the second stage into the third or, on the other hand, by refusing to go beyond the second, we create problems for ourselves. Those who attempt the latter, thanks to deferred gratification, have usually scaled peaks of superior achievement, while often disdaining those left behind. They may have scintillating minds and even a scintilla of virtue, but they lack the generosity and desire to lead that would empower them to use their acquisitions to better others. When one does not deploy one's virtuous self-ownership and resulting attainments in the service of others, it quite manifestly and almost necessarily turns bad. Then it serves but to feed one's competitive pride and leads to the forfeiture of one's brotherhood and humanity. Such is the case of many professors, who cunningly cloak their intellectual "deflowering" of youth behind specious efforts at illuminating them with sophisticated and sophistic reductionism.

Then there's the more interesting and common case of those who, perhaps overly sentimentally or emotionally, want to put forth love, romance, and dedication (or perhaps more truthfully, want to be on the receiving end of others' love, romance, and dedication). They, nevertheless, find that their grasp exceeds their moral reach. They lack the wherewithal to redeem their rose-colored daydreaming, however truthful and noble their dreams may be. Because they only barely know and own themselves, sooner or later they find it impossible to give of themselves completely, with no strings attached, especially when flooded with a welter of negative feelings.

These unwitting emotional sluggards confuse the death of "liking" with the demise of loving. They thus shun the voluntary, deliberate, self-forgetting services that alone express and develop true love or dedication. What such people lack is sufficient self-acquaintance and mind-directed virtue. They run up against the metaphysical impossibility of wanting and trying to give what they don't really possess. Their hearts may be in the right place, but their minds and habits are not. Their deficit is the opposite of the superior achievers.

We seem made for ecstatic self-transcendence and self-forgetfulness. Somehow, there must be a more refined, higher form of enlightened self-interest that lifts us, however temporarily, to something approaching this bliss, euphoria, or ecstasy. Are there circumstances, psychological or emotional, that the ancient sages overlooked, in which we can catch glimpses of any super-enlightened self-interest?

## SOME CLUES

Here are some telling "highs" that point to our being made for self-giving:

1.  SOLDIERS IN WAR: a soldier or sailor doesn't take serious risks or expose himself to death for a cause or his country, but rather, quite uncharacteristically, for his "buddy." He finds himself doing heroic things quite beyond himself. (This may be why veterans like to congregate and relive by recalling their joint, surprisingly "happy" ventures.)

2.  UNLIKELY HEROES: What happens to men at war can also overtake quite ordinary people who stumble upon accidents and are instantly transformed by those dire circumstances. Remember

that commercial flight in our nation's capital during a cold spell that crashed through ice on the Potomac River? There was at least one driver on a nearby bridge who repeatedly dove through the hole to rescue passengers, struggling visibly beneath the ice, which was too thick for them to crack their way to freedom. After fetching three or four, the man tried again, only this time to succumb to the same hypothermia and asphyxiation that took the lives of those unrescued.

3. REAL ROMANTIC LOVE: it lifts the couple beyond themselves and prompts their instinctively doing the most atypically unselfish things. They move about "on cloud nine," oblivious to all but their beloved.

4. THE MOTHER OF A SICK CHILD: she so unstintingly and not fully consciously sacrifices herself for her all-needing child.

5. *Franny and Zooey*: In this J. D. Salinger novella, a formerly self-centered brother surprisingly puts himself out to get his sister out of herself and thus helps her to avoid a nervous breakdown.

Now, you may object that these "highs" are brought about by adrenaline (1 & 2), sexual attraction (3), maternal instinct (4), sibling empathy or compassion (5). They are, admittedly, rather unusual emotional conditions brought on by passing circumstances and thus don't and can't last. But while they last, the person so visited finds himself uncalculatingly engaging in self-forgetting, self-sacrificing other-love, and loves it. There are many other such emotional peaks: breaking a sports record, response to unadulterated beauty in music, the synergism that takes place when voices come together in song, the inspired cooperation that allows a team to perform far beyond its ability (as in the U.S. hockey victory over the U.S.S.R. at the Olympics in Lake Placid in 1980).

Are we euphoric because we're totally caught up in the other and his or her needs; or are we generously obsessed with the other because of our emotional state? But does it really matter? Surely these peaks provide enough teasing evidence to suggest that we are made for free, disinterested self-giving. Maybe these fleeting, emotional, almost compulsive highs are intended to show us how generous we can be and how beneficial such generosity is for others no less than for ourselves. And doesn't that strong hint point to a third and final moral stage, wherein we would freely and virtuously commit ourselves to loving and serving others? And in this super-enlightened self-interest might we not find, paradoxically, our ultimate fulfillment? It may just be that we're never happier than when making others authentically happy themselves.

## Love so Rare

Why did the classical thinkers miss the point? There was not much romantic love abroad, for one thing; there was, on the other hand, lots of male chauvinism. Obviously J. D. Salinger hadn't come on the scene; they were keen on heroic honor and glory, but didn't exactly draw the full conclusion. Except for Socrates, Plato, and Aristotle, there's nothing in the historical record to indicate that the rest of humanity discovered that they're made for self-giving. There may have been individual exceptions, who kept it to themselves or didn't have the means to get the message much beyond a narrow social circle. In any event, for over two thousand years men and women have been without a complete, objective map to human felicity valid for everyone.

But if enlightened self-interest (the second moral stage) is scarce, much more so is the super-enlightened kind (the third moral stage). True, absolute love for others is very likely something we have neither generated nor even received, though we may think otherwise. Our usual loves are still too contractual and reciprocal. However much we might give of ourselves to others, we still hold on to the hope of some repayment, even if only from an approving conscience. For a time at least virtue makes us feel good about ourselves; it seems to be its own reward. Authentic friendship (a rarity indeed) is the closest most of us get to disinterested self-giving. But even at friendship's highest reaches, we still find mutual expectations and reciprocities at work. To such an extent is this true that we cannot conceive of a totally one-sided friendship. Such might, however, come close to being the no-strings-attached gift of self.

Now, can anyone claim that such one-sided, loving service of others doesn't work or spell fulfillment? It might just be the case that we, however advanced in age, have never authored such generous deeds ever. It's not that we've tried such a heroic life and found it wanting. Rather, we must shamefacedly admit, we may never have tried it.

The progressive discovery that we're made for others should manifest itself in ever greater fulfillment: we're more and more acting in accord with how we're built, and we're rewarded accordingly. In turn the discovery of how beneficial to oneself is self-sacrificing love undoes most of the reservations we might have about God and organized religion. Are not the rejection of and reservations about the Christian religion largely protests against the personal sacrifices it eventually requires of its followers? But if, for the sake of their own ethical fulfillment, people are already freely eliminating from their behavior whatever is counter-productive, are they likely to balk at any talk of further forgetting and thereby transcending themselves?

Now a commitment to live on this higher plane will not prevent our occasionally backsliding into merely enlightened self-interest or even into hedonism. We are weak and inconstant and easily duped. But the more we succeed in living up to this commitment of utmost generosity, the more fulfilled, happy, constant we'll be. Ours will be more like a slow-burn ecstasy, bliss on the installment plan.

HERE WE CONCLUDE the theoretical part of this ethical program. The following chapters are intended to show how we might grow in self-knowing, self-owning, and self-giving in the thick of our ordinary occupations. In each I generally heed what has proved to be a helpful sequence. First comes an attempt to document "how things are" in the hopes of uncovering pockets of unexamined, self-defeating behavior in most major areas of our routine life. The next section is devoted to "how things should be," showing how the triple program of knowing, owning, and giving oneself can be achieved amid the various haunts of ordinary life. The third section gets practical: "how to get there."

Many are those who think (self-servingly?) that to grow in truth and virtue, one must, at least temporarily but for a fairly major chunk of time, absent oneself from the usual rat race and betake oneself somewhere akin to a cloister or an ivory tower. And since this is an almost utopian prospect, given the pressures and commitments of most established adult lives ("we're trapped"), one can but muddle through with only very rare stabs at anything approximating the good, virtuous life. Thus, many mistakenly think that life's myriad but mundane trifles hinder authentic fulfillment. Let's hope such skeptics have more than just a pleasant surprise coming.

# INTERLUDE:
## A MORAL MAP

T HE FOLLOWING CHART aims to serve three purposes. First, it represents an attempt to synthesize the book's ethical program. Second, it tries to show how interconnected are all our moral commissions and omissions, plus the penalties that ensue from being selective. Third, it seeks to compensate for a rhetorical tendency in the text to assume that erring is universally human. As a statement of fact over the long haul, that is doubtless true. But we should not therefore conclude that we cannot not err. Were we to read and heed correctly the three levels of "pre-moral conditions," ours could be, with enough interest and struggle, the "positive response," though the "negative response" accords more with our relative undevelopment.

That our being, with its various principles, does not come knit together in a harmonious whole should come as no surprise—nor need we ascribe the consequent proneness to err to some primal catastrophe that somehow bent or wounded our nature. Physically, emotionally, intellectually, we're to grow during at least the first two decades of life—why should our ethical growth be any different? Why blame original sin for our culpable moral irresponsibility and indolence? The more positive responses we put forth, the more developed and fulfilled we become; and the more clearly etched we see our natural constitution to be, the easier the moral struggle becomes. If we so continue to choose, we can take (as indeed some undoubtedly have) "the road less traveled" at each successive fork.

# UNENLIGHTENED SELF-INTEREST
## (FIRST MORAL STAGE)

### PRE-MORAL CONDITION

Early on, moral ambiguity and immaturity hold sway: a jumble of minor attractions and aversions; little reflection; hope rests largely in prospective goods; minor good deeds and misdeeds mainly cancel each other out.

With age, experience, and puberty, awareness of more subtle goods, plus onset of venereal and other mega-pleasures; recognition of social nature: claims and counterclaims; happiness deficit rising; fears grow as attachments grow; learning from moral hits and misses, personal and vicarious, arises; possibility of divorcing pleasure from instinctive function makes itself known; fewer prospective goods left unsampled, thus shrinking hopes.

### POSITIVE RESPONSE

Some vital dissatisfaction and conflicting moral directions noted; need for priorities; learning to sacrifice short-term goodies to long-range goals; some recognition of others' moral claims; some minor fears and aversions overcome.

Reflection leads to discovery of instincts (preserving self and species) shared with brutes and a specifically human appetite for bliss as source of moral tension; proper roles delineated for imagination, mind, and will; unless mind and will assert themselves, behavior is barely reasonable, voluntary, and beneficial; proneness to err stems from desperate will, bullied by whetted instincts, plus wild imagination; they override truth-seeking mind; when instinctive objects are not needed, stimuli are shunned, lest self-dominion be lost.

### NEGATIVE RESPONSE

To the extent unhappiness is admitted, other people or circumstances are blamed; search for pleasures and flight from pains intensify; claims on others are inflated; reflection crowded out by noise and busyness.

Above trends wax; with diminished returns, keener, even kinky, stimuli needed to stay even with earlier indulgence; more excuses spun to explain away bliss deficit; "entitlement" to maximizing pleasures and to minimizing pains; temptation sought as "proof" for determinism, or responsibility-lessening pantheism resorted to; reason pressed into shrewd servicing of laziness, pride, hedonism, self-pity; others are exploited for same ends; some paranoia; tendency to live in and for future.

# ENLIGHTENED SELF-INTEREST
## (SECOND MORAL STAGE)

| PRE-MORAL CONDITION | POSITIVE RESPONSE | NEGATIVE RESPONSE |
|---|---|---|
| As a result of self-knowing, the need is faced for deeds consistent with our basic orientation (how we're built) and vice versa; we can easily dupe and deprive ourselves by falling short or going overboard in 4 major dimensions: a) pleasures; b) pains or fears; c) others' moral claims; and d) assessing moral choices; still fewer manifest goods left to try (though more subtle); most facile hopes have been unmasked. | Self-owning is added to self-knowing, whereby appetites, will, and mind submit to reality; these habits (moderation, fortitude, justice, and practical wisdom) grow by repeating like deeds; facilitate doing good and hinder vice; the 4 virtues integrate animal and human needs and powers into an autonomous whole, fulfilling our definition; establishes character, personhood; frees from subhuman reactions and reflexes; opens mind to reality, to rewards received from disinterested love (family); thus curbing self-centeredness; self-domination also makes possible the quest for a non-manifest object to satisfy specifically human appetite; contrary to conventional wisdom, usual occupations, tasks and duties offer excellent occasions to grow in self-knowing and self-owning; also virtue veterans become responsive to goodness, beauty, true culture and hopeful of ever higher, lasting goods. | Above trends continue to wax; reluctant deferral of instant gratification and resignation to some self-imposed privations—for sole goal of concrete advancement; minimal legal debts are paid, barely any moral claims; mind turns into shrewder prospector for competitive advantages; these tendencies often accompany and hone superior natural gifts; such persons, empowered by quasi-virtue, often turn into single-minded achievers: the proud stuff of superiority; uncommon achievements, aptitudes, leave behind also-rans and barely-rans; the fulfillment scheme of such depends on prowess (academic, professional, financial, athletic, artistic) and the likely adulation it will draw; throughout, a tendency to use others, however subtly, breeding misunderstandings and resentments. |

# Super-Enlightened Self-Interest
## (Third Moral Stage)

### Pre-Moral Condition

To the degree a self-knower and self-owner has united and enriched his/her being with virtues and knowledge, skills and achievements, a new option becomes available: whether to put those endowments and acquisitions at the service of beleaguered others.

### Positive Response

Self-knowing and -possessing underwrite self-giving, finding ultimate purpose; sublimation experienced; subject and object of self-giving are enriched, undoing tension between altruism and self-love; self-givers transform all relations; no more moral trifles or dead-ends, thanks to alchemy of love; to maintain this pitch of dedication, self-givers need guidance and fellowship; this habit can weather all tragedies, setbacks and unrequited loves; self-givers desire to live it to the full for others' sake and to teach this fundamental truth of the human condition to their peers; mind can now undistractedly prosecute search for bliss; relative self-givers can now recognize any absolute self-giver; self-forgetting and -sacrificing brings about, paradoxically, the fullest development, fulfillment and happiness, short of discovering who or what can satiate our appetite for ecstatic bliss.

### Negative Response

By refusing to go beyond the call of duty (justly recognizing one has received others' beneficence), one become love-impotent, however astutely this sterility is camouflaged; moreover, when proud feats prove unfulfilling, nongivers turn skeptics and cynics, taking perverse delight in a negative proselytism that draws the "naive" away from the rewards and demands of reality, above all of human nature; life is seen as "no exit," only mirages; having abandoned all hope, such deflate their expectations to spare themselves more disappointments; supremely lonely, they are left with a cancerous pride that guts all their achievements; hence, they seek to drag others down to their misery.

# PART II

# SELF-KNOWING
# AND
# SELF-OWNING

# 6

# INDISPENSABLE
# QUIET TIME

> Silence is man's chief learning.
> — Palladas, *circa* 600 B.C.

LET'S START WITH THE CONCLUSION. You owe it to yourself to adopt the ironclad resolution to find fifteen minutes for quiet reflection each day, every day for the rest of your life. Hundreds, thousands, of both sages and saints, from East and West, have recommended this practice as the most fundamental step in our fulfillment, both here and hereafter. If you never make any other resolution, make this one and keep it, come what may, however busy you find yourself, however barren and fruitless the practice may at times seem. Keeping it will not always be easy or pleasant (maybe not even most of the time). At last count humanity had accumulated 28,931,706 excuses for at first skipping it and then, eventually, dropping it altogether. The determination and resourcefulness with which humanity fights the recommendation, tooth and nail, should, in itself, be a clue to its absolute necessity.

The need for setting aside time exclusively for reflection and meditation is magnified by contemporary trends that give no sign of abating. If anything, these circumstances will likely keep on growing and spreading. As brainwork has replaced brawnwork and as the perspective of years has shrunk to nanoseconds, the chances for the kind of informal, spontaneous thinking and reflecting on one's life and role have sharply plummeted. Ours may well be the first generation since the dawn of time that has tried to get along without any provision for contemplation. How persuasive are the results?

Morality is non-manifest truth, for which we must go exploring and prospecting. In many cases these ethical truths, often paradoxical, must be first experienced before we can see and understand them. It may very well be the case that the only things truly worth knowing and loving are incommunicable and therefore must be discovered by each of us on his own.

## NATURE ABHORS A VACUUM

Which is it to be: activism or contemplation? But must we choose? Most of us think so, and we place our bets on busyness. We can be as occupied and hard-working as we like, but if we're interiorly fighting our work or merely putting up with it as an unavoidable, onerous means to some end that lies elsewhere, little good or virtue will come our way. That's actually the best way to cultivate a split personality: obliged to do something unappealing only in order to be able to do something else that really sparks our interest. Further, if we outdo workaholics in both quantity and quality of work, but only in order to run away from either personal problems or troublesome relations with other people, we're nothing more than cunning escapists. Behind a flurry of activity often lurk dissatisfaction, psychological dislocation, even perhaps an ulcer or two. It's not output or efficiency or even artistry that fulfills or builds us up. How can mere externals make us happy?

Yet we seldom think along these lines. Rather, we stay on the surface, we react, priding ourselves on our spontaneity; we harbor a lot of unexamined, often conflicting motives. Other-directed, we run with the pack, go with the flow. Afraid of rejection, we grovel for crowd approval. We also shun quiet and solitude. If we can't physically be with others, we find electronic substitutes: radio, music, TV, the Web. . . . Or books. Or solitaire. Or pets. Or hobbies. Another help to avoid reflecting on oneself is to work up a huge case of indignation against (take your pick): the reigning political party, predatory capitalists, leftward drift, environmental polluters, fluoridation, the IRS . . . you name it. The important thing with an all-consuming cause is, first, to see the enemy behind everything undesirable and then to blow it up so that it fills our mental and emotional screen.

Now it's not exactly true that in such a state we don't think. In a way we're thinking all the time, but in an exaggerated, defensive fashion. At least we're almost always talking interiorly with ourselves. Sometimes even aloud (something men do more than women). We encourage and excuse ourselves. We find good reasons to exempt ourselves from legal and even moral duties. We compare ourselves favorably with other people. In our semi-paranoia we pity ourselves. We're also kept busy inflating our good points, while sweeping self-incriminating evidence under the rug. Almost unconsciously each of us chatters away with himself: "Take it easy; you've had a hard day; you deserve some of this or that. Oh, poor body, yes, how you suffer. . . . Of course, anything you say." Exaggerated? If so, why do we cringe in chagrin and disbelief when shown a snapshot of ourselves or when we hear our recorded voice? With our incessant mono-logue, we all fabricate a cocoon to shield us from criticism or corrections and to keep reality at arm's length.

## FEARS FROM WITHIN AND WITHOUT

So much of our life is reactive. We're hemmed in by all kinds of fears from both necessary and unnecessary evils. Consequently we confuse happiness with obtaining freedom from fears and restraints. Since when are we justified in calling ourselves reasonable animals? At best, we are but half-rational and half-voluntary. We lead most of our lives enveloped in a foggy miasma. In our untruthfulness we believe and hope too much in ourselves, while loving ourselves beyond any objective merits. Activists that we are, we surround ourselves with all kinds of defense mechanisms against quiet, solitude, and reflection. How we resist digging inside, making our own acquaintance! We're mortally afraid of discovering that we do in fact dupe ourselves and therefore some time will have to renounce our pursuit of counterfeit goods. How we fight the prospect of seeing our false, bloated personality deflated. In our century alone we've witnessed the relative death of humanities, liberal arts, classical ideals, leisure, contemplation—all crowded out by a feverish, Faustian activism. Yet how persecuted we are by the fear of what others think. As sociologist David Reisman maintains, since the 1950s Westerners' internal gyroscope has been on the blink. We've gone from being traditionally inner-directed to other-directed, desperate for the crowd's *imprimatur*.

And then, despite all these depressing shortcomings, we have the nerve to believe we're superior to others. Don't we spend half of our time cutting others down? So obsessed are we with attaining a competitive edge over others that we're truly driven to outshine them in one of many different dimensions. In fact, it really doesn't matter which dimension. If we're not bright, at least we don't put on airs. If we can't dance well, at least we're king of the hill when it comes to mixing Martinis. We see the speck in all others' eyes, but not the two-by-four in our own. How we dismiss any negative feedback that gets through. This failing is commonly called pride.

How easily we detect it and how readily we detest it in others, yet how hard it is to see in ourselves. Especially since it *does* feed on what it tends to motivate: positive things like intellectual prowess, virtue, and achievements. Now we humans are not all equal (except under the law), be it in talents, opportunities, or accomplishments. We sometimes can and do become better than others in one aspect or another. Now there's nothing wrong in acknowledging these relative perfections. What, however, is completely unwarranted is for us to turn a very finite perfection into a universal superiority and to start looking down on others. We feel compelled to build our own pedestal out of the unmasked shortcomings of others, which we're "obliged" to reveal to all comers.

## TRUTH HURTS BUT HEALS

Our sorry mental world, in sum, is a stew of "necessary evils," escapism, and shallowness—all amid a self-centered and self-excusing monologue. Wasn't it something like this that moved Socrates to proclaim that "the unexamined life is not worth living"? Among its other liabilities, an uncritical attitude toward life leads us to commit the same stupid mistakes over and over again, thus frustrating as many times our craving for happiness. Instead of righting ourselves by accommodating reason and will to reality, we tend to employ them in the opposite direction, to everyone's detriment. Surely we can and must do better than that. The challenge is to become objective, truthful, to detach ourselves from false idols by undeceiving ourselves.

That, in any case, is one of the fundamental premises of ethics. We must face the truth, awkward or otherwise, and pattern our efforts at moral reform on it. Unless we know ourselves, we cannot later own and give ourselves. This self-knowledge is threefold: to own up to our mistakes, to see *how* it is that we can and do err, and, finally, to see the benefits that come our way from seeking ever higher, better goods that accord with our usually underfed being. If we're ultimately to be happy, we must progressively know the truth and try to live it, to live up to it. Otherwise we defraud both ourselves and others. We also create imaginary hells for both parties. Neither do we wean ourselves from addictions to overblown gratifications. While thus pampered, we're also besieged by equally exaggerated fears. Given the toll exacted by self-ignorance, we're all sold on the need for self-knowledge, but why is it that we're so slow to grow in it?

Only truth therapy can liberate us from ingrained habits that may spell, eventually, No Exit. What makes or breaks us is our inner world, the relatively unknown and unvisited world of heart, motives, and intentions. You see: we humans establish contact with the macrocosm, the world outside and around us, only through the very own personal microcosm that each of us is. If we get ourselves wrong, we'll get everything else wrong too. Only by righting ourselves can we get all else right too. A crucial question: Around whom or what does our interior conversation revolve? We must sit down and make our own acquaintance, however painful it may be to discover that we are so immature, undefined, and confused. Rest assured, though, we'll reap much more pain by running away from the bearable pain of deliberate self-knowing. And surely admitting that we're not happy in our own self-deceiving and self-defeating clutches is a piddling, though necessary, price to pay for the admission ticket to true happiness, a bliss that need not end.

## THE HARDEST WORK THERE IS

Thoreau also said: "Oh, if we were to live but one day deliberately." Another call for reflection comes from Edmund Burke: "We don't need so much to learn new truths as to remind ourselves of old truths." Won't courageously facing my own bad news open the door to welcoming any good news? Somehow or other the truth makes us free, undoing all kinds of limiting untruths and half-truths and dissolving many kinds of self-cheating behavior.

Yet another reason for reflection: all fundamental truths are subtle and must therefore be sought inferentially, mediately. Till then, the world presents itself with ambiguities unending. In this prospecting for incommunicable truths, it's everybody for himself. I can't do your thinking and loving for you; nor would you ever let me. With subtle, fundamental, demanding truths, experience prompts us to be ever reselling ourselves on them and recommitting ourselves to them—time and again.

All this higher knowing and loving eventually gives way to the mastery of self-possession. We can thus reach a plateau of serene unflappability (but diametrically opposed to passive states of nirvana). We achieve a state of relative immunity to exaggerated pains and pleasures, while enjoying much more what real pleasures there are. We're also much less harassed by any of the pains or toils that life may deal out to us. Moreover, true self-knowledge, however painful, allows us to stop taking ourselves so seriously. We end up diminishing problems and banishing tragedies from our existence. The freedom that is self-ownership allows us to set our own agenda, to go on the offensive in setting or, even better, discovering aims truly worth living and maybe even dying for.

## HOW TO MEDITATE

1. *Constancy–Every Day*: Finding some daily time to get acquainted with yourself is all-important. Whatever else you might treat lightly or superficially, you can't afford to be anything other than always faithful to your daily quiet time. Initially perhaps you might just have to take my word (and that of the thousands mentioned earlier) for its absolute necessity. But if you log at least thirty consecutive days of earnest, conscientious effort to know yourself, you'll no longer have to take the recommenda-

tion on trust. You'll be irreversibly committed to it yourself; consequently, you'll never skip it on this side of the grave.

2. *Prime Time and Place*: Don't devote leftovers of time or energy to this crucial, make-or-break practice. Its value towers over that of anything else you might pursue; so prize it accordingly. Give it your very best effort at the very best time, when you're most alert and uncluttered and when this quarter-hour is least likely to be interrupted or pushed aside. Don't leave it to the very end of the day; nor should you do it in bed (unless bedridden with some illness). Free yourself as much as possible from distractions, as an aid to concentration. So where to do it is almost as important as when. Some suggested whens and wheres: in the library or chapel during a free period in school; right after a quickie lunch; stopping off at some quiet, recollected place on the way home from school or work; in your room, following dinner and before starting to study. Another ironclad rule: no more than fifteen minutes when you're visited by good feelings; no fewer than fifteen, when you're utterly blank or as dry as the Sahara. So, time yourself.

3. *Topics*: How you're living each of the cardinal virtues: moderation, fortitude, justice, prudence (practical wisdom); how you're treating your spouse, parents, and siblings; how you're discharging your duties and chores; how you're exploiting your classes and study schedule, plus your general use of time; how you're acquitting yourself in your various friendships; your reactions to feedback and criticism in general; what things make you happy—and the opposite; any worries, problems, concerns; reviewing previously made (and jotted down) resolutions; dreaming about your capabilities and promises— and the practical steps to develop them; recent failings, mistakes and how to avoid them in future; prospecting for and examining any clues to the existence of any invisible world; unmasking pride, envy, cynicism, thoughts, and words rashly

critical of others; trying to understand others by imaginatively putting yourself in their place; our most common excuses and rationalizations; commitments unkept and loves unrequited; best ways to rest and relax and recreate yourself; learning to pinpoint and avoid situations or things or people that prey on your weaknesses and drag you down; probing your bad moods and anger; helping others to bear their burdens; where and how do you procrastinate. . . .

4.  *Some crutches*: There will be times when we simply can't ditch distractions, or our mind is wildly in a muddle, or we're just plain exhausted and we can't put two words, let alone ideas, together. At such times it may be good to have on hand a book or two that serve up pithy sayings intended to get us to meditate, reflect, and contemplate; many such exist. See the appendix, entitled *Ancient Sage Sayings*, of over two hundred points of wisdom to get us to think. They're all from ancient Greek or Roman sages and are aimed at getting us to be true to, and to develop, our being's hunger for bliss.

Here are some more ways to grow in self-knowledge:

*Examining one's conscience*: Almost all classical humanists recommended this brief but daily exercise before going to bed. Some three to five minutes should be enough for this daily bookkeeping. It should conclude with a concrete resolution for the next day, whereby we try to plug the most threatening hole that may have occurred in our protective dikes. In its simplest form, we could ask ourselves just four questions: What did I do? What didn't I do? What could I have done better? How did yesterday's resolution go?

*Particular struggle*: it's unwise to tackle too many reforming fronts all at once. Moral pundits recommend only one at a time, for a month or so, before moving on to another. We'll soon notice that any headway in one area tends to spill over positively onto others.

*Heeding feedback*: whether with friends or at work or especially at home, each of us does elicit criticism (perhaps implied, but, more often than not, less than constructive). Now our first instinct is self-protectively to dismiss these gripes or whatever, above all from one's children. Operating, however, on the principle that where there's smoke, there's usually fire, we should at least take mental note of these jibes and assess them now and then in our quiet time. Others may just know us better than we do ourselves.

*Seeking advice*: whenever we're on the threshold of taking a major step that has long-term consequences—change of job or city, going back for more schooling, marital plans, and so on—let's seek the advice of those whose opinions we've learned to trust.

# 7

# RESPECTING PLEASURE

I can't get no satisfaction.
— M. Jagger, 1967

Prosperity doth best discover vice,
but adversity doth best discover virtue.
— Francis Bacon, *Essays*, 1625

Prosperity is the touchstone of virtue;
for it is less difficult to bear misfortunes,
than to remain uncorrupted by pleasures.
— Socrates, 414(?) B.C.

IOLOGISTS TELL US that cold-blooded animals take on the temperature of their surroundings. This they do unconsciously and automatically. If, say, you dropped a frog into boiling water, it would instinctively and immediately jump out. But not so if you very gradually warmed up the water. It doesn't notice that the heat is slowly rising; no defense mechanism is triggered. Drowsy and lethargic in the lulling water, the amphibian gives up the frog ghost before it can react and becomes a set of well-cooked frog legs.    Much the same thing has happened to most humans in the proliferation and democratization of pleasures during the second half of the twentieth century.   Awash in what feels good, we constantly indulge ourselves, when not in fact committed to  full-blown hedonism.

Since, thanks to osmosis, we've all become pleasure addicts, to a greater or less extent, we may not be aware of our newfound dependency on it.  Or we fail to see the problem.  After all, don't we pay our taxes, refrain from robbing banks, and cut our lawn regularly?  Where's the problem?  There's little, if any, gross or base immorality in our lives.  We're hardly scofflaws.  Where's the harm in embracing the never-ending cornucopia of conveniences, gadgets, comforts, and palate-pleasers brought to us by Yankee ingenuity and the American way of life?  Isn't, after all, the pursuit of happiness enshrined in our very Declaration of Independence?  To do less would strike most of us as downright unpatriotic, if not puritanical.

## HARMLESS PLEASURES?

To enlighten those who may doubt that unbridled gratification can be harmful, we could do worse than to turn to history, even limiting ourselves to the past century.  Our great-grandparents certainly didn't have it so easy as we.  They had to scrimp and save to put food on the table, keep a roof over their heads, and find clothing to cover their backs.  They were industrious and frugal, enterprising and reliable, endowed with guts and grit.  To do otherwise never occurred to them, because hard conditions left them no other options.  They didn't choose virtue; it was, so to say, thrust upon them by inimical circumstances.  Our predecessors didn't abstain, forgo, delay, and sacrifice as a matter of principle, but of necessity.  Their virtue, then, was often but a veneer of—not an informed, deliberate, freely chosen way of life.  We're authorized to make that claim by what happened when circumstances turned gentler and kinder. What seemed like virtue broke down fairly quickly.

In any case, we their great-grandchildren seem never to have spotted an indulgence we did not hotly pursue. But please note that for now we can skip over the obviously detrimental extremes of outright major addictions to sex, alcohol, smoking, gambling, or drugs. We're referring to the pleasure-plucking that is neither illegal or immoral, but which nevertheless can stunt our moral and spiritual growth. Such goodies can even define who we are. We resemble nothing so much as an octopus with those hundreds of suction cups glued to as many attachments.

In any case, what we like and choose, to a greater or less extent, does interfere with our knowing and loving aright. All those zillion pleasurable things "we simply can't do without" leave us not only exhausted but also impotent when it comes to appreciating objective goodness, beauty, and truth. We've unconsciously donned a set of blinders, when not a strait-jacket, that can't help but affect the development and fulfillment of our being. The "harmless," if multitudinous, toys our times have dumped into our uncritical laps at least hinder heeding the call to be reasonable animals.

## AFFLUENCE: TRUE TEST OF VIRTUE

When all is said and done, the urgent question has become: Can we live the authentically "good life" amid growing affluence, freedom, and education without capsizing or imploding? If "softness makes cowards of us all," can we, even amid the greatest opulence and chances for self-indulgence, somehow conduct ourselves so as to avoid becoming soft and cowardly? Today and tomorrow (for the clock's not about to be turned back), must it be the case that "whatever body wants, body gets"? Must our epitaph read, "He malled and he perished"?

For example, take a young man, call him Guy, who is toying with the idea of marriage. Yes, he likes, even loves, his prospective mate. They seem to share enough interests and values, yet they don't so overlap as to preclude sparking and complementing each other. While a mild agnostic as to whether true love is hatched in heaven, Guy sees no reason, current or foreseeable, why his love won't last and even, down the road of course, why he won't father a child or two. Under the sway of this romantic picture, reinforced doubtless by physical pulls and pushes, how could Guy view his marital prospects as other than rosy?

What, nevertheless, makes the prospects for lifetime commitment highly improbable is an ensemble of many tacit, prior pledges. This web of allegiances has become such a part of his life that its relevance to making a successful marriage can be so easily overlooked. What or who are these obstacles—those "old girl friends"?

Guy *must*, for example, work out twice a week; talk with his mom on the phone for an hour every Tuesday; shower in 117.9° water; hew to a painstakingly crafted career plan; breakfast exclusively on "Cap'n Crunch"; vacation in Club Med style twice a year; shop Brooks Brothers; read *Sports Illustrated*; attend a certain number of concerts during the year; take this, drink that, eat the other; TGIF with the boys every week; religiously salivate weekly over NFL football (or any other pro sport); drive *the* car that expresses his personality. . . . The instances and composite may be somewhat exaggerated, but the pattern is undeniable. The world is full of Guys today. The attachments may differ, but the result is equally constraining.

"But," all those guys might ask, "what's so bad about all those things? Surely many of these advances are true goods. Are you huffily turning your back on the American way of life? Is it hermits you'd make us?"

## IT ALL JUST SORT OF, LIKE, HAPPENED

In and of themselves none of these things or interests is wrong; no standard, legal or moral, is violated. Objectively their possession or exercise is quite peripheral and, therefore, as Guy assumes, inconsequential. Even all together, though the load is staggering (for listed are but a few of Guy's countless "toys"), one could, if artful and nimble, stave off suffocation. What, nonetheless, does prove to be the matrimonial prospector's undoing, leaving him impotent in the venture of the free self-giving that spells love, is his unquestioned "need" for all these baubles. Guy, after all, is an obedient child of his age. Never weaned from affluence and countless conveniences, he came into adulthood bereft of any critical sonar. No one ever warned him—quite the contrary—that all about him, the merest whims were being covertly elevated to the realm of knee-jerk necessities. It all just sort of, like, happened.

But can't Guy wake up or grow up? For poor Guy actually to do so, he would have to forswear an unwitting lie. In his thoughtlessness he exaggerates the objective worth of all his ac-coutrements, especially their "necessary" contribution to his happiness. If he were to cultivate a take-it-or-leave-it attitude (grateful for their presence, but unruffled in their absence), Guy could move unharmed and unfettered amid the greatest opulence or penury.

The untruth we glimpse, but hidden from Guy, is confirmed when, threatened by the possible disappearance of his props, he turns sad over the likewise overblown hardships to ensue from losing them. Why grow despondent, Guy asks, if they were merely incidental to his well-being? (Note the unacknowledged incon-sistency: toys are "harmless" while being acquired, "indispensable" once landed.) Guy then musters up uncommon energy to fight off their possible loss. The components of his playpen aren't bad in themselves; what's bad and fallacious and stunting is his seeming inability to do without them. They've become non-negotiable fixtures of his mental and moral landscape. Quite literally, he's stuck on them.

The more Guy squanders love on trifles, the less remains to invest in worthier objects, if in that state he can even discern higher goals. Guy ought to unmask and renounce his "harmless" dependencies and addictions, partly through reflection and partly through voluntary self-privation. Unless he does, he'll remain a moral pygmy and ethical novice, though he might be the last to realize it. He may sincerely desire to love his intended spouse, but with what? At the very least he's so over-committed to amassing and protecting his fiefdom that little energy and time remain to demonstrate his affection. But more deeply, Guy, even when spared grosser addictions and proverbial vices, so little owns himself that he can barely summon up enough self-dominion to seek—let alone achieve—the disinterestedness that supports genuine love. Guy must start by respecting his body, his corporeal nature.

That means, first, that he should come to accept pleasure as a reward for doing what he ought as regards his legitimate bodily needs. Thus, Guy should eat and drink enough to satisfy objective corporeal needs; neither more nor less; the same goes for sleep and rest, for relaxation and recreation, for shelter and clothing and the like. But not all pleasures were created equal, nor do they all represent equal mortal threats. For example, the easy separation of prodigious sexual pleasure from its corresponding reproductive function would seem to pose a particular danger for us. Freud himself warns us that this is the mother of all addictions.

It's truly amazing how little we need to survive and even thrive. We need to impose truth on all our appetites, especially the one that seeks after bliss. But first through reflection we must see how appetitive, reactive, and pre-rational is so much of our comportment. Without our fully realizing it, we may be engaging in self-defeating behavior. What mainly needs straightening out are our mind and will so that they don't demand of lowly appetites or instincts what they can't possibly deliver. We also need to be brutally frank with ourselves regarding all that cornucopia of goodies and toys that drags not just Guy down. If we lie to ourselves here about the objective worth of these largely inconsequential things, we set ourselves up for some whoppers.

## MODERATION MULTIPLIES PLEASURES

So, let's be truthful about satisfying objective bodily needs, while gratefully accepting pleasures that come with such satisfaction. Let's in fact knowingly and voluntarily do exactly as the animals: no more and no less than what's needed to get by. And let's shy away from divorcing pleasure from functions. When we do aim for more than pleasure, paradoxically there come our way many simple, overlooked pleasantries, plus ever higher ones. True hedonists, ironically, should be the first to sign up for temperance.

This virtuous moderation lifts our behavior into the reasonable, voluntary realm, wherein we deliberately choose what we're to do. It gives us self-possession, dominion, freedom. But, again, this self-ownership via virtue is not an end, although it is an indispensable intermediate end and condition for us to begin to satisfy our appetite for euphoric happiness. See virtue, then, as a bodyguard against deceit and pleasure-exaggeration. It frees up our mind and will, so they in turn can be about their respective quests for unalloyed truth and absolute goodness.

If we don't embark on this higher search, we'll have hell to pay, at least figuratively if not literally. We must be constantly and eagerly on the lookout for what will really fulfill us. If we don't vigorously and hopefully go beyond piddling goodies, again and again we'll be tempted to equate happiness with pleasure-grabbing. We'll repeatedly fall for the sirens' songs, not having learned anything from previously experienced shortfalls and dissatisfactions.

## THE STUFF OF SELF-MASTERY

Our primary need, then, is to know what's going on inside insofar as this affects our behavioral choices. We must be savagely honest in our self-scrutinies. This indicates, as we said, the need, daily if not more often, of examining our conscience and prudently reflecting on options, past and future. We must come to see what really makes us happy, not just seemingly and deceptively. But this daily quiet time isn't only for unearthing and berating ourselves for our missteps. Man does not live on virtuous self-discipline alone. Above all, we have to dream, time and again, about the prospect of what or, more probably, who might really make us blissful. We are also to examine open-mindedly the quests of others as known to us through history and biography, in a continual search for what really works. We are gradually to put together our very own pantheon of heroes. A certain amount of this reflection and reading should acquaint us with truths, both negative and positive, of both ourselves and all others.

Then, we must go on a disciplinary diet with regard to exaggerated goodies and "needs." We need to go on the offensive, an unmasking campaign. This requires a bit of study to formulate a plan of self-privations. If we rank and divide up the challenges, we're more likely to succeed. We're also to avoid situations that prey on our weaknesses and do us in. This never-ending and progressive program in virtue will help us to respect both bodily functions and rewards for what they are and to be true to both. Pleasure comes with a built-in escalation which leads to outright addiction. If we don't learn to give the body less than it "needs," it will turn traitor. He has most who needs least. To seek pleasure directly is to see it ever escape our clutches; there's the source of almost all our boredom.

Now, to toughen yourself up, here's a proved four-part plan: Don't create needs or have luxuries. Never view your possessions as exclusively your own. Don't complain when true or apparent necessities are missing. Be generous with the needy.

## MORE FIELDS TO WEED

More fields in which we can "kill what's killing us": posture, comfort, ease; air conditioning or heating; Miatas; no 180-degree head swivels after glamorous women; no X-ray vision; what we hear, taste, smell and touch. Yet let's never forget that this self-discipline isn't so much a noun as an adverb: *how* and *why* we do what we're already doing. There are worse ways to discipline ourselves than becoming a voluntary slave to duty and perfection. We are pack rats. Also those fifty-two credit cards betray our obsession with security . . . . Greed makes us blind. But the right approach to goods consists neither in having nor in not having, but in being virtuously and truthfully detached.

Yet, let's forget the downside. Now is the first time in the history of the world that virtue has truly become a free proposition for nearly everybody. Let's make a virtue of affluence. Let's show the world we can be effectively, interiorly, temperate and detached while seated in the lap of luxury. Detachment, however, is not disdain for things. Yes, let's all shoot to make a million dollars per annum and to give most of it away where it can truly benefit others. Moderation underwrites almsgiving, magnanimity, liberality, while allowing us to put forth the powerful example of self-possession.

*More ways*: Keeping busy; economizing on time; making things last; taking care of them. The best examples of detachment and moderation are parents who spend their lives for their children and who with their effort and constancy, often without complaining of their needs, bring up their family, creating a cheerful home where everyone can learn to love, serve, and work.

While in our quest for truth we should come to realize that these goods are gifts and not things we're entitled to. Rather let's enjoy them as due rewards for being about our vital business and in no way scorn them. Meanwhile and above all, let's never abandon the search for what can truly make us permanently ecstatic: "in search of the eternal buzz."

# 8

# CHASTITY: WHY AND HOW

> Pure and disposed to mount to the stars.
> — Dante, *Purgatory, Divine Comedy*, canto 33, 1321

> There has been only one sensual experience
> which has carried spiritual undertones,
> and that is the ecstasy of physical passion
> when one is young and when it is associated with love. . . .
> Efforts to protract it . . . in middle age or old age
> usually produce horror and distortion.
> — Malcolm Muggeridge,
> "A Dialogue with Roy Trevivian," 1969

FIRST LET ME SAY I'm not about to lecture or harangue you, nor to take away your toys, nor even to try to sell you on the cold shower. I do want to share some personal observations and experiences, and the advice I give myself, if not always heed.

If the improbable and nearly impossible subject of chastity must be raised on the eve of the year 2000, I can think of no better auspices than those of Augustine. As you know, the young man from north Africa was no stranger to lust, mistresses, and illegitimate children. Yet Augustine, even as he felt his pagan lifestyle slipping away, still tried to keep God at arm's length with his famous request: "O Lord, grant me chastity—but not quite yet." No wonder those words have been aptly dubbed "The Undergraduate's Prayer."

A physician friend of mine was also made aware of the dangers of raising the issue of chastity. One day a leather-clad aspirant to the Hell's Angels motorcycle clan burst into his office and proclaimed to the whole waiting room, "Where's the doc? I think I've got the clap!" He was quickly ushered into one of those tiny rooms and seen by the doctor. "Yes," affirmed the physician, "you have not only gonorrhea, but three other venereal diseases as well. Have you ever tried chastity?" "Doc, I'm desperate; can you write me out a prescription for that?" When the motorcyclist learned that chastity was not available at the local drugstore, the doctor nearly ended up in the hospital himself.

Let me first say that the pro-chastity case I wish to lay before you makes no appeal to religion or other arguments from authority. Neither will I try to scare you with a catalog of venereal diseases and other dysfunctions that might very well invade your once private parts as a result of promiscuous couplings. Rather, my whole case appeals to the most enlightened of self-interests, personal to be sure, but ultimately that of the species also. Stated negatively and very simply it is this: we can't be happy, unless we freely and lovingly give ourselves to others. Nor can we love others unless we come to own ourselves, which spells the need for chastity, among other self-liberating virtues. Yet the benefits aren't only personal. When men, the prime sexual predators, finally turn themselves inside out and thus become capable of loving disinterestedly, a truce will be called in the current and ever worsening war between the sexes. For then the fully alive Man whom women have only secretly dared to dream about will be on their very doorstep.

Men dream about increasing both their sexual thrills and conquests, while women dream about romance. Behind the quest for Mr. Right is the hope of finding a dashing knight on a white stallion who overcomes all adverisities and social conventions to rescue her from an unappreciated and humdrum existence and whisk her to his pinnacled castle, there to worship and ravish her. While that's a tall order, men committed to chastity and never-ending courtship will attract droves of equally virtuous women, who in turn will gratefully overlook and help to supply what's missing in their Prince Charmings.

By now it should be clear that I am not some sort of latter-day Puritan. All cockeyed views that brand sex as something vile elicit from me only scorn. Neither surrendering to our sexual instincts nor fearfully fleeing them works, because neither accords with the way we're built—something you'll discover if you really comb through your experiences. We can't just let instinctive sex be; we must do something with it, even within marriage. The only authentic option is to humanize sex, endowing it with freely chosen purposes which allow both parties to grow (rather than shrink). This can be in a good marriage or in an equally dedicated single life where the drive is harnessed to more expansive self-giving.

## IS CHASTITY POSSIBLE?

Let's face it: chastity comes across as a strictly negative thing. Those who would program us to "just say No" are partly to blame; even worse are their confreres who, especially in the past, exaggerate the ills and guilts of unchastity. The rest of the blame can be apportioned among those who equate pleasure with happiness, lust with love, humanity with animality. Many of the latter seemingly want to be overpowered, to forfeit their freedom and, above all, any responsibility for their libidinous abandon. Indeed, those who don't ever get beyond instinctive lust are truly sex-driven.

What is patently dishonest is for those who welcome sexual stimuli and thus go about in a state of semi-arousal to claim that chastity is a foregone impossibility. How would they, of all people, know? The "need" to engage in sex is a fabrication on the part of those who, admittedly, cannot say No to the greatest sensual pleasure because they choose not to say No to its more resistible preliminaries and to lesser gratifications. As Freud himself said, sexual indulgence is the primary addiction; all other dependencies, on such as alcohol, drugs, and tobacco are but derivatives. Are we saying alcoholics shouldn't hang out in bars? That's right: such would seem to be an indispensable first step if they want to dry out and stay that way. The whole problem with undomesticated, knee-jerk sex is that it weaves a web of selfishness that, if not undone, locks us in our ego-cage, perhaps permanently, and inflicts harm on others. Here are two letters that appeared in Ann Landers's column. They reveal that all's not well in Playboyville. The first is from a young man, who tells about his "first time":

> I was 16 and the girl was 15. I really didn't like her much but I wanted to see if I could score. I was the only guy in my crowd who didn't have anything to his credit and they used to tease me about it.
>
> It was a crummy thing I did. I lied and told the girl I had been crazy about her for a long time—a real snow job. The whole thing lasted five minutes. When I took her home I didn't even kiss her good night.
>
> I never called her for a date after that and I'm sure I hurt her feelings. I used that girl for my own selfish purposes and to this day I'm ashamed of myself.
>
> Sex without love is lousy. I hope every guy who reads this will remember what I'm saying. I wish I had learned it earlier.

Now the girl's perspective:

> I am 16 and a junior in a well-known private girls school in Washington, DC. Like nearly all the other students here I

have already lost my virginity. Although most people consider this subject a very personal one, I feel the need to share this part of my life with girls who are trying to decide whether to have sex for the first time. In all the years I've been reading your column, I have never seen the honest-to-goodness truth about this subject and I think it's time somebody spoke out.

Take my word for it, girls, sex does not live up to the glowing reports and hype you see in the movies. It's no big deal. In fact, it's pretty darned disappointing. I would have waited at least until I got to college had I known what it was going to be like.

I truly regret that my first time was with a guy I didn't care that much about. I am still going out with him, which is getting to be a problem. I'd like to end this relationship and date other guys, but after being so intimate, it's awfully tough.

Since that first night, he expects sex on every date, like we are married or something. Our whole relationship seems to revolve around going to bed. When I don't feel like it we end up in an argument. It's like I owe it to him. I don't think this guy is in love with me—at least he's never said so. I know deep down that I am not in love with him either and this makes me feel sort of cheap.

I realize now that the first time is a very big step in a girl's life. After you've done it, things are never the same. It changes everything.

My advice is, don't be in such a rush. It's a headache and a worry. (Could I be pregnant?) Sex is not for entertainment. It should be a commitment. Be smart and save yourself for someone you wouldn't mind spending the rest of your life with.

## WHY THE DOUBLE STANDARD?

Now for a bit of analysis: Chastity comes much harder to men than to women (except for those male-mimicking *femmes* who've become fixated on sexual pleasure). It's no secret that the undisciplined male sex drive is monotonously predictable and frivolous. For men from 13 to 93 years of age, nothing ever seems to change, except perhaps the immediate source of gratification. Man's arousal is so physical, indiscriminate, effortless, and imperious. As a male colleague of mine recently wrote in an access of refreshing candor: "I've never yet met a woman who didn't attract me." The outcome, furthermore, is invested with about as much drama and suspense as the other functions of human plumbing. For men, release from sexual tension comes across as psychologically peripheral and largely phenomenal, that is, as no big deal. Left to their wanton ways, most men find sex one big, obsessive game with few or no ulterior motives or meanings.

If women before weren't sufficiently familiar with these male facts of life, the sexual revolution of the '60s has spawned plenty of damning evidence. "Whatever men say or do," bemoan today many chastened (if not chaste) women, "they have only one thing on their mind. They're such animals, completely incapable of genuine relationships, of lasting commitments." The result is that women are fast giving up on men and marriage. Instead they're betaking their exploited selves to the comfort of the feminist sisterhood. There some become lesbians, while others try to content themselves with Harlequin romances, stealthily and pantingly devoured behind plain, brown-paper wrappers.

Are these disenchanted women overreacting? Perhaps a tad, but beneath the surface lies a valid complaint. Ironically enough, it took the recent female abolition of the double standard regarding sexual freedom to reveal men's native lust. Till then there'd been a bit of hypocrisy on both sides of the bed. For millennia, as popular wisdom has it, men by and large have put up with romance in order to get sex, while their counterparts have put up with sex in order to get romance. Now it doesn't take a certified psychologist to foresee what would happen if the romancing prerequisite were to diminish or even disappear. Wouldn't the result resemble an addicted sweet-tooth turned loose in a candy store?

Newly liberated women read the double standard, not as a tactical device to elevate and domesticate the "naked nomad" that is man (in George Gilder's apt phrase), but rather as an oppressive hindrance to their own experimentation and kicks. Then the next logical step for these newly liberated women was to jettison any remaining inhibitions and try to ape male recreational sex. Well, we've had a generation or two of free-and-easy sex, of the "just do it" school. We were told something we implicitly and eagerly obeyed, namely that if we just brought sex into the open, everything would be fine. So, up with directness, sex-ed, freedom, instinct, naturalness, the undraped body beautiful. And down with taboos, fears, repression, guilt, dirtiness, authority, kids. Men gladly heard that sex is but a game, with unlimited players—and free to boot. Initially at least, women just as gladly heard they could follow men down into the sweaty trenches dedicated to Venus. All long-standing prohibitions and injunctions were soon swept aside in the pell-mell dash. But has the vaunted sexual revolution brought us any nearer to the bliss we can't help but seek?

## HARVESTING THE SEXUAL REVOLUTION

It didn't take women long, especially with Masters and Johnson in the wings, to realize that there's pleasure to be had for them, too. But female accommodation of casual sex makes men, if anything, less and less fit for love, romance, and marriage. Sooner or later, with a literally withering laugh at his endowments and endurance, sexually superior women are today kicking the bums out into the dark night of impotence, if not brothels and bathhouses.

Can't men and women, especially we men, somehow dislodge insatiable lust from our fevered brains? The problem is less one of stimuli and testosterone than of muddled minds and unreinforced wills. We were sold a no-fault view of sex within a more or less deterministic scenario of human nature. The whole fraud becomes more plausible when viewed historically.

As the influence of religion waned in the nineteenth century, so too did fire and brimstone as reasons to brake the fierce sexual drive. Rigid social conventions and nascent science were both then pressed into service by our prissy, neurotic Victorian forebears to provide a new set of threats to unbridled sexual indulgence. Need we mention those physical devices designed to nip lust in the bud? "Stunting your growth" was another of the many cooked-up physical and psychological harms sure to befall the unrepentant masturbator and fornicator. But when many such practitioners outgrew their parents and more abstemious peers, pseudo-science took a well-deserved nose dive. Or better said: "real" science in a swing of the pendulum was then conscripted to defend the utter harmlessness of doing what comes so naturally. Where was the physical harm? After all, how could human doings be either good or bad, when our behavior is determined by gene or circumstance or both? Down with all value judgments. Can't we manipulate our plumbing at will?

It was almost as if the moral guardians of the twentieth century surrendered to the injunction: "If you can't beat 'em, join 'em." White-haired grandmothers, such as Dr. Ruth Westheimer and Dr. Mary Calderone, soon took to the roads and airwaves to spread the new, condescending, maybe even demagogic message: "That's all right, Sonny (or Missy), you can't help it; so just keep on playing with yourself—and no harm done." In their well-intentioned but misguided efforts to rid humanity of psychologically crippling sexual guilt, liberationists incited us to stunt, not our physical, but our moral and spiritual growth. Isn't that, after all, what the feminists and other disillusioned women are angry about today? For whatever reason, we men are deemed to be such moral midgets, ethical eunuchs, and perpetual adolescents that we're incapable of transcending our sexual kicks.

What courses are open to us? George Gilder, the author of *Sexual Suicide*, later retitled *Men and Marriage*, wants to turn the clock back to the day when understanding but wary women imposed some sexual restraint on men by largely limiting their sexual favors to marriage and its procreative aftermath. But making of necessity a virtue is no real solution. Making men wait till marriage or thereabouts does not necessarily make them, once the knot is tied, less lustful. Even the most conscientious and virtuous of husbands find it very difficult not to treat their wives as sexual objects. It was men's lack of interior self-dominion—debunked moreover as an impossible ideal—that largely spurred the feminist revolt of the '60s and beyond.

The '90s are calling for another revolt, but this time in the opposite direction. So, all you rebels out there, how about for once pushing for internalized, genuine male chastity for all the right reasons? Appearances to the contrary notwithstanding, we men just might be able to harness our sex drive or, when not, at least to acknowledge the harm we do others and ourselves. Have we so soon forgotten the social, cultural, and personal rewards from sublimating Eros promised us by even Freud? *

## TAMING THE BEAST

Yet chastity can't stand alone, not even when cultivated in the larger garden of, say, the four classical cardinal virtues. Acquiring good moral habits for the sake of smug self-perfection, as many ancient Greeks and Romans did, cannot fulfill us. "Know thyself" should disclose how little we shortsighted hedonists own ourselves and how much we gyp ourselves. Yet efforts to reclaim ourselves out of enlightened self-interest only make ultimate sense when we also take the paradoxical step to "give thyself." If you haven't yet experientially discovered this fundamental law governing the human condition, you don't know what you're missing. Here's another formulation of the super-enlightened self-interest that

* See Chapter 18 for more.

eluded the likes of Socrates and Seneca, Aristotle and Cicero: "Generosity fulfills and selfishness backfires." Still another: "You're never happier than when making others happy."

Love, you see, is freely giving oneself. The real thing is the missing elixir. Without it people and institutions can't help but misfire. Were there more of the genuine article today, especially on the part of men, would there be so many angry, frustrated women, not to mention millions of love-starved children? But lustful pleasure masquerading as love, even within marriage, is an unstable, contradictory thing. Such *ersatz* love is no longer free but conditioned and necessary; neither is it so much giving as getting and using. The only thing sham love can father is mutual masturbation.

What we can't seem to get straight is that true love is the absolutely hardest challenge facing us. Love's no overpowering feeling or state; it can't be flicked on or off, nor is it triggered by circumstances outside our control. At best a temporary set of emotions—falling in love—may sometimes overtake us and lead us to act as if we were truly loving. But might not the purpose of this emotion, so long as it lasts, be to teach us how the genuine love of self-forgetfulness and self-transcendence is to express itself? Otherwise how would we know and aspire to the deliverance of bliss? Genuine other-love (disinterested attention to the other's best welfare) takes time and reflection, training, and self-mastery.

## LUST INTO LOVE

Thanks to this therapy of truth and virtue, we emancipate ourselves from a host of pre-rational attractions and semi-voluntary aversions. Only then are we able to love: to give of ourselves to others with no strings attached. We can't give what we don't have. When people aren't already striving to be reasonable and freely autonomous, there's no way they can acquit themselves in the thick of a superficially undertaken marital commitment. They're simply unprepared for its challenges and demands; they can't help but default. We have to master the alphabet before we can aspire to write, let alone to become writers. We must be on the way and committed to becoming fully human and consistently true to ourselves before trying to acquit ourselves at the love game. And a big part of that, though not the chief part, is sexual self-dominion or chastity. How else will we ever transcend instinct in order really to make love—not just sex—and not just in bed?

Now, you're probably thinking: "But doesn't nature do us a dirty trick by ushering in puberty ten, fifteen, even twenty years before it becomes feasible to get married today? Isn't that too long to be just saying No? Most people by then have long since thrown in the towel." But you can as easily turn the argument around. Isn't it advantageous to have a longer apprenticeship in virtue, love, and chastity, given the seriousness and demands of marriage? See adolescence and beyond as at least a trial-and-error period, when one ought to be learning how to live, especially from one's own and others' mistakes. Since our failings are largely due to weakness, at the very least we should be learning which circumstances prey upon our weakness and therefore should be avoided.

The adolescent danger is to fall into defeatism before beginning to fight—or even before finding out that any struggle is called for. Puberty comes in like a lion and with it the possibility of a whole new *genre* of pleasures. A virtueless, weak youngster has few reasons and resources to abstain from orgasm, be it alone or accompanied. Stimuli welcomed, plus the accompanying flood of predisposing hormones, make of habitual masturbation a foregone conclusion at least for non-resisting boys. Many teens, not to mention their elders, have never tried to figure out why and how to refrain or what to make of the emptiness and even bitterness ensuing from sexual indulgence (the oft-noted *tristitia post coitum*). Many others, however, have learned how and when to struggle to be self-possessing and even self-giving. Such youths, moreover, spare themselves many a temptation by happily engaging in more demanding but also more deeply fulfilling activities. When, nevertheless, lust does manage to sneak through their outer defenses, they also have acquired enough moral strength and savvy to slam the door immediately and beat a hasty retreat, instead of foolishly staying around to dialogue and to see what may happen.

Now Aristotle claims that misbehavior born of weakness (as opposed to supposed entitlement) can be remedied, certainly repudiated. Actually, given the intensity of sexual pleasure and the abundant, though largely avoidable, stimuli, solitary sex may be the least of our failings. Here's the only final, fatal one: Dismissing the negative mental, moral, and emotional evidence born of sexual self-indulgence, while still clutching to unenlightened self-interest. Behold the Big Lie that spells disaster. Again Aristotle: "Such a [self-indulgent] man is of necessity unlikely to repent, and therefore incurable, since a man who cannot repent cannot be cured." *

So, don't reject out of hand the prospect of cultivating virtuous self-acquaintance and self-ownership and thereby becoming capable of love. That's the way we're made; nothing else will really work. Sure, there will likely be lots of fits and starts, hits and misses, but let's learn from both. But if there's no chastity before marriage (or at least the desire and struggle to be continent), there certainly won't be any chastity, love, disinterestedness afterwards. What will abound is a soon-eroded veneer of other-love and a lasting hard-core of self-love.

## SEX AS GIFT, NOT ENTITLEMENT

The quickest way to ensure that pleasure eludes you is to pursue it directly, hoardingly. Why? Because pleasure is governed by the

* See Appendix, number 144.

law of diminishing returns. On the other hand, the best way to see pleasure grow and last is to go beyond it in furtherance of real love. Thus, married couples who don't stop at their respective kicks can continue to enjoy their sexual embraces far into their golden years.

Webster's Dictionary says that chastity implies "refraining from all acts, thoughts and so on that are not virginal or in keeping with one's marriage vows." Put positively, chastity entails a lifelong struggle to reserve sex only to expressing love for one's spouse and any future children. The acquired ability to shout Yes to what really matters and fulfills presupposes a myriad of whispered No's to exaggerated pleasures, fears, and "needs." Male chastity looks to skirting physical arousal during waking hours, except as freely willed incarnations of marital love. On the other hand, female chastity, except where a fixation on venereal gratification has taken root, is usually a more interior, diffuse thing: avoiding near-irresistible romantic day-dreaming and scheming, triggered by such things as rivalries with other women, fashion photography, soap operas, heart-throb novels, primping, and the like.

## A FORETASTE?

There's one last thing to be said about sex—maybe the most crucial. The euphoric bliss which accompanies sexual climax, whether the marriage-sanctioned kind or not, does indeed promise more than it can deliver and proves much too fleeting for our taste. When, however, this ecstatic joy is not the companion of, and reward for, the absolute gift of self to one's spouse and any resulting children, it becomes the most obvious instance of wrongly seeking the right thing. (It's the self-getting that spells counterproductive immorality, as we saw in the first chapter.) But its one silver lining may be to whet our appetite for bigger, better, lasting euphorias for which we seem to be made. Would therefore the sexually inexperienced be at a disadvantage for not having their appetite for bliss triggered sexually? Not at all. As C. S. Lewis documents in *Surprised by Joy*, there are many other occasions, often hauntingly unexpected and even mysterious, for experiencing these breathtaking joys.

And doesn't that seemingly insatiable hunger point to the probable existence of something or someone that could very well bring about ecstasy unending? So, don't knock sex as a tease that deceives; stop idolizing sex as if it were something divine. Sex can never be the end-all and be-all of human existence. Rather, see sex as a foretaste, an apéritif. It's doing all it can in pointing beyond itself to bliss unbounded and ineffable. Yes, let's passionately seek utter joy. The only tragedy would be to seek it—and to keep on seeking it—where it can't possibly be found.

# INTERLUDE:
## 45 WAYS TO BE CHASTE
### (THOUGH 10 MAY BE ENOUGH)

C HASTITY PRESUPPOSES a decision to reserve sex for intimacy or reproduction—and only within marriage. The challenge to be chaste differs somewhat between men and women. Men get quickly aroused in an unmistakably physical fashion; women less so on both counts, unless hooked on masturbation. Most women's fantasizing is more globally romantic; men's almost exclusively erotic. Day-dreaming, panting over heart-throb novels, or drooling over fashion photography usually triggers her undoing; unbridled looking or just slipping into a sensual mood often undoes him. How women dress greatly affects men; what men whisper greatly affects women. Of the following tips some are aimed more at men, others at women; some have to be recast to be relevant to relations with one's spouse, though there are eleven just for married folks. In any case it's good for all parties to know what challenges others face.

Child and family psychiatrist James Egan stresses that parents must be very direct, unambiguous, and unapologetic to their children about remaining virgins till the day they marry. This is of enormous help to young adults, who often need just such reinforcement to do what they suspect may be the right thing. This can even be couched in terms of not following the Gadarene swine over the cliff. One empirical finding that usually grabs the youthful attention: there is a direct correlation between the incidence of divorce and the number of premarital partners. Expect to find one divorce for every two or three bedmates.

Another argument for the parental quiver: no chastity before marriage, no chastity (or fidelity) afterwards. How on earth can tying the knot at thirty years of age transform sexual veterans of fifteen years' wanton standing into model husbands and wives? "Such expectations strain even the most gullible credulity," adds Egan.

These tips presuppose a commitment to be chaste and only make sense when oriented to that goal. To achieve it, we all need not live every one these recommendations—only enough for each of us quite distinct individuals to attain and harness sexual self-dominion in the cause of self-giving, marital or otherwise. Though abiding by "ten" may be enough, we can hardly expect to reach minimal chastity by going in directions opposed to the remaining suggestions we choose not to adopt.

The effort to be sexually self-possessed should be neither an exclusive nor obsessive endeavor. By far the best context is to be cultivating the four cardinal virtues and consistently practicing the loving self-giving they make possible. If we live in accord with the way we're built and oriented, chastity often recedes into the background, duly occupying the fourth or fifth place in our ethical exertions.

The first twenty-five suggestions, perhaps weighted somewhat in the man's direction, have been arranged in ascending order of importance and also in categories that link tips to specific failings. Thus readers can more easily know which pitfall they are avoiding and why.

IDLENESS (the failure to avail oneself fully of time, talents, and chances to do good):

1.  Read yourself to sleep with something light and unprovocative.

2.  Go to bed physically tired. Keep busy; work hard; husband time; crowd out day-dreaming. Here as in so many other areas

the best defense is a good offense: being about our business, pursuing a star worth hitching our wagon to.

3. Multiply voluntary manifestations of affection and kindness, especially when absent sexual attraction: roommates, friends, family, even non-friends. Acquitting ourselves of the debts of friendship and fraternity predisposes to chastity.

4. Flee self-pity; replace with deliberate favor-doing or intensified study or work.

CURIOSITY (excessive, provocative interest in others, especially their bodies):

5. Skip lingerie ads.

6. Remove glasses outdoors except when driving or playing softball. Since the eyes are portals for so much that later comes back to haunt us, discipline them by abstaining from looking at whatever attracts the gaze.

7. Race over racy passages in novels, even by respectable authors. Similarly, close or avert eyes during steamy scenes on TV, in movies. Likewise skim or skip lurid descriptions of sex crimes.

8. Don't scrutinize and calibrate the opposite sex.

COMFORT (the negative desire to evade pain and effort):

9. To lessen jostling and possible arousal, even involuntary, men might find it better to wear briefs (as opposed to boxer shorts), even under pajamas.

10. Men: if you're hard on yourself, you'll keep it soft—and vice versa.

11. Don't under- or oversleep. In bed, lie on your side instead of your stomach. Bolt from the bed once awake or awakened.

SENSUALITY (the positive desire to feel warm and fuzzy):

12. Touch yourself only for hygienic purposes—and then minimally. Don't over-towel yourself following shower. Study not one's privy parts. Leave the tape measure with the sewing kit and the yardstick in the tool room. Leave comparative anatomy to doctors.

13. Frequent family beaches—or take up spelunking or beekeeping.

14. Correlate lust with alcohol intake. Eat a bit less than what you "need," not giving your body all it asks for.

15. Modesty and dispatch in the locker room. Neither walk around in the buff at home.

16. Men: at the first hint of arousal jump from bed, turn on light, run around the block, raid the refrigerator, call somebody (even if just the weatherman), get distracted with something, even dig your fingernails into your palm to displace the pleasure obsession . . . and that as often as necessary. The same medicine works in the event of pesky memories, skin flick recollections, fantasizing. . . . If you begin to struggle only after the body swings into action, you're pretty much a goner. You must begin earlier, on the periphery, with little things.

17. Men (and some women?): appeal to date's maternal instinct and plead your weakness: get her to promise to slap you when your hands get out of hand. Minimize or, better, cut short any intra-date activity pointing to passion unstoppable.

VANITY (excessive interest in our body or appearance):

18. Stop admiring physique in mirror.

19. Stop drooling over red Porsches or Miatas.

20. With opposite sex in general, stop compulsive flirting; if anything, seem a bit severe, uninterested, unavailable.

PRIDE (the presumptuous belief that we are immune from temptation; that we can get away with sexual self-indulgence with no harm to ourselves or others; that we can do as we wish, answering to nobody or nothing, and still be happy):

21. Stop telling yourself: "I can take this . . . no problem with this adult . . . I'm no longer an impressionable teen." Decades later, most men can still call up at will obscene images ingested during adolescence in such lurid and complete details that you'd think the whole pornographic binge took place yesterday.

22. The more you distrust yourself, the less you'll be ambushed by instinct. Don't be so stupidly brave as to dialogue with, or declare one's immunity to, awakening instinct. Flee: the sooner the better. As time goes on, your early warning system will grow more sensitive to what occasions the arousal that's practically impossible to turn down.

23. Yet, the ongoing effort to be chaste and continent should not be the primary or certainly the only front of our moral struggles. When things are going well in more important areas, chastity becomes easier. More important are seeking truth, enterprising benevolence, duties, friendship. . . . When we acquire a taste for greater joys, we reach relative dominion over sex.

24. Don't go to bed worrying whether you'll revert to old ways; that's the sticky fear that issues in needless relapses and complications.

25. If despite precautions you succumb, begin all over again, pinpointing what went wrong—and what to avoid in future,

and when to start avoiding it. Above all, try to ascertain your heart's status. Most, if not all, of our unchastity is of the weakness variety; weakness that is coterminous with the human condition till death do us part. But fragility is no license to remain unchaste, but a call for whatever steps lie within reach (or at least the desire to do so).

NOW SOME TIPS applicable mostly to women (that men should be familiar with):

26. Dress as well and elegantly as you can, but no less modestly. The more you display, the more you cheapen yourself and incite the male sex drive—with its untoward effects. So avoid clinging, translucent, scanty apparel.

27. Keep your balance and sense of humor over exaggerated fears of losing out in the matrimonial rat race. Stop comparing notes with, and keeping scorecards on, your friends and acquaintances. Despite appearances, when it comes to settling down, good matrimonial prospects prefer character over curvature.

28. Beware of spending too much time or money on cosmetics and primping.

29. Unless you prove a good conversationalist (the opposite of a compulsive chatterer) on dates, his actions will undoubtedly speak louder than your words.

30. Don't be so insecure and gullible: men, especially when aroused, will say and promise you anything and everything to get what they can't help but want.

31. Pull the plug once and for all on reading all those trashy romances. Only a Supreme Being, if he, could satisfy such hungers for romancing and wooing.

32. No soap operas, not even on prime time. They're worse for you than his *Playboy* or *Penthouse*.

33. The cuddling or nuzzling that's only wholesome affection for you will likely ignite his instinct.

34. Fall not for unruly men who trigger or objectively need your maternal instinct.

FINALLY, here are some tips for married couples:

35. Engage your spouse in good conversation, often, naturally and confidentially (this is an antidote to the blasé assumption that couples who share moral principles have little problem communicating with one another).

36. At least verbally, tell your spouse every day that you're very happy to have him or her to love for the rest of your days.

37. Especially when one's spouse is absent, the husband must curb his eyes with other women, limiting himself to seeing, rather than looking at, them. The wife, on the other hand, must rein in her romantic imagination as often as necessary with the men she encounters. Neither should get chummier with members of the other sex than they would normally be with colleagues and friends of the same sex; in fact, they should be more reserved and somewhat distant, telegraphing unavailability.

38. Reject right then and there even the slightest thought that you shouldn't have married one another. If, moreover, you entertain thoughts of infidelity, right away plan and start implementing affectionate deeds for your spouse. (In some cases, if the chemistry is right, the only way to rid oneself of the residue from near infidelity is to share it with one's spouse, pleading both weakness and the need for understanding and more love.)

**39.** Mix socially with principled, like-minded couples. On the other hand, personally abstain from (and likewise help your spouse by competing against) the wiles of popular culture.

**40.** Wives should not physically convey sexual availability to their husbands by various states of undress, when in fact they're not particularly ready, willing, and able.

**41.** In business social conversations, especially during travels, refer often to your spouse and children by sharing light, positive anecdotes, while maintaining appropriate discretion. (Here's how one man, while traveling abroad on business, handled an importunate female associate: "When I got married, I gave to my wife the right to my body, or at least to my sexual capacity. So, here's her telephone number. Ask her if she'll temporarily waive that right. And I'll abide by your joint decision.")

**42.** Have a good, playful, fairly frequent sex life, overcoming tiredness and other logistical hardships, for the other's sake. This is especially important for the husband, lest he begin to stray. Of course if the husband abounds in displays of physical affection and considerateness and intimacy other than intercourse, his wife will be much more inclined and find intercourse more pleasurable.

**43.** It would be good for the hubby to invest in a portable razor, so that while driving home he can divest himself of his five o'clock shadow before crossing the threshold. If at all possible, he shouldn't downdress to be more comfortable until after dinner.

**44.** An even more crucial investment for him is to see that his wife is both well-dressed and well-coiffed. Here's one area where he can justifiably splurge.

**45.** Spouses working outside the home, especially men, must repeatedly fight tooth and nail against the insidious temptation to be or even to seem too busy for the other spouse and children. Maintaining the proper balance between family and work involves candidly inviting your partner's suggestions, help, and mercy.

## PRIVATIZATION?

These days privatization is in the air, practically everywhere. Well then, how about privatizing again what we used to call our privy parts, though maybe for better and more articulated reasons? The recommendation does not stem from prudery. Rather it arises from the corrosive toll exacted by all that hyperstimulated and rampant prurience infecting the human race. Ask Madison Avenue, the producers and purveyors of popular culture, or even the bikini-clad whether partial and even complete nudity sells. It does, for the simple reason that it grabs the attention (largely male), excites, and leaves the consumer panting for more. Here we're not talking about peep shows, topless bars, or pornography. Most of us agree their sole purpose, since they undermine self-dominion, directly contradicts both individual and social well-being. No, let's focus on just the so-called "innocent" unveilings, which may not be so harmless as once thought.

If you teach at a junior or senior high school, according to the *Wall Street Journal*, you may have noticed the latest trend among teens and even hormonally precocious pre-teens. They smell, especially after physical education, even those not worshiping at the altar of "grunge." The reason is simple: no showers, particularly among boys. Why so? Maybe they abhor being the object of homosexual lust (though how could they ever say so?). Or maybe they find the whole locker room scene of braggadocio and steamy, undraped bodies, even their own, to be sexually provocative, making chastity all the harder.

Whether or not this same-sex nudity affects heterosexuals personally, it can be—and most likely is—provocative for those who, while homosexually inclined, are struggling to abstain sexually.

Why add unthinkingly to their already considerable troubles? Can't towels serve more than one purpose?

Likewise, if you're a psychiatrist or psychologist dealing with homosexuals, you soon discover that a contributing factor can be a sexual inferiority complex. Into this can easily fall young men of uncertain sexual orientation or those with late-developing or smallish sexual endowments, primary or secondary. While dressing and undressing, both boys and girls impulsively tend to gawk. Invidious comparisons, especially when verbalized, are often enough to sow doubts as to the late-bloomer's heterosexuality.

Yet a third related caveat: young children of either sex accompanying mom or dad into the latter's locker room at health clubs, YMCA/YWCAs, neighborhood pools, and so on. Even the permissive *Washington Post* was left shaking its head. Recently wrote its Phil McCombs: "I'm undressing. Now I'm naked. Nearby are several little girls. A few are as old as 6, going on 7. Some are naked too. There are little boys around, and older boys. A few of them are naked, fully or partially. There are also other men around, and—you guessed it!—they are big and hairy and naked." This set McCombs to worrying about the exposed children's physical, mental, emotional, and spiritual well-being. Real are the dangers of molestation (which may only take thirty to ninety seconds), pedophilia and premature "hyperarousal" (which often masquerades as a "learning disability") during what is supposed to be their "latency" period. He also found out that most child psychologists frown on younger kids' exposure to nudity, even at home.

Let's not be presumptuous or naive in this matter of curbing, when not eliminating, sexual stimuli for all ages. We get into trouble by unthinkingly toying with, or creating, temptation for either ourselves or others. We don't see the harm, because the incitement to lust is often a delayed reaction. But then, ironically, we dub chastity impossible. . . .

These are ways to keep sexual passion at bay. They and any others are tactics, means, that only make sense when one's sold on the goal of limiting sex to marital expressions of other-love. You can scoff at them if you like, but if you're to convert the sow's ear of sexual instinct into the silk purse of genuine love, you must do something. You cannot remain supine. See chastity as the best insurance policy against the siren songs and seductive scents of bogus blisses. Sexual self-mastery resembles nothing so much as the regimen and training that lift raw athletic talent to the level of expertise and artistry. The secret is to filter out sexual stimuli, lest our despotic drive be incited, precluding the ability to act humanly, reasonably and freely. When that's not done, I would almost have to agree with those who claim they'd go crazy without sex (though they'll probably go no less crazy with just sex). But one can, with adroitness and wariness, put out the sparks one by one. It also helps, immeasurably, to be oriented toward higher, more selfless goals whose rewards are already being savored.

# 9

# Fending off Fears

To see what is right and not to do it is want of courage.
— Confucius, *Analects*, *circa* 590 B.C.

Fear of danger is ten thousand times more terrifying
than danger itself.
— Daniel Defoe, *Robinson Crusoe*, 1719

Life is difficult.  This is a great truth, one of the greatest truths.
It is a great truth because once we truly know
that life is difficult—once we truly understand and accept it—
then life is no longer difficult.  Because once it is accepted,
the fact that life is difficult no longer matters.
— M. Scott Peck, *The Road Less Traveled*, 1978

OUR INSTINCTS SET US UP to shy away from harmful things.  Fears are barriers cautioning us against putting our life or health at risk.  With animals these reflexive repulsions work almost infallibly.  It's only with humans that things can go awry and usually do.  Our venal mind, especially our wanton imagination, at the promptings of an immature, bossy will, tends to blow prospective pains out of proportion. Driven by our overriding appetite for happiness, we tend to exaggerate the drawbacks of any course of action.

Many of us tend to minimize little cowardices and anxieties. With a shrug we mutter, "We're only human, right? At least we're not traitors or pathological quitters. Besides, aren't most failures to be strong-minded or strong-willed quite puny and, so, unimportant, even forgivable?" Yes, but tiny cowardices soon add up to major capitulations. Conversely, the fewer pleasures we "need," the more moderate, that is, we are, the fewer fears that they may disappear will haunt us.

How our imagination works in the face of dangers can be seen in an example. Put a ten-foot plank on the ground and enlist a passer-by to walk its length without falling off. He does so with ease and aplomb. Up the ante by securely fastening its two ends to seven-foot stands and ask your volunteer to repeat the test. He manages the challenge, yes, but barely: he breaks out in a sweat while traversing it more unsteadily. How so? He has just as much room to walk on as in the first test. But his imagination now pictures the risk of falling seven feet to the ground. Then, a third test. Secure your plank across a thousand-foot chasm and invite him to cross it. Not him; he might fall! Try as you might to persuade him, even with a big wad of bills, he refuses totally. Now, let a raving lunatic brandishing a knife jump out from behind a boulder and rush at you. There is but one escape. Almost without thinking, you both race for your lives across the plank and pull it up after you. Whence the courage to accomplish what a moment before seemed utterly "impossible"? His imagination again worked the moment he realized an even greater danger threatened.

Yes, let's not exaggerate fears to the point of paralysis. But the story also points out that crippling fears can be overcome by even greater fears. To budge us off dead center, we might try picturing to ourselves, engaging the imagination, the long-term threats and hardships ensuing from our current surrendering to minor dangers. Would that we could represent to ourselves, while making our own, the final, disgusting "picture of Dorian Gray." Here's another task for our quiet time.

## COWARDS MULTIPLY TROUBLES

We traditionally call fortitude the virtue which detects and deflates these pains and fears. But when we don't exercise this reasonable self-mastery, everything gets bent out of shape. Thus the effort to eradicate whatever is unpleasant in life brings in its wake three worse liabilities. First, we find ourselves less and less capable of expending energy in even the most worthwhile projects and ventures, such as our careers, or of making the kind of durable commitments that alone can make friendship and marriage not only survive but thrive as well. We lower our sights more and more to conform to a languid disposition. As a result, we become blind to most of life's bigger, better things, all requiring effort.

Second, we easily capsize emotionally and psychologically in the face of major, unavoidable suffering or tragedy. How? By dint of having unreasonably run away from facing minor pains and fears, while unthinkingly allowing wants and whims to be turned into non-negotiable needs, we can become cowed pushovers. But worse than our shrinking morally is the confining self-lying behind it. By falling for the illusion of exaggerated hardship, we end up fabricating baseless fears. When we don't confront and accept the exertions we *can* put forth, practically every exertion comes across as little less than torture.

Third, as Shakespeare says in *Julius Caesar*, "Cowards die many times before their deaths; the valiant never taste of death but once." Just as whoever most directly and single-mindedly pursues pleasures finds they most slip through one's fingers like eels, so too whoever most tries to elude suffering, paradoxically, suffers much more— and uselessly besides. Most human "disasters" are at best exaggerated annoyances, when not figments of an uncurbed and overwrought imagination. Such a mental landscape can ever more readily resemble pandemonium (in the original sense of "infested with demons"). The more things we cannot do without, the more threatened fiefdoms we must anxiously protect. We thus indulge in a fake fear-generating process that can issue in paranoia. Indeed, most mental disorders are fears run amok.

Closer to home and more universally, in this business of self-discipline we get pushed around by many masked failings and fears, however reluctant we are to expose them. Cowardice goes by many aliases: impatience, flightiness, superficiality, inconstancy, mental and physical laziness, inattention, procrastination, dilettantism, self-pity, softness, fearfulness, spinelessness, timidity, defeatism, irresolution, pusillanimity. . . . The problem isn't with our self-preserving instinct's sending out an indiscriminate warning signal. The exaggeration comes, not from our animal side, but from our supposedly reasonable nature: our overactive imagination, our too inactive mind, and our overeager craving for happiness. Like the paranoid or hypochondriac, we distort mere inconveniences into mortal threats. When we insufficiently test possible exertions against the touchstone of experience, we become not only unrealistic, but in effect unwitting masochists as well. This failure to ponder sufficiently both ends and means weakens our commitment to both. Much of our fickleness stems from not selling ourselves time and again on the arduous good we originally aimed at. Without these re-commitments, any goal's attractiveness wanes over time. Our mind is supposed to be our greatest friend and guide, but how can it be, if we don't take the trouble to use it? A weak, soft person is not only cowardly, but impractical to boot.

## UNMASKING FEARS

Our analysis of fear and cowardice points in the right direction. Reflection and thinking should make us more courageous and patient, by making molehills out of mentally magnified mountains. No less valuable is an enterprising, generous, devil-may-care attitude eager to embrace hardships small and large, especially the former. Here experience can be a most valuable teacher. Here also the best defense is a good offense. You see, before actually experiencing a new hardship, we're likely to overestimate the toll it will exact. Such inexperience leads to overcautiousness. Consequently, the more fears we unmask and reduce to their proper dimensions, the freer and more objective we'll be. Yes, let's look before we leap. But when untested challenges come along, it's also good for us to leap first, lest we not know what to look for. Theoretically, for instance, we know that skipping lunch won't kill us, but when actually abstaining we're still plagued by fears or doubts. Now these misgivings only disappear when we've compiled a track record of lunches skipped with no harm done (except to our girth). We'd keep many crippling fears at bay if we were to commit ourselves to a deliberate program of welcoming at least some hardships.

That seems to be the tacit purpose behind a number of "growth" institutions. Practically everybody praises the character-building to be had from such more directly body-building activities as sports and athletics. Both moral and physical stamina can be had from such things as scouting and Outward Bound. The same two purposes were obviously served formerly by rites of passage. Many is the man (even woman?) who signs up for the armed services as a "cure" for a lack of self-discipline. Is that why many men claim that their stints in uniform, even during warfare, were the greatest years of their lives? Then, for junior offenders the idea is catching on of modeling their incarceration on boot camp. Almost all serious religious induction programs, regardless of the particular creed, prescribe a minimum of deliberate, ascetical exposure to pain, for spiritual and intellectual gains.

## HONEST ABE NO QUITTER

Tell Abraham Lincoln that success in life can be had with but a snap of the fingers. He was nine when his mother died; sixteen, when his best friend went insane; nineteen when Sarah, his beloved sister, died; in his mid-twenties, when Anne Rutledge, his fiancée, died. At his first run in 1831 for a seat in the Illinois legislature, Abe was defeated. In 1834 he won a seat. In 1843 his try for the U.S. Congress failed. Three years later he was victorious. In 1848 his re-election bid ended in defeat. In 1850 his second son died. In 1855 and 1858, he failed to win a U.S. Senate seat. In 1856 he ran unsuccessfully to be his party's candidate for U.S. vice president. His perseverance gave the country its sixteenth president. For a more contemporary figure, take Martin Luther King Jr. Thanks to his vision, patient leadership and moral strength, racial minorities have achieved a greater degree of equal opportunity in American society than they ever had before.

Ideally, pleasure or pain should not be the reason for either doing or skipping a particular deed. Such incentives and rewards or warnings are attention-getters that should be subservient to the thought process of discovering objective goods and adhering to their pursuit. Only by subjectively making objective duties our own do we grow in virtuous self-ownership, emancipating ourselves from the pulls and tugs of instinct. The result is the freedom to act humanly, as increasingly reality-conforming animals. The acquired habits of courage and endurance (the two faces of active and passive fortitude) don't make up the highest of the cardinal virtues or the most essential quality to our ratifying human nature, but they come close. And the softer life becomes, the more we need courage. See this hardiness (or even manliness, rightly understood) as the protecting bodyguard for pursuing our ultimate end. Without it, it's nearly impossible for us to aim at any arduous and long-term goal. Only thereby do we shed our cry-baby, hysterical, and immature reactions to necessary effort and difficulty. Only thus can we authentically size up the sober side of reality and chart adequate efforts and plans.

How far from utopian vegetating are the thrilling, sweaty, all-out exertions of the game and chase! Such exhilarations reveal our nature's secret craving for activities that don't instrumentally lead to anything else; play, in other words. Exhaustion is not our bane; indolence is. We revel in activities that aren't steps but end, in and of themselves. That may well be another clue to what awaits us, when and if we do find something worth at least living for.

## Guts-Building

There are three secrets to growing in courage, patience, and perseverance—the stuff of fortitude. The first is to generate and sustain a healthy state of positive tension, which prevents fears from getting a toehold in our psyche. It's the disposition we call "beginning the day on the right foot" and trying to stay "on our toes" for the remainder. It's decidedly *not* the nervous, steeled resolve to virtue which cannot possibly be maintained even over the medium term. But it does involve turning a deaf ear to self-pity, preferably by getting happily involved in doing something absorbingly beautiful and beneficial.

The second is to do so with and amid the manageable trifles of each day: all those things and details we otherwise tend to slight, sparing ourselves in the process. Let's try to be consistently brave and persistent in meeting these relatively slight challenges. It does little or no good to override our fears on some, perhaps dramatic, occasions, if we alternate such self-discipline with thoughtless softness and self-pampering. The challenge is to build up over time a good habit (some have likened virtue to a "groove" in our nature) by continually exerting ourselves. We grow in our ability to conquer major fears by deflecting and even ignoring minor ones.

The third short-cut to quieting exaggerated fears is to expose oneself deliberately, on a daily basis, to three or four bits of pain. When we thus meet self-administered pain head-on, we rediscover that the suffering is not so bad, nor are we such weaklings after all. Otherwise, given our ever more comfortable settings, we can unwittingly fall victim to objectively baseless, though subjectively heightened fears. This discipline is far from masochism; rather it's all about realism. We thus whittle down corporeal or emotional threats to their proper dimensions, so that we're free to accept or decline them, as the case might be. This pain-shrinking discipline, for example, could take the form of a less than "just right" shower, taking the stairs at work instead of the elevator (or not resting against its walls), some vigorous calisthenics, walking in the shade in winter and in the sun in summer, a demanding posture for an hour or two, choosing the least comfortable chair, and so on. When there are enough of these self-denials, we find it that much easier to do everything else in a self-demanding fashion; then self-denial goes from being a noun to an adverb, thus enriching while facilitating all our undertakings.

What follows are some more ways to reinforce both our will and commitments:

1. Unearth, confront, admit, and catalog your cowardices. How and where does softening the blow hinder your pursuit of goals? Are you, for instance, as professionally ambitious as you ought to be? Married men should ask themselves whether by not exerting themselves enough they've made it necessary for their wives, contrary perhaps to their wishes and inclinations, to work outside the home. Are you obsessed with security and financial worries?

2. Face and cut any attachments to inflated "necessities." Be especially honest in spotting any non-negotiable "idols" that lead you astray. Are there mere things you simply can't do without?

3.  Also own up to commitments and promises you're currently welshing on. Are you afraid of rocking the boat at work, at home, with buddies? How much of your behavior is dictated by the fear of rejection? Do you overly fret over how others react to you? If so, buy one of those posters that reads: "You wouldn't worry so much about what others think of you if you realized how little they do."

4.  Come up with a list of four or five ways to practice guts-building self-denial. Keep track of both hits and misses.

Now, let's get more practical and incisive.

5.  Cut down on your news intake from the newspaper and TV; fifteen daily minutes should be enough.

6.  How about fasting for a day, cutting back for a week, a month? If a smoker, do you ration cigarettes? Every meal should entail at least one instance of self-denial: skipping sugar or butter, delaying water, eating more of what you don't like (or less of what you do).

7.  How about skipping all snacks between meals?

8.  Have you ever tried to forgo TV for a weekend? a month? a year?

9.  Why not drop hard liquor altogether, limiting yourself to beer and wine, both in moderation of course? In any case, each of us needs to fix a numerical limit beyond which we don't go in our quaffing.

10. Delay the AC or heater in the car; if not the whole body, wash at least your hands in cold water.

11. Exercise restraint in listening to the radio and music, even when commuting, especially when others are in the vehicle.

# 10

# WHY STUDY?

Each man has his own vocation. The talent is the call.
— Ralph Waldo Emerson, *Essays*, 1841

A little learning is a dangerous thing.
— Alexander Pope, *An Essay on Criticism*, 1711

Intellectual passion drives out sensuality.
— Leonardo da Vinci, *The Notebooks*, 1490-95

FOR MOST OF US most of the time our studies seem like one big necessary evil. Here we examine study in its dimension as work and, more particularly, its contribution to our moral growth, especially in fortitude. That's why whoever is no longer a student but engaged in professional work can and should substitute "work" every time the word "study" comes up.

Ideally, through our studies, each of us discovers and develops talents and dispositions that add up to our very personal and possibly unique calling in life, plus a whole world of truth, beauty, and goodness intimately allied to our ultimate goal in life. The former discoveries make it possible for us to commit ourselves lovingly to our very mission in the workplace and to find therein creative energies and vistas that redound to our own and others' benefit. However necessary and commendable these fruits of study and work, they do not occupy us here. In this and the following chapter, we're interested, rather, in uncovering and developing the moral qualities and personal rewards of diligently applying ourselves to all the tasks, chores, duties, and toils entailed in being, first, a student and, later, a professional. The question addressed here is: How does studying and working hard and well promote at least my enlightened self-interest?

Why study? Why is it necessary? To get good grades in order to get into a good college, in order to advance to graduate school, in order to set ourselves up for a successful career, in order to make lots of money in order to land a good spouse and raise a modest family; maybe even to learn some things. . . . Study thus adds up to a basic link in the chain of the relatively unexamined life, a necessary step and means, maybe even an intermediate end. But it's not the final end or purpose, not what's to fulfill us, not something to live for. No, not even for the nerds and geeks and workaholics. For them, work and study only seem to be their consuming passion, but are really little more than escape mechanisms. By submerging themselves obsessively in their studies or deals or tasks, they shut out much more intractable problems of a personal, familial, and social nature by indulging in what we might call an achievement narcotic.

Much closer to the ideal missing in our lives is the passionate dedication of, say, artists who eat, sleep, drink, breathe for their elusive masterpiece. Most of us find ourselves somewhere in between.

We've unmasked some bogus pleasures and some exaggerated fears by confronting them and curbing our imagination. We've acquired a certain readiness to defer gratifications in pursuit of higher objectives. Willy-nilly, we've acquired a certain self-discipline and self-dominion in meeting some of the demands and requirements of our studies. We've even basked now and then in the higher pleasure of superior achievements wrought by working hard and well.

Yet we still see studies and work as an unavoidable discipline or program to be imposed on ourselves, though somewhat against our inclinations. Studies remain something alien and imperfectly digested that impinges on our fulfillment, on what we confusedly think is our final aim in life. If we didn't have to study, we probably wouldn't or at least not at the present tempo and intensity.

## WHY WE STINT

Why do we see study as a necessary evil? It crimps our style, loves, whims. Studying is hard, unpleasant, exacting, and tedious. How can we love toil? Studies sit athwart our pleasure-seeking, softness, laziness, selfishness, wanton freedom, unthinkingness. The demands and requirements of excellence in studies and work tend to generate lots of self-pity, amid clenched fists and gritted teeth. And that accumulated self-pity can eventually erupt in wild pleasure-grabbing. The situation is not dissimilar to those who go on a severe diet and who actually lose, say, thirty pounds. Yet they can't keep it off. So much so, that within a year, experts so tell us, nineteen out of twenty have regained at least the pounds lost, if not still more.

And because studies represent an onerous, foreign body getting in our way, we therefore hold back, cut corners, act defensively, lighten the load. We don't interiorize our studies, making them our own—something we really want, however trying. More particularly, we waste class-time, only paying half attention. The same divided interest invades our homework. Our mind all too often wanders to what we think we really want or love. Actually we don't understand the need and purpose of labor; consequently we're not free to choose it as a good. We thus deny ourselves the satisfactions and joys that come from achievement, mastery, and dominion. We don't get inside our subjects or endeavors enough for them, in turn, to get inside us, motivating us to ever higher Everests of achievement and success. The result is a split personality: half wanting, half not wanting.

## BOTH END AND MEANS?

But, besides being a necessary means for ulterior purposes, can study or work be something more, even an all-consuming end? If so, we may well find ourselves on the threshold of a discovery that could prove to be enormously beneficial. Can effort and toil be converted from something negative we must reluctantly but maturely shoulder and tolerate into something we might well live for, handsomely rewarded with a superior, if not supreme, happiness all the while? The toil we defensively shy away from may be an inestimable treasure well worth sacrificing for. Our voluntarily, freely embracing all the demands of our studies, not holding anything back, may make of us the "aristocrats of love" that in our heart of hearts we secretly yearn to be.

It isn't a question of more and harder classes, homework, assignments, duties. Chances are nothing need change in what you're currently doing. What's needed is a change—a 180-degree revolution—in heart or motivation. Such a new motive should lead you to work smarter, more intensely, more productively, more wisely, more excellently, and much more fulfillingly. In other words: since you have to study anyway, why not make the most of it, capitalizing and exploiting it for everything it can possibly yield, even an authentic bliss which need never fade? It may call for more intensity and single-mindedness, more commitment and stubbornness, more patience and perseverance, higher goals and greater expectations and hopes, but won't they all prove more than worth while, if in so doing you're left as happy as can be?

When we seriously commit ourselves to study as perfectly as we possibly can (setting high goals and planning practical steps and means), our subsequent efforts can be a great source of self-knowledge, the first ingredient of genuine self-improvement. And none too soon. For we hem and haw, we backslide, we're terribly fickle and inconstant; we're so superficial and soft. We cheat and then try to rationalize it. So divided is our mind and heart that we might, just might, wring twenty-seven minutes out of every hour. "Good enough"; "just enough to get by"; so run our mantras. This self-knowledge business should get us to face all the unpleasant and embarrassing personal shortcomings and self-fed lies revealed by a plan and reflection on our wavering efforts to live it. But when we do our best for all the right reasons we're rewarded with a higher, more lasting gratification in exchange for feeding our being what it craves.

## WANTED: BRAVE STUDENTS

Moreover, studying well can be a great, and possibly the best, source of virtuous self-ownership. It can make real, full persons out of us. Such industriousness, moreover, can cure practically everything that ails us: our laziness, softness, shallowness, ignorance, self-centeredness, critical-carping spirit, pride, unfairness, petty addictions, compulsions, boredom. All-out diligence is the gym where we can acquire by practice, little by little, all the virtues that will, finally, ensconce us in the driver's seat. It will likewise emancipate us from the downward-tending crowd, from our nagging appetites and instincts.

We'll acquire the stamina and grit, guts, to aim high, no matter what the cost or duration of the efforts. We'll come more readily to give others what is due them, recognizing their legitimate and objective claims to our attention, if not honor and love. Our exaggerated and self-defeating self-centeredness will also shrink. And, finally, we'll grow in practical wisdom, learning from our deeds and thinking them out beforehand; we'll become much more adept at wisely juggling means and ends. All this deliberate and voluntarily chosen virtue-making will increasingly unify and integrate ourselves. Then we'll no longer be pushover sissies in the face of the imperious demands of our body. Besides freer, we'll become more honest, especially with ourselves, unmasking our almost incessant self-deceptions and self-excusings. We'll become more objective, open-minded, knowledgeable, wiser.

We're talking about truth and virtue therapy; sure it hurts a bit for a time, but it works. As we submit ourselves to this cure, we come to see its need and purpose; we sell ourselves on it. We see that it's good for us, and consequently it's something we want and need and thus impose the more freely and knowingly on ourselves. We discover that work works, if we truly work at it. We thereby fortify and develop our character and nature. And here, as elsewhere, nothing succeeds like success. As we come progressively to taste the benefits of this self-completion, we boldly and assuredly make our own the superior kingdom of enlightened self-interest. We become self-motivated, increasingly sold on the rewards of this so-called "immanent" self-enrichment.

But still the combined self-knowledge and self-ownership that we glean from industrious, diligent application to studies do not yet spell utter fulfillment, only a necessary and indispensable step and condition thereto. They make it possible for us to attain to the third moral stage of super-enlightened self-interest. We labor to know and own ourselves, so that ultimately we are enabled freely to give of ourselves to others, the only way to genuine self-ful-fillment.

Can study or work actually be made into the free, disinterested, no-strings-attached self-giving that defines true love? It can be, if we're willing to pay the price, to sacrifice ourselves for this su-preme good. But we must throw ourselves totally into what we're doing, aiming for nothing less than excellence. We thus crowd out self-pity, in effect killing the very things holding us back. Let's study hard and well to improve ourselves as much as possible, but not only for ourselves, above all for others.

We are thus able to put our knowledge, savvy, competence and insights at the service of others, those closest to us first, but ever farther afield. We can then serve, lead, help, solve intractable problems in the workplace and public square. In doing so, we're also teaching others, if they wish to know, how we humans are built and how we're to live. They'll be able to observe that we lead a very demanding life, but somehow, mysteriously, intriguingly, doing so doesn't get us down. On the contrary, it fulfills us: we're the happiest people around.

## LABORS OF LOVE?

Being and doing the best for others' sake, while truly serving them, is a real, absorbing labor of love, even when others misread us. For us, love's labors are never lost. Whether or not we actually benefit others, we always benefit ourselves by genuinely giving ourselves. We'll find it easier to understand others. We'll raise the fine art of friendship and loyalty and favors to new heights.

Now this self-sacrificing and self-forgetting way of life is the very opposite of usual notions of fulfillment and happiness. But contrary to all the world's maxims, it does work, handsomely so. Do it, and you'll see. But not only you. Show others an infectious good example of true mirth and gladness. Eventually your superior and durable happiness will work its charm and melt the resistance of others. Since their strongest appetite is to be happy, if your formula delivers more than theirs, eventually they'll beat a path to your door to get yours.

Now if we so diligently toil, our studies, while remaining means to various ends, also fully become an end, an embodiment of our love for others (which coincides with authentic self-love). For when we gladly, unreservedly, give ourselves via studies and work, in fact it becomes play, something we do for itself, with no ulterior motives. Thus, as in any sport, we can play our hearts out. Study can become a totally consuming game for us, crowding out all defensiveness. But we'll never discover that this is the way to live if we hold back, if we indulge in a martyr's mentality or victim's complex.

## STEP BY STEP

As said earlier, it's not a question of adding or changing anything in your routine as a student. What you do should remain the same; your change of heart need only affect the why and how of your studies. You'll turn yourself into a leader only gradually by dint of many small, insignificant labors. We must stoop to conquer, progressively refining and improving everything that we do as students. "Divide and conquer," the Romans told us, was the way to win wars; it's also the formula to become an ever better and fuller and happier person. Some practical suggestions follow:

1.  Make and follow a written-out study schedule for the week's seven days: a definite but minimum number of hours with fixed times to start and finish. You may go beyond it, but not fall short.

    If your assignments that day do not exhaust the minimum, spend the rest of the time reviewing or planning and drafting future papers. If you cheat, penalize yourself by adding the missed weekday hours to your weekend quota. Don't forget that a good, strong, punctual start is half the battle.

    Also make sure that yours are good study conditions: quiet, good lighting, at desk or table, in a neat, orderly place, trying to minimize distractions. No television or phone calls or snacking or (for most of us) music. Then chain yourself to a not fully comfortable chair for periods of two full hours or so.

2. Lead off with your hardest, least friendly subject, instead of leaving it till last when you're most tired. Begin each evening's study binge with a list of priorities and what all you're to do; then follow that order, one thing at a time till it's finished; then to the next one and so on.

3. Don't be a dilettante, flitting here and there. Work with intensity, generously acquiring blisters and tiredness.

Work manfully, professionally, as if you were earning one hundred dollars an hour. Squeeze sixty minutes out of every hour and sixty seconds out of every minute. Don't worry about getting exhausted. We should be aiming to end each day squeezed out like a lemon. Your first all-nighter will likely signal that finally you've hoisted your big toe onto the threshold of maturity and responsibility.

4. Exploit classes: be alert and pay attention; intervene; ask questions; let your ignorance show; be pro-active; take good notes; watch your posture, lest you fritter what little attention and stamina you can muster. Get help from professors and smarter classmates; often your smart peers can explain things better, more sympathetically, than teachers.

5. Don't forget that with each new body of knowledge, there's the invariable learning curve.

It's pure grunt work and drudgery, uphill all the way, until you acquire a certain dominion and facility. So, be patient; pay the price, one step in front of the previous, doggedly moving up bit by bit. Pay attention to little things: neatness; double-checking work; proofreading papers. Keep a dictionary handy to look up then and there any unfamiliar words and to jot them down where you can later and repeatedly review them until they're lodged in your word-bank. Never forget that "tomorrow" and "later" are adverbs of the defeated; rather, make your motto "today, now."

It's amazing how much work we can get done on the eve of a vacation. If then, why not so every day?

6. Yet, students shouldn't be masochists. Strive to get seven to eight hours of sleep a night, which means you have to economize much more on the finite chunks *earlier on.*

We all need distractions, preferably somewhat planned: rest and recreation, games, sports, exercise. Make room in your schedule for everything, including social activities and the like, while trying to keep everything in its place. The goal isn't to become a hermit or grind or misanthrope, but someone who's learning to work smarter, more productively, getting more and better work done in less time, if possible. Once we've really made studies our own thing and dedicate ourselves to them with uncluttered mind and heart, we learn so much more. (Once I became acquainted with this vision of things, in my freshman year at college, my grades doubled and my study time was cut in half.) Try to go through three drafts of your papers, with enough time in between so that you can be critical of your previous attempts.

7. Approach your studies as athletes approach their game, sloughing off failures and past negligence.

Don't grow tragic over failures; it takes a heap of repeated failures to clear six feet on the high jump. Those excel who plod through their studies each day with constancy and cheerfulness, fully aware that mastery is the cumulative result of lots of little things. Learn from your mistakes, instead of bemoaning them. Own up to situations that prey on your weaknesses, and resolve in future to skirt them.

8. *For college students:* Once they find themselves on the much less structured college campus, even the best high school students tend to come unstuck, at least temporarily.

There are just too many distractions, good and bad, for these often homesick and emotionally confused young adults. At the very least they waste lots of time in bits and drabs during the day; this obliges them to burn the midnight oil and, consequently, they must function, and that none too well, with too little sleep.

This sorry state sets them up not only for "bingeing" on their seventy-two-hour-long weekends, but also for lots of self-doubts and recriminations. Solution? Here's what I suggested to a Princeton freshman home for the year-end break: "Why not try to get all your studying done before dinner, thus freeing up the evenings for sports, avocations, laundry, correspondence, socializing. . . . ? Like adults in the workaday world, try to work and study diligently from 9 a.m. to 6 p.m., thus professionalizing your day. You'll do better in your studies, you'll crowd out self-pity, you'll be able to acquit yourself of social duties to family and friends off campus; you might just eke out fifteen minutes for that "indispensable quiet time."

Another pitfall collegians, especially entering freshmen, need to eschew is that of excessively worrying about how they're coming across to their peers. Outside the familial nest, where they met with more affirmation and validation, it's understandable that their fear of rejection in their dorms is exaggerated. What was laid out in the preceding paragraph is very relevant to this problem. If they're thinking and studying about only one thing from 9 a.m. to 6 p.m., they'll not only crowd out those debilitating and distracting worries, but also by their solid academic record establish a solid basis for the reputation and respect they hope to earn from others.

## LEAD BY STUDYING WELL AND HARD

9. The pursuit of excellence in studies lends itself to self-giving in an immediate and obvious way.

We can tread in the footsteps of Socrates, Plato, and Aristotle. For them, sharing their knowledge with others in ways that were engaging, unobtrusive, and attractive was a natural overflow of the wisdom they had achieved. When we see others struggling to understand or solve problems that we've already mastered, why not, as discreetly and in as uncondescending a way as possible, offer to show them how? Ideally, each of us from afar should appear very busy and dedicated, but up close as approachable and amiable as possible. Otherwise we slam the door on those who might approach us for help. We might also offer to study together, being very careful that this comes across as something beneficial to both parties: "two see more than one." Now making available to others the fruits of our blood, sweat, and tears in studies is compatible with a healthy rivalry, so long as it doesn't become too competitive and cut-throat.

We don't want to offend others' sensibilities by coming across, even distantly, as a know-it-all. When you're the one asking for help, always keep in mind that your helper is doing you a favor, but also, less obviously, you're doing him a pair of favors. The first is a chance to be generous; the second a chance to master even better what he knows by trying to explain it to you.

10. Finally, we must also call to mind, to keep up the commitment and energy level, the bountiful consequences that will follow immediately and in the long term.

For one, it's making us more human, more friendly, more helpful, more understanding of others' shortcomings and foibles, more likable and approachable, more of a gentle leader of our peers. For another, we're now learning the fundamentals and principles on which, with time and greater knowledge and wisdom, we'll build our own very personal contributions to the good of our profession, community, family, and the like. Through virtuous self-dominion and self-discipline, we'll be able to practice the secret of creativity: alternating total immersion with total disengagement.

Then, this will help us to come up with solutions, both theoretical and practical, to nagging, seemingly insoluble problems and dichotomies, even social and political.

We'll avoid being mini-persons, with cramped, stereotypical minds and hearts. We'll be able to rise above the polarities that distance people both politically and socially. We'll become readers, hooked on great ideas and people and books. We'll open-mindedly keep on growing intellectually and virtuously. We'll become capable of establishing a marriage and family. We'll give off light and strength to our friends, colleagues, relatives, and acquaintances. The power and attractiveness of a fully ratified and "finished" human being can be truly astounding. And all because one day the then girl or boy decided never to say No to the call of academic excellence and personal self-development.

# 11

# WORK WORKS

Man is so made that he can only find relaxation
from one kind of labor by taking up another.
— Anatole France, *The Log*, 1859

The end of labor is to gain leisure.
The aim of education is the wise use of leisure.
— Aristotle, *Nichomachean Ethics*, 340(?) B.C.

M OST OF US WORK ONLY because we have to, for a
variety of reasons. To earn money, of course; to put
food on the table; to buy all those things we need and
others we don't; to allow us to underwrite all those things we're
interested in; to hold up our end of the marriage contract. . . .
Were you or I to win a huge lottery prize, most probably we'd
gladly abandon all this toil and labor business.

As we said in the last chapter, it would be ideal for us all to be
passionately committed to and engaged in our life's work, having
achieved a perfect fit between talents and schooling and our professional calling. But in the absence of that perfect dovetailing

(which, due to a host of oftentimes negative and involuntary circumstances, probably less than a majority actually achieve), we aren't to mope through the rest of our days, as if we missed the boat, as if we can only count on frustrations from here on out. With even the most inhumane and stultifying of jobs (and maybe more easily, for just that reason), we can still virtuously build self-ownership and exercise self-giving. On the other hand, those who achieve a perfect fit between talent and niche—an opera singer, say—can easily (and quite frequently) fall victim to cancerous pride. It's immeasurably better to go through life loving a job we don't like than to like a job so much that it occasions our moral undoing.

Very rare is the person who works just to contribute ideas or beauty or solutions to the common welfare. Somewhat less rare is the person who works largely to find fulfillment therein: some doctors, some teachers, some volunteers, some nurses, many mothers. Yet even among these latter, idealism soon enough peters out. What a pity that we spend most of our time doing mere chores, because there's no getting around them. If adulthood largely consists in realistically agreeing to do what we have to do, no wonder, then, that most adolescents try to prolong their playful irresponsibility as long as they can, sometimes into middle age.

## PENAL SENTENCE?

And if work is just a means to something else, why not try to soften the blow, so long as we don't jeopardize what we most covet in life? Next to talking about the weather, the most common theme of workaday conversations is to grumble about our job. It's all very sad that, despite what we may have read in *Reader's Digest*, our adult days are spent as though working off a penal sentence. Could this also be why many adults smugly display their cynicism and take almost perverse delight in puncturing the dream-filled balloons of any remaining youthful idealists?

Where have all the heroes gone, where the pioneers, where the romantics, where the conquistadors? About the only remaining fan clubs are those of professional sports titans. But even there, isn't it the physical prowess or the wealth of pro athletes that commands admiration? Most of the novels sold today invite escape into a male world of derring-do or its counterpart of bodice-ripping, harlequinesque romances. Anything to help us forget the drab, boring, flat drudgery of what occupies at least half of our waking hours and even some of our nightmares. Is it any wonder that some of those trapped by uninspiring jobs seek all too fleeting release in sex, booze, or drugs? Is this all there is?

Well might we wonder if something hasn't gone haywire. And that wonder is compounded as we witness the rest of the world, lemming-like, aping Americans in our inexorable, homogenized middle-classdom with all its calories, toys, baubles, and gadgets. Sure, we can tell ourselves, especially when callow and ingenuous, that we're different, that we'll somehow escape the rat race, that our superiority will be recognized, that *our* honeymoon will last, that we'll nab a Nobel and so on. Yet isn't that the very same line all girls and boys feed themselves?

When we come to think of work in these bleak, objective terms, it's enough to run out and embrace the next nihilistic, European deconstructionist to come along. But we seldom think so radically. Instead some of us try to drown out the interior whining and desperation by working frenetically and thrillingly shooting for megabucks. Or we dabble in a succession of sports, hobbies, and other avocations, when not dreaming our way to a lower handicap. Or we slave away for years in anticipation of retirement and then, alas, find ourselves without the body or acquired interests to enjoy the so-called golden years.

## ALL WORK CAN BE

Can things be different? It's largely a question of attitude and the vision sustaining our motivation. Wouldn't it be great if we could find in our job the same fun, excitement, thrill and blessed fatigue that come from giving one's all, and then some, to an athletic contest? Wouldn't it be great if we could find in our job a life-absorbing ideal? Work can be all that, provided we drop our defensive, self-protective attitude toward it. The problem is we never really make work our own. It just sits there astride our path as a constant bother, an external imposition. And the main reason we don't internalize work is that we don't see its intrinsic relation to our own welfare—perhaps because our notion of personal fulfillment is all wet.

"Work five, play two," reads the matchbook hawking some beer or cigarette. That about sums up the uneasy truce between the two major contenders for our time and interest. We work in order to have the money to play; working harder will let us play even harder. Oh, sure, we also work to support the family, to keep out of mischief, to fill the time, to generate an achievement or two that will justify our existence, to have a ready answer for the cocktail-party query, "what do *you* do?" There's nothing wrong with any of those reasons, but why settle for so little? That very same work—provided we're constantly pushing to do it ever better—can also be motivated by two far superior reasons. We can also work for the best of self-loves (self-owning) and the best of other-loves (the self-giving that generates an ever better service to others in their real needs). So true is this that, even if we were misguidedly to fail professionally, we could still justifiably tell ourselves that behind the regrettable (and soon to be remedied) failure lie two other, more important successes. Namely, the contribution our work made to enriching our character and benefiting others.

So, if we came to see we're made for working in this fashion, simultaneously improving the job, ourselves, and our clients or customers, we could go very far indeed. The argument leads back to our appetite for bliss. We can't help but desire to be happy; moreover, our happiness is intimately linked to making others happy by freely serving them, a self-giving made possible by the self-dominion that in turn is made possible by cultivating virtue. Well, then, why not attain both ends by generating lots of "good work well done," in the words of Dorothy Sayers? We'll even get paid for doing so—let's hope, handsomely so. Still, as John Ruskin tells us, "The highest reward for a person's toil is not what they get for it, but what they become by it."

Working the way we ought can equip us to love as well as to express love itself. Besides work's end-product, work can be both a means to self-giving and the end of self-giving itself. A little self-knowledge soon discloses it's our body or instincts or glands or whims or the crowd that calls the shots as far as much of our behavior is concerned. Consequently, we must appropriate, conquer ourselves by virtuous living. Now it just so happens that working well calls for all the virtues you can name. We can acquire and perfect them by working unstintingly—and to that extent we grow in self-dominion. If love is defined as the free gift of self and we can only give what we already possess, it surely follows that we can love only to the degree that we own ourselves. Thus, working selflessly kills the selfishness killing us.

Diligence starves and strangles our moodiness, flightiness, softness, ignorance, irresponsibility, infantile fears, sensuality, self-centeredness, so many psychosomatic aches and pains. Work works (wonders), if we work at it. It's really the closest thing to a panacea available to us. Instead of cussing our work, we have to love it for all it can do for us and others. Work then goes from being seen as a necessary evil to a peerless privilege and good.

"There is no limit to how far most people would go to avoid the real labor of thinking," so said the inventor of the twentieth century, Thomas A. Edison. This extraordinary man was granted 1,093 patents for his inventions: a patent for every ten to twelve days of his adult life. His secret? "One percent inspiration and ninety-nine percent perspiration."

## IMPROVE THE WORK AND THE WORKER

So far the virtuous benefits born of working well have been personal ones, those accruing mostly to the "worker." But the goods surely don't end there (though without them, you won't be motivated to go anywhere). The quality of your work's end-product will also grow. Since today in one way or another we've all got service jobs, the virtuous, industrious "worker" will also serve more and better, more cheerfully, with a greater disposition to detect what customers or clients really need and to come up enterprisingly with the goods. That means your service will be more exclusively focused on addressing others' needs, thereby relegating both your company's and your own personal needs to some back room. Colleagues and clients alike will wonder why you're so productive, friendly, helpful, cheerful, despite your demanding, taxing tempo and intensity. You'll thus be playing out before their inquisitive and even acquisitive—certainly envious—eyes one of the biggest secrets of life: how and why work has a direct bearing on ultimate fulfillment.

Your exemplary life of toil and loyalty cannot go unheeded. Till then others may have erroneously thought that happiness consists in maximizing ease or pleasures, all in the service of self. Till then, too, your bosses may have thought that maximizing short-term financial profits was the name of the business game. They never really dared to put customers first, while letting the profits take care of themselves. Working virtuously, unstintingly, is a win-win proposition. What's good for you is also what's good for your clients and your business—and more, much more.

## CAN'T HAVE IT ALL

Before we can transform work, however, a first requirement is that our job consist of good, honest, needed work: a service, not a fraud or sham or shameful stimulus of baser drives. A second requirement—a huge challenge today—is to keep our work within finite, humane bounds, lest it gobble up all our energy and other responsibilities. Downright cruel are the time demands of many professions, such as law, medicine, high finance, accounting, and consulting as practiced today in large organizations or firms in large cities. Professionals, both women and men, should be realistic and humble enough to realize that they can't have it all, all at once, but only piecemeal, progressively. Sixty- to eighty-hour weeks have proved beyond any doubt that all work and no play indeed makes Jack and Jacqueline dull and exhausted everybodies in everything. Such peremptory, structured work, in the application of one of those perverse Peter Principles, tends to expand to fill every available nook. So much so that their practitioners should seriously consider deferring marriage until they're firmly established (having made partner, for instance).

In any event people with such jobs must strenuously set limits and religiously heed their schedule in ever renewed defense and furtherance of higher, though less structured, priorities and allegiances (one's own spiritual and physical well-being, family, friends, interests, and avocations). If our job is riding us, and not vice versa, there's no conceivable way that we can make it into something more than an obsessive chase after labor's fruits and rewards (money, power, fame), draining the job of any intrinsic value. It simply can't be all for the work and nothing for the worker. Practically the only way to avoid the Faustian exchange of soul for success is to bring the topic repeatedly to one's quiet time and therein pledge oneself anew to convert it into an incarnation of the best of self-loves and other-loves. Otherwise, frenzied work tends to metastasize more and more, with all the ensuing ravages (personal, familial, social).

A third requirement is to make sure good, humanized work is done well, with our eyes fixed on excellence and our commitment to others' objective needs. That calls for such qualities as order, organization, neatness, economizing on time, heeding priorities, punctuality, finishing things completely, alternating immersion with detachment (the best formula for creativity), banning shoddiness, checking everything over before pronouncing it "finished", keeping abreast of developments in one's particular specialty. . . .

## How to Internalize

Much remains unsaid on the broad and rich subject of work, rewards you'll keep on discovering up to retirement and beyond. For now, let's see what we can do to start working better. Here are habits that will directly contribute to your self-ownership, the stuff of courage and patience:

1.  Paradoxically, the single most practical thing you can do is to dream habitually about all the treasures hidden beneath the unattractive surface of plain toil.

    Because work is hard and tiring, emotionally if not physically, we tend instinctively to shy away from its demands. Therefore we can't be surprised to find ourselves, on or off the job, often pronouncing "that's good enough" over a slipshod task. That's why we must sell ourselves time and again on all work's concealed benefits, while learning to turn a deaf ear to negative feelings, distractions, and rationalizations. Working all-out is the best favor you can do for all parties.

2.  Then, stop complaining, both exteriorly and interiorly, even when you're the butt of unfairness or just lack of appreciation, or when the job objectively leaves much to be desired.

So long as you're stuck with a flop of a job (slights, annoyances, and all), make the most of it. Much more is at stake than a paycheck or an understanding supervisor or peer recognition. If you crowd out self-pity and plunge yourself into what you're supposed to be doing, most of work's disagreeable aspects recede, if not disappear. Honestly now: when was the last time you heard of a documented case of someone dying or going absolutely batty from work-induced exhaustion?

3.  Spend the first minute of your morning's and afternoon's work getting set. That means principally two things. Take a deep, long breath and re-commit yourself to the regimen. Then figure out what needs to be done and in what order. Then, anchors aweigh.

4.  Be punctual in starting your work and leaving it at the end of the day. Also arrive a minute or two early to all your appointments.

5.  Keep a list of priorities. Usually do first what you dislike or tend to delay the most. You'll find it's neither quite so bad nor time-consuming as feared. Beware of never getting around to very important long-range objectives, sacrificed on the altar of what's immediate and urgent.

6.  Do one thing at a time and finish it. When completed, fetch and address the next project. Try to minimize distractions and interruptions. Perhaps for certain periods you can let others or the answering machine take messages. A neat, uncluttered, organized mind, not to mention one's work area, is always a big plus.

7.  "Serve order," said an ancient sage, "and it will serve you." And for that, "a place for everything and everything in its place." That's much easier said than done, but whatever reasonable time we "waste" on order will multiply our time.

Also keep in mind that if we're habitually orderly, we won't have to set aside half an hour here or there to straighten everything up. There simply won't be much clutter.

8. Be and appear to be very busy from afar and very accommodating up close. However important or pressing what you have in hand, people still come first, even if you must smilingly promise to get back to them as soon as possible.

9. Don't be such a perfectionist that you neurotically preclude ever making a mistake, but at the exorbitant cost of scant output. But *do* proofread everything before sending it forth, even if your computer has checked the spelling, punctuation, and so forth.

10. Time is a treasure: so seize and husband each workday's hours and minutes, keeping "down" times to a bare minimum. It's always amazing how much work you can get through the week before you go on vacation. Well, then, why not see each weekend as a two-day vacation—and try to recapture that pre-vacation tempo and intensity every week of the year?

Never put things off, except when you've very deliberately scheduled them for later. Surfing the Internet or the Web can be a big time-eater, just like getting bogged down in articles and reports coming across your desk. How true is the old saying: "If you want something done, go to a busy person." The implication is that only busy people know how to squeeze still more out of their loaded but still finite schedules.

## Humanizing the Workplace

The above recommendations look largely to the "worker's" personal growth. Now, some that go farther afield:

11. "Profit" and "professional" success are not dirty words, when honestly achieved by someone who wants to lead by serving better. Each of us should be aware of how diligent and painstaking are the best professionals in our field—and then try to match, if not best, them. For the sake of advancing both our company and family, we ought to seek both promotions and pay raises, but let's make sure they're fair and square. Heed annual evaluations and precipitate, by inviting, partial ones in between.

12. Everything we can do to foster profit-sharing plans, employee stock-ownership, and the decentralization that brings decision-making as far down the line as possible will benefit not only the company but each of those who make it up.

13. Don't sit around waiting for the top executives to pull a full-blown inspiring corporate culture out of the hat. Neither can you afford to become an ever narrower specialist, while leaving the "vision" thing to others. Don't wait for your superiors to ask for your suggestions. Right where you are, reinvent your current tasks in an unending search for an ever better service or product, however slight. Energize your co-workers with your enthusiastic efforts to outdo yourself. Of such enterprising, demanding stuff are the too rare qualified candidates for CEO made.

14. Good managers should know both their people and their respective missions so well that they can deftly help each to see how personal goals can be furthered by and through the pursuit of corporate aims—and vice versa. The trick is to get the enlightened self-interest of both the company and employee somehow to mesh. It can be done, though never improvised.

15. Whatever your corporate rung, help your colleagues and any underlings to become team players, fired with the shared calling

to build, grow, make, create, and coalesce—all in the venture for successively better mousetraps.

16. Be as frugal with corporate money as you are with your own, especially on business trips and while partaking of assorted other perks, lest the next downsizing become your retirement party, among other reasons.

17. Don't fall for the coward's trap of thinking that ever more data and feedback will make your hard decisions for you, exempting you from personal risk. That way lies data (and soul) overkill. If at root you don't relish, and grow on, meeting challenges, abandon the private for the public sector.

18. Smile as you work, even when alone. You will, if you forget about yourself and earnestly try to please others (clients, co-workers, family) by trying to make of your individual toils a masterwork.

# 12

# GETTING OTHERS RIGHT

> You just don't understand.
> — Deborah Tannen, title of her best-selling book, 1990

WE GET OTHERS WRONG.  We slight them; we use them; we misunderstand them.  Usually without realizing it, we see others as stepping stones to our own ends. Or, perhaps more often, certainly more seriously, we misinterpret their actions toward us and see them as stumbling blocks, as threats or obstacles.  Now it's no secret that others are seldom putty in our hands: they resist being exploited or misunderstood.  They may even become vindictive, trying to get even with us.  In fact, many, if not most, of our problems come from our faulty interaction with others.

That's too bad, because others play a crucial role in our development.  We are essentially social animals.  "No man is an island"; neither is there really anything like a self-made person. Physically and intellectually we mature only gradually, all the while dependent on others.  It take years and much outside influence for us to grow morally and spiritually. *The Lord of the Flies* is one account of how near-teens degenerate when left without mature guidance. Ultimately, the problem is that we tend to misinterpret or estrange the very people whose contributions are most necessary to our growth and fulfillment. On the other hand, as a defense mechanism we tend to congregate with user-friendly copies of our character, with both its good and bad elements. Thus, we instinctively shy away from those who could help us most and insulate ourselves with others who confirm us in our runthood.

What do we most need from others? What is our biggest deficit? We homunculi most approach infinity in our capacity for self-deception. As we have seen, we tend almost automatically to kid ourselves. Consequently we need others to help us undeceive ourselves. Now, almost necessarily do these needed truths hurt in their acceptance and assimilation. "Knowledge," as Elizabeth Barrett Browning warned, "by suffering entereth." Therefore our greatest social need would be met by finding ourselves within a relatively small group of loving authority figures (parents, school, church, mosque . . .), who *dare* to help us, little by little, to acknowledge these truths. Unfortunately such truth-teaching authorities are hard to find these days. There seems to be a shortage of courage on the part of those obligated or commissioned to train us ethically. Instead we're practically overrun by those who would pander to our most self-defeating whims. Such "pimps" gleefully teach us what we *want* self-servingly to hear, rather than what we *need* to hear and heed.

## THE ART OF UNDERSTANDING

Thus it's crucial to get our own subjective house sufficiently in order, lest we fail to acknowledge, again, that we each tend to be our worst enemy. Only then can we hope to recognize, and thus successfully avail ourselves of, those who would be our true and *truthful* friends. When ultimately we read ourselves aright, we make it that much easier to read others right.

Understanding is what we mainly owe each other. While we may all too often think we can peer inside and figure out what makes others tick, the sobering truth is that we readily indulge in the snap assessments and rash judgments that do violence to others' rightful ways of being and doing. And our tactlessness is soon requited, befouling our relationships. Even close friends admit it's very time-consuming, painstaking, and rare to know each other well. Each of us is unique, with a very personal history of nature and nurture, an unrepeatable amalgam of chances and privations. So much so that each of us offers no little natural mystery to even the good-willed gaze of others. When it comes to knowing and understanding others, therefore, let's first admit our ignorance and then act accordingly: gently, tentatively, thoughtfully, respectfully. But we must also work at putting ourselves in others' shoes. Understanding at least those at our side involves two aspects: interacting inquisitively with them and, in their absence, reflecting at leisure on what we have learned. It's the challenge of playing the detective or the puzzle solver; it's the novelist's knack of engaging a keen eye and receptive ear.

Before we (and they) can even begin to share the truths that others cannot readily reach by themselves, aren't we each first obliged to respect the truth of others' existence? To recognize, that is, that each is an autonomous, self-directing person whose motives are often opaque to us? To acknowledge that each of them is entitled to as many mistakes as we are? Don't we in all fairness owe all others understanding and consideration? In social relations "to understand all is to forgive all" may be, for most of us, a peak too high. But doesn't "to understand much is to forgive much" come closer to the mark of the basic fairness we should be shooting for? Now all this account-settling doesn't come easily or automatically.

## A CHAIN REACTION?

Over ninety percent of all human troubles and needs would disappear if all of us were truly, disinterestedly understanding and loving of one another. Unfortunately we're not—nor is there any power, earthly or otherwise, that can compel us to love, willingly to serve, one another. In fact to the extent that love is anything less than free, to that degree it stops being love. So, there's precious little each of us can do to get others to recognize and address our objective needs—and vice versa. What then, to leave our mutual interactions to mere reactions and accidents of fate? Probably not that, either. Might it not be, rather, that we're morally bound, if not by love, at least by justice to work towards understanding and respecting others, as a bare minimum for the mutual service we owe one another?

We're very good at picking out, from miles away, the shortcomings and failings of others, while somehow their good points and positive deeds are all too readily hidden in the fog we generate. With ourselves, however, the opposite is true. We clearly see to the point of gross exaggeration our good side (such as it is), while we expertly explain away, if ever acknowledge, our own weaknesses and misdeeds. All this accentuating the positive and covering over the negative in ourselves leads us competitively to ignore others' assets and inflate their liabilities. The same perverse process takes place in everybody walking the face of the earth. What we should, therefore, be trying to do is to mete out to others what we so generously bestow on ourselves. (Perhaps then they'll do the same in our regard.) How much better, in other words, would the world be, if we were all (or at least some of us) to live the so-called Golden Rule. Now we are in fact bound—not by optional love, mind you—but by strict justice so to do: dealing with others just as we'd like them to deal with us.

## FLESHING OUT THE GOLDEN RULE

Four sources are at hand to disclose how we might improve our dealings with others. First, ask yourself how you would best like to be treated. Then, recall the slights and even injustices that, conversely, have come your way and what should have been in their place. Reconstruct, besides, the pleasant surprises that landed on your doorstep as a result of others' going out of their way to do right by you, and then try to repeat them. Finally, look at how you relate to yourself as a model for how you are to relate to others. Readers are left to draw both conclusions and objectives from the first three sources, which depend in part on your very personal experiences and expectations. Let's explore the fourth together.

You love yourself automatically, necessarily, in the sense that you desire the best for yourself. To will your own happiness is nothing optional, but an instinctive drive, as we saw earlier. Yet your self-love is compatible with even the remote possibility of having authored the most heinous crimes and dastardly misdeeds. It is not predicated on finding anything good, meritorious, attractive or lovable in yourself. You've finally discovered someone who loves you unconditionally, unreservedly, irrevocably: Yourself.

Now this self-love, when unenlightened by the mind's reality-reading radar, will lead us into trouble. But, conversely, this self-love, when submissive to reason, can generate much true self-knowledge and self-understanding. Relying on inside information to which no one else is privy, our mind and will, when paired and cooperating, can ferret out good excuses or objective, mitigating circumstances to explain why our behavior sometimes falls short of our principles. This good self-love justifiably allows us to tolerate in ourselves without neurosis or anxiety a more or less large discrepancy between what we'd like to be and what we actually are.

Now then, if we are to treat others just as we would like to be treated, isn't the understanding way we treat ourselves the very way we'd like others to treat us? At the very least, since we have no inside information of others, shouldn't we habitually make that extra effort to be understanding, to give others the benefit of the doubt, to find excuses as readily for them as for ourselves? If we only manage to do so, say, half the time, one thing is certain: people will be trampling on one another to become our friend and boon companion. The next best thing to knowing oneself loved unconditionally is the security of knowing oneself understood, if not always, at least most of the time. With whosoever understands us so, the "need" for poses and masks disappears; we relax; we can be ourselves; we no longer need all those defense mechanisms. What further steps should this deliberate, virtuous effort to understand others lead to? Fifteen suggestions follow.

## "UNWRONGING" OTHERS

1.   If you can't praise, keep your mouth shut.

2.   When others' shortcomings surface, be quick to defend at least their good will, especially if the allegedly guilty party is not present to explain his apparent misdeeds.

3.   When others do wrong, especially if they wrong you, try to find or make excuses for their disappointing actions.

4.   At least once a week we should ponder on, sifting them in time reserved for reflection, whatever wounds, barbs, and slights have come our way, to gain perspective. Our initial reaction was probably exaggerated, and the provocation may have been unintentional: just an inconsiderate lack of tact.

5.   Why not make a mutual pact with your best friend (or spouse or favorite sibling) for each to tell the other periodically whatever personal habits or traits stand in need of improvement, especially if such misdeeds unwittingly alienate others?

6. Try to have a wide variety of friends, with definite, even angular, personalities and characters, to compensate for the tendency to collect only carbon copies of yourself.

7. Don't judge others, unless you're bound to do so. Never do so when upset.

8. With those "who get your goat" or otherwise repel or annoy you, try acting as if you liked them and soon you possibly will (or if not, at least they won't bother you so much). Your more positive attitude may be what they need for their hidden good points to surface.

9. Try to stop sizing up others and pigeon-holing them; such rash judgments are almost always false and usually very unfair.

10. Listen, listen, listen; ask, ask, ask; observe, observe, observe.

11. First impressions may be right or less so, depending on one's mood and underlying attitude. So, the best thing is to sift them later and at leisure, with a dose of self-mistrust.

12. Married couples (and even friends) need to argue now and then to clear the air and give vent to pent-up resentments, "having it out," as the expression goes. Just spare your kids, neighbors, and relatives the emotional fireworks—and make up soon thereafter.

13. What, among other benefits, are friends for, if not to serve as a sounding board for one's questionable reactions to others?

14. If A is harming or maligning B, however intentionally, one should screw up one's courage and do whatever is necessary to get A to desist.

15. Our ongoing efforts to understand others and to make them understood to others will net us a bunch of candidates for friendship.

# 13

# ACKNOWLEDGING
# DEBTS TO PARENTS

The joys of parents are secret,
and so are their griefs and fears.
—Francis Bacon, *Essays*, 1625

O UR MISGUIDED, unenlightened self-interest tries
to get reality to conform to it, as we've seen. This
distortion sows troubles aplenty, both with self and
others. We misread others, and they misread us. Consequently
everybody is more or less paranoid: exaggerating the threats that
others represent. Now, it's notorious that this persecution complex is most alive and fanned within tight social units, and there's
no tighter unit than the family.

Consequently, much of the challenge is to convert children's
self-centeredness into the just, realistic recognition of what they
have received from their parents. On the other hand, the challenge
facing parents is for them to recognize and respect the truth that
their children are, with age, increasingly autonomous agents—not
potentially embarrassing extensions of themselves. Parents have
to work at truly educating their children, so that each interiorizes

169

the principles of enlightened self-interest. Such children are then able to understand who their parents are and where they're coming from.

## TOO CLOSE TO SEE

Our perception of things closest to us is proverbially very poor. The most notable instance is ourselves—something we never seem to get rightly focused. Closely related and just behind are our parents, no matter what our (or their) age. We very much tend to take them for granted, however loving and disinterested they've been to us—or not. Part of the problem is that we start off on the wrong foot. We were only dimly aware of their most heroic and wholly one-sided efforts in our behalf, until we attained the use of reason around, let us hope, six or seven years of age. And even since then, in the best of cases, we've probably recognized only the proverbial tip of the iceberg.

What is so painfully obvious to the parents themselves can be almost hidden from the kids. Children can unthinkingly assume that their parents are naturally masochists, that they derive secret kicks from never forgetting to cook dinner or to do the laundry or from the ulcer born of wearing oneself out in a fiercely competitive marketplace. That's why without melodrama children must come to see all the blood, sweat, and tears; the sleepless nights and zillions of dirty diapers; the anxieties, fears, and disappointments; the tiredness and boredom overcome; the huge emotional and financial investment; the years of unstinting, unrequited giving; the great expectations and high hopes; the interests, friends, hobbies, and wishes unpursued, the books unread, the dresses unbought, the concerts or ball games unattended; the scrimping and saving. Children are also invited to see as well the exalted beauty and heroic goals of the marital calling whereby two people freely, lovingly, and permanently pledge to sacrifice themselves in a joint venture of making a family, with very uncertain prospects.

## DECIPHERING TOUGH LOVE

Selfish and self-deceiving as we are, we get habituated to being the object of parents' self-sacrificing love and everything that follows in its wake, as if we were entitled to gifts (a clear contradiction in terms). Another important way we read our parents wrongly is to misinterpret their necessary interventions to correct, discipline, and punish us as the opposite of love. Finally, we usually overreact to their shortcomings and foibles, as if the latter disproved their abiding, general good will and justified our small and large rebellions. Were parents totally loving, unflawed, and unerring in their judgments, we'd more fairly and easily honor them for their countless disinterested services. The catch comes when parents either fall short of the virtuous mark or exceed their bounds. Imperfect children of imperfect parents are heirs to lots of mutual resentments and recriminations.

Not only are we less than objective in this child-parent relationship, but we abound in overemotional responses, both positive and negative, which further becloud the whole picture. Sometimes there's so much overlaid acrimony that we don't want to acknowledge any debts at all. Throw in a lot of sibling rivalry, and you have a cauldron seething with a veritable witch's brew. Moreover, if we react to others' reactions (rather than, more humanly, more deliberately, acting), everything is at hand for a truly vicious circle. Such is human weakness, familiarity *does* breed contempt, with our eagle-eye for others' peccadilloes and our utter blindness to more serious failings in ourselves. Given the potential for, and reality of, perpetual disaster on the home front, the wonder isn't how were we ever born into such a dysfunctional family, but, rather, why our parents didn't throw us out on our ear many long years ago. Or why they ever had us in the first place. Welcome to Family Chemistry 101 or, better yet, Filial Fairness 101.

## ACKNOWLEDGING ALL THOSE IOUs

Before going any further, it's crucial to clarify what's at issue. We just spoke of "fairness": in other words we're dealing with the duties of justice—obligations (truths) children are bound to recognize and discharge with respect to parents. For now, we're not talking about loving them (which means going above and beyond the call of duty), something doubtless worthy and laudable. Neither are we talking about necessarily paying our parents back. The debts we're dealing with have to do with recognizing the truth of what our parents have done for us. We owe them that recognition, acknowledgment, honor, and respect. The need to settle this account still holds, even when parents have long since passed away. For its main purpose is to get at one's personal truth by acknowledging, however belatedly, their countless contributions.

But justly recognizing the source of all those endowments is also something we owe ourselves. Whatever we owe others, we owe it to ourselves to be just and truthful. And the truth is we owe others much more than we habitually and self-servingly think. Even more: since most truths involve relationships, striving to be just is usually a prerequisite to all-important truthfulness. To cure it is to cure ourselves, at least in part. And a big part of that cure is to free ourselves from our cramped self-orbit, the strait-jacket woven by our unenlightened self-interest and the untruths it has sired.

What is far harder than paying back actual IOUs is to recognize and do something about all those unbidden things and benefits that have come our way out of others' disinterestedness; gifts, in a word. Since our benefactors were not bound to be generous—true love must be free in both the giving and receiving—for their own sake they perhaps have no desire, certainly no right, to be repaid. Such is the one-way gratuitousness of genuine love. But what about our recognizing their highly voluntary love for us? Ought not such unowed gifts elicit from us even greater appreciation and response than the usual, physical claims of others? Yet in the absence of any claims put forward, it's so easy to take both giver and gifts for granted. Surely our doing so, however, will do us and others no minor harm. Such insensitivity violates not only morality, but sanity, truth, and fellowship. Yet these social truths have subtle and unenforceable claims to recognition and reverence. When these are ignored, we make it that much harder to get beyond the closed circle within which each of us is otherwise trapped.

## SOURING ALL OTHER RELATIONSHIPS

This lack of response also blocks many from discovering and relishing anything possibly greater than parental love. Before such breakthroughs can take place, children must first acknowledge the more obvious and tangible favors received from parents. Unless these are addressed, junior is pretty much a goner. The debt to one's parents is so huge that the failure to acknowledge it cannot help but befoul and vitiate all other ties. We have here an early, basic rapport that flavors all subsequent relationships. It's not the most important bond, but if left distorted, it will skew all our relations with others.

Truthfulness cannot be exercised piecemeal. All our parents' countless services and efforts—whether born of justice or love— just stand there. Were we cavalierly to ignore or sidestep them, we would shackle both our ability to know things and people as they are and to love those most deserving of our love. Prying ourselves away from our selfishness takes place, if at all, by recognizing what we've received so one-sidedly from our parents and honoring them for it all. Good, disinterested parents are bound to help their children acknowledge the many benefits they've received so unilaterally. Why? Because dad and mom need a pat on the back? Not primarily. Rather, because kids blind to their debts cannot grow. Period.

Progressively recognizing and honoring the compound debt with one's parents is the built-in occasion for shifting one's basic orientation away from obsession with self. That one has been— first unconsciously, then less so—the undeserving and unreciprocating object of so much blood, sweat, tears, time, money, attention, and anxiety on the part of one's parents is simply too immense an investment to ignore without bad will. Moreover, most parents are neither so generous nor subtle that they fail to call junior's attention now and then, especially as he grows older, to what has largely been a one-way conveyor belt. Partly for their sake, but especially for his, parents so hope and pray that their child will come to recognize this debt and set about doing . . . what?

## How to Repay

Junior could never totally repay his parents (nor would he be expected to), especially since he owes them his very life. Obey them in everything? Probably not that either, and for two good reasons. First, most parents are too protective and possessive and somewhat lacking consequently in perspective. Fewer, but still many, parents misguidedly overstep their legitimate bounds, even with the best of wills: interfering, meddling, sometimes worse. To conform to erroneous parents would be to compound the problem.

Second, what parents ultimately most desire for their offspring is that they become free, thinking, autonomous, responsible, principled, even virtuous adults—though maybe not so soon. There's the rub. Especially when parents see their still half-free and half-thinking children making up their own minds in fairly long-term directions without being fully conversant with, or committed to, their own best welfare. Ideally, children must strive, as early, freely, and wisely as possible, to take responsibility for their decisions, deeds, and mistakes. To pass the buck to parents, caving in to their wishes, would run counter to what both child and parents desire in their heart of hearts. So, a child must learn to manage his own life with as much self-determination as accountability, seeing parental desire as but one of many counsels.

## MAKING IT A TWO-WAY STREET

What can children do to start setting matters right? Try some of these: Esteeming parents, pleasing them, understanding them, venerating them, being considerate, loving them, availing yourself of the talents and opportunities they've handed on—above all, by growing. Life represents their greatest gift, which ultimately points to committing yourself to the loving self-giving that echoes your parents' and makes theirs worthwhile and rewarded. Unless junior comes to respect his parents truthfully and love them disinterestedly, he's not likely to learn to love or even to know anyone but himself, alas. Do you now see that recognizing one's debts with parents is humanity's passport to reality? Here are some more strategic tips:

1.  Parents may err in directing their children—too much or too little—but children should never doubt what motivates them: a good-willed desire for what's best for their offspring. Keeping this fact in mind makes it easier to understand and forgive their excesses or shortcomings. Parental over-insistence on behavioral externals and non-essentials is easier to take when children try to see it as stemming from loving possessiveness, however misguided.

2.  Explicitly recognizing parental sacrifices by grateful word and deed, especially by good use of time and talents and heeding their legitimate wishes, makes it less likely that parents will usurp their children's increasing right to self-determination. The more responsibly children use their growing freedom, the more their parents will respect it—and them.

3.  Without an on-going effort at mutual understanding, requiring time, quiet, and reflection, parents and children alike tend to react to one another, especially to each other's foibles—the familiarity that leads to voiced contempt.

4.  Yet, despite everything, how are children to handle parental impositions that exceed proper bounds, such as choice of studies, career, spouse . . .? The more children honor, respect, please, and obey their parents in all other areas, the easier it will be for them to exercise, tactfully, their autonomy in these. They should neither dismiss parental wishes nor slavishly heed them. When all else fails, a temporary compromise or rupture may be the only way out.

5.  Now we won't go far (or last long) in acknowledging the above practical consequences of our parental debts, unless we eke out time now and then to reflect and meditate, because these truths are often elusive and subtle, unknown or long-forgotten, obliging us to infer or recall them.

## HOME FRONT PRIMER

Now for some more tactical pointers:

1.  To minimize needless fretting, children should make every effort to inform deferentially their parents as to their whereabouts and plans, especially when those plans come unstuck.

2.  Children should never assume anything, especially when it's so easy to clarify matters ahead of time by simply asking.

3.  Children need to learn to deny themselves the self-serving option of being able to say, "Oh, I forgot." Isn't that what reminders are for? Moreover, they should be helped to see

that mom doesn't habitually forget to cook dinner or that dad doesn't forget to go to the office.

Heeding these first three tips is the best minimum for showing oneself responsible and hence deserving of less parental micromanagement.

4.   In their parentally inculcated desires to be ever less a parasite, children must learn to pick up after themselves—and then after others, especially less responsible younger siblings. The goal should be to leave things as neat, if not neater, than they found them; this especially applies to all-family rooms, bathrooms in particular.

5.   There must be some way of teaching kids to make their beds, to hang up their clothes (or to refold and re-stow them), to keep dresser, desk, and closet orderly, to have a place for everything and then to put everything back in its place. Somewhere along the line, wouldn't it be great if they were to learn that the state of their drawers and closet mirrors the state of their mind and heart? This rule is true at least to this extent: external order and priorities reflect internal order and serenity, while facilitating both. It's never very helpful, nor even perhaps possible, to live genuine virtues piecemeal.

6.   One good way for children to assume a growing share of the household burdens is the resolve to be the first to answer the phone and door, not to mention voluntarily doing their chores without having to be nagged.

7.   Teens and near-teens need to be informed of (perhaps even docked for) their approximate share for such outlays as water, electricity, and gas, as another spur to their sense of responsibility and frugality.

8.   Parents would be well advised to be long on affection for their offspring, but short on money. Get them somehow to imitate

a ten-year-old boy known to me whose family lived at a busy intersection. He baked and sold enough cookies to idling motorists to underwrite two whole weeks at a sleep-away camp.

9. By making it always something approximating a special occasion, parents should make it very hard for their children to miss family meals and very easy to want to linger with mom and dad afterwards.

10. On occasions dad may very well find it beneficial to record stealthily on audio-tape kid-caused ruckuses, assorted poutings, complaints, and other intemperate eruptions and, then, without preaching, play it back alone to the offenders, to help them hear how they come across.

11. If at all possible, parents should never run errands, especially in the car, without the company of one child. This is a wonderful opportunity for the personal dealings that ideally lead to deep parent-child friendships.

12. Drill-sergeant tones and commands must be kept to a minimum. That's why parents will see to it that the strongest order on the home front be preceded by a "please" or enveloped with a "would you terribly much mind to...?"

13. As much as possible, dad should involve the children, preferably one by one and one on one, in such tasks as home repairs, upkeep, car maintenance and cleanliness.

14. Gracious, grateful, positive, affirmative, courteous, tactful, freedom-respecting parents may just rear chips off the ol' block.

# PART III

# SELF-GIVING

# 14

# BEFRIENDING FRIENDS

What is love? two souls and one flesh;
friendship? two bodies and one soul.
— Joseph Roux, *Meditations...Love and Friendship*,
*circa* 1870

THERE'S A SUSPICION ABROAD that of all the endangered species, friendship might be the closest to extinction, especially among men. There are plenty of people we might call "friends," but on closer inspection we should more truthfully call them acquaintances, buddies, or even chums. Now if we had ever been a partner to a genuine friendship with its endearing give-and-take, we'd quickly know the difference. At best our "friends" are but embryonic friends.

The saying goes: Family you don't choose—only friends. But do we even do that much? Isn't it truer that for the most part friendships just happen? We rub elbows; with some we get along better than with others; we rub elbows still more with those found to our liking; common interests are discovered and pursued; we do things together; we confide in them and they in us. Throughout, enough bonding is taking place to dub the relationship friendship. And so perhaps it is (though barely): a usually tacit but reinforcing web of intimacy and reciprocity that waxes or wanes with time, changing circumstances, and inevitable stress.

Who are the would-be friends we've collected along the way, if indeed we have generated any? Usually they're people with whom we've shared good times, interests, escapades, or even trials. We find them non-threatening; we're comfortable together; we're similar to one another. In practice friendship often boils down to a mutual admiration and protection society. Rarely, however, is it a deeply personal, one-on-one thing, especially for men. We males tend to coalesce and travel in packs, gangs, groups, wherein dirty jokes, sexual exploits, and booze-lubricated adventures serve as the binding agent. The Boy Scouts, National Guard, the armed forces (especially the Marines), unofficial athletic teams, the neighborhood watering hole (that is, the local bar) are all instances of this male herd spirit. We anonymous ciphers seem to find validation, reinforcement, security, and strength in these clusters of like-minded peers.

## FINISHING THE JOB

So, you might be wondering, what's wrong with having junior friends? Hardly anything at all. Let's just finish the job, instead of leaving it a quarter or a half or even more incomplete. That's the only point. Friendship is good, even great, as far as it goes. In all too many cases, however, it doesn't go far enough, and is nowhere near what it can be. We arrest friendship's development when we let it remain in the realm of herd instinct, instead of more deliberately "growing" it.

Always present is the unwitting but real danger of not coaxing friendship beyond self-love. We naturally like ourselves, and so, by extension, we tend to like those who resemble us, at least superficially. Being and moving in the company of the familiar, these pals represent, as it were, an eagerly sought vote of confidence in our personality and character. As for who and what we are, we all duly feel somewhat uneasy. We thus seek and need affirmation in our incompleteness. To a greater or less extent we're all other-directed. At work here too is the primal instinct of self-preservation.

With arrested friendship, we also witness the possible "tie that binds," the homogenizing pressure that drags us down, that exacts conformity to group fiat. We can so easily find ourselves limited to, and deprived by, the company of look-alike mini-persons. We find ourselves then branding those who fall outside our inner circle as not only different, but threatening and inimical. The inclusions and exclusions of so-called friendship thus become a source of joint, defensive impoverishment, instead of enrichment.

Our description of immature friendship discloses the usual motivation behind this mutual admiration society. It's not so much that we "desire" friends so much as we "need" them. Nor is it less true that our friends "need" us. We band together, because we find it mutually convenient. The intent behind most friendship is therefore a fundamental urge, however unwitting, to receive and to exploit. We often use others for our unenlightened aims, however much we must apparently "give" to prime the pump, to bribe personal benefits out of others, and so forth. So long as this contractual relationship among moral diminutives proves mutually helpful, it lasts, though in a barely commendable fashion. But when, as invariably happens, friends start going in different directions, both geographically and morally, it takes very little to undo the prior pattern. Were there, however, more self-knowledge and self-definition, our doings and choosings, both personal and social, would (or could) be much more thoughtful, enterprising, and beneficial to both parties.

As you've probably noticed, females seem more inclined to have friends (and enemies)—or something approximating the authentic article. That's not to say they can't be catty and gossipy and, arguably, more inclined to bear grudges. But till "friendship" turns bad, affection, intimacy, and mutual favors seem to come more naturally to women. Aren't they always whispering secrets and compliments to one another? In general, females display fewer signs of a psychological or spiritual identity crisis. Not for them self-doubts; biology—the ability to make babies and nurture them—does seem to be destiny for them. Women engage in far less anti-social behavior than do men.

## Male Identity Crisis

On the other hand, men don't seem to know where they're headed or how to get there, except to prove themselves with at least the appearance of derring-do and sexual conquest. They are mortally afraid of being called or thought a "sissy." Yet their fathers in some cases may be uncertain role models, perhaps only sporadically showing how real men act. Further, most schooling takes place under a succession of females. In fact, education can be seen as an attempt at emasculation, but certainly feminization. So men overcompensate with exaggerated machismo and homophobia, while insisting on smoking Marlboros and drinking excessively.

Men are very competitive and seem to think that the more fellow males they put down, the higher will be the resulting pedestal, from which they can lord it over others. Schoolboys are notoriously cruel and unjust and very given to practicing ostracism. We men shun showing affection or intimacy, especially with members of the same sex. We tend to affiliate upward to natural male leaders, whom both sexes tend to admire. With the tight-knit and reduced nuclear family, we've found no substitute for the absent uncles and other masculine role models to initiate boys into manly lore and ways with various traditional rites of passage (hunting, fishing, camping, drinking). Formerly it was clear that men were hunters,

fighters, pioneers, cowboys, providers. But, in today's highly ur-
banized and unisexed world, what are men supposed to be or do?
Now this collective male identity crisis, highly exacerbated in
our day, works against our striking up true friendships. Such
relationships, especially with other men, come across as too personal, soft, threatening, long-term, unexciting. And with women?
Then sexual attraction almost always gets in the way, often making
us devious manipulators. A current dearth of platonic friendships,
finally, deprives us of the lessons and rewards of the meeting of
minds (as opposed to bodies) that defines true friendship. As a
result, men are largely bereft of experiencing relationships that
are not somehow sexual, be they hetero- or homo-. Then, no
wonder love boils down to "making love." How impoverished and
stunted we men end up!

## TURNING UNENLIGHTENED
## FRIENDSHIP AROUND

When it comes to friendship, chance seems to rule. Everything
remains somewhat fuzzy, unexamined, rudimentary, unsatisfying,
impermanent. We tend to fall into and out of a succession of
short-lived relationships with equally superficial companions, if
not mere bedmates. We all tend to "use" our "friends," whether
female or male, for our own questionable ends. Rather than
"befriending" others, today's young people tend to do little more
than "network." But surely we can and are called to do better
than just "getting ahead." And the sooner we admit we have few,
if any, friends (and certainly don't deserve much better), the readier
we'll be to start at ground zero. Otherwise we run the very real
risk of letting both sexual lust and grubby greed call all our social
shots. Here, too, we must begin with self-knowledge.

Only by acknowledging that our friendships are stunted,
however painful the admission of self-love's limits may be, are we

thereby freed to start cultivating the real, deep, genuine thing. And none too soon. We will continue to distort and vitiate friendship until we've acquired virtuous self-dominion, since we cannot give of ourselves unless we first take possession of ourselves. Yet the painful admission that we're semiconsciously using others, often as accomplices to our base doings, should point us in the right, virtuous direction.

As we more and more become self-knowing and self-owning individuals (therefore with character and personality), we emerge into personhood, capable of knowing and loving aright. We then become capable of bestowing and receiving the mutual esteem and support, the kindness and confidentiality that define friendship.

Once we've discovered who we are and what we're about, we're much more likely to discover and attract like-minded and like-hearted peers, with whom we can share ideas and ideals, joys and sorrows. Friendship is nothing if not grounded on common interests and tastes, ideally on common virtues. We appreciate the favors our friend does for us, while we're strongly tempted to reciprocate, to generate favors in turn. I better both myself and my friend by improving our friendship, and vice versa. We relax in the other's presence; we let our hair down, remove the mask and open ourselves to the other's approving gaze. Neither is using the other, but each basks in the understanding and consideration the other disinterestedly offers.

We all somehow desperately need someone in our corner, who delights in us, whose allegiance is not revocable. Friendship, indeed, is rare, mutual, asexual love; many ancient sages liken it to "one soul in two bodies." It motivates us to grow spiritually and morally, lest we prove unworthy of the other.

Friendship is a most precious treasure, well worth waiting and working for. One of the biggest threats to marriage is the absence of, and even incapacity for, friendship between the couple. In its absence, in George Santayana's melancholy expression, "They walk alone together." Ideally, before getting married each future partner should have experienced the joy and reward of genuine friendship with someone other than his or her spouse-to-be. Having been enriched by that experience, each is therefore better able to aim for something similar, if not better, within marriage. Surely the best marriage would be one where two souls become one body *and* the two bodies become one soul. The best and most lasting friendships are those that develop between fellow aristocrats of love.

## AT LEAST ONE DEEP FRIENDSHIP

The program is simply this: let's *really* befriend our current "friends," however many or few. For now, don't worry too much about making more friends. Let's first rescue and vivify the friendships we already lay claim to. Once we learn what all true friendship entails, then we'll know when, why, and how to expand our circle of friends. We must realistically start with those at our side. It's not that easy for us to mend our stunted and stunting ways, however exalted and globe-girdling any newfound resolve. For one, let's avoid the self-deceiving trap that befell Lucy in "Peanuts," when she declared, "I love humanity; it's people I can't stand."

We must also get over the shortsighted belief that what's good for others is bad for me and vice versa. In fact, what others need and expect from me is paradoxically what's best for me. I'm designed and built to give of myself with no strings attached. Now that truth is far from self-evident; it actually flies in the face of conventional wisdom. Therefore at first sight this selfless generosity would seem to spell misery rather than happiness. There's probably no way short of actual experience to grasp this deepest of truths: selfishness backfires and generosity fulfills. Or another formulation: You're never happier than when making others genuinely happy.

Interestingly enough, when we build our character and strive to become full-fledged, virtuous persons, we needn't seek or strike up friendship. Then indeed, but only then, does friendship arise spontaneously, for like attracts like.

Here's a ten-point program for having almost too many friends:

1. Understand your friends by trying to stand in their shoes. Review each now and then during your times of reflection.

2. Make excuses for them as readily as you do for yourself, especially when they're not around to explain or defend themselves.

3. Listen, ask, and remember well. Know their pet peeves, favorite drink, birthday, anniversary, assorted hot buttons, favorite pro teams, preferred colors, and so on.

4. Help them with their burdens, especially when your aid can go unrecognized. Ideally, make it seem as if they're doing you a service.

5. Ply them with favors (but don't keep count). Cater now and then to their likes and dislikes.

6. Be truthful, even when it hurts. We especially owe others, above all our friends, the deepest, most transcendental truths that are hardest to come by.

7. Exchange letters. Let there be non-directed phone calls, but not too lengthy.

8. Overlook and foregive their shortcomings.

9. Be genuinely grateful.

10. Sing and drink together.

# 15

# FOR FOLLOWERS
# TO FOLLOW

The only thing necessary for the triumph of evil
is for good men to do nothing.
— Edmund Burke, 1794

Very soon, only too soon, your country will stand
in need of not just exceptional men, but of *great* men.
Find them in your souls. Find them in your hearts.
Find them in the depths of your country.
— Aleksandr Solzhenitsyn, addressing the U.S. Congress, 1976

IN HIS *Republic*'s famous cave allegory, Plato asserts that almost
all of us find ourselves enchained in a huge cave, with our
backs turned to its opening and our eyes fixed on its back
wall. Outside the cave's entrance is perpetually maintained a large
bonfire; between it and the actual entrance people do various things
and walk back and forth, projecting their shadows onto the back
wall. All the cave dwellers, never having been outside the cavern,
are persuaded that the shadows they see projected represent the
sum total of reality. They don't even suspect that what they're
witnessing is a mere shadow world. Now and then a few cave

inmates manage to escape, as a reward for their virtue and truthfulness, to the outer world, where things are truly seen for what they are. Their amazed discovery strongly tempts them to return to the cavern to set its remaining inmates straight. However, they find persuasion both arduous and slow, given the human propensity to prefer the familiar, however deficient, to what is the feared unknown.

Things, 2,500 years later, have not changed all that much. Few are those who achieve a grasp of reality, and their efforts to get their peers to abandon unreality, the shadow world of uncertainties, are only partially successful at best. What can be done to expedite the recovery of those who don't know better?

## MY BROTHER'S KEEPER?

Need we even bother? If those who escape do so on their own steam, as a result of personal initiatives that ratify their being, must not any future escapees do likewise, on their very own? Even if we wanted to, could we actually help them in any way? While we doubtless cannot do for others what they must do for themselves, is it exactly true that our escape, such as it is (still so recent perhaps and therefore unsettled), was wholly the work of rugged individualism, a strictly solo performance?

None of us has lived in such a vacuum that outside influences, be they good or less so, could never penetrate our cocoon. Perhaps we've had the enormous luck to run into exceptional persons who sharply contrast with the crowd by their uncommon vision, generosity, virtue, or happiness. Perhaps we saw and appreciated enough to envy them their good fortune. None of these exceptional people was perhaps intentionally putting forth edifying good example. But might not they have had a fertilizing impact on us, at least enough to get us to start questioning whether our way of living left something to be desired? "Might there not be a better, more fulfilling way?" we may have covertly asked ourselves. "Might not these objects of envy deserve closer scrutiny and fuller imitation?"

## UNCONSCIOUS LEADERSHIP

Agreed: there is very little we can do for misguided and benighted others. Chances are, they're not very receptive to arguments or presentation of evidence, especially if the tone wherewith they're exposed to a new train of thought strikes them as presumptuous. We all dread having to hear, "What gives you the right to criticize the way I live?" We also probably know personally, or have heard of, religious glad-handers whose conversion efforts quite plainly backfire, maybe even making matters worse than they had been. We can't do others' thinking for them, nor can we administer their freedom or dictate their loves. We could write books, but would they buy them?

The truism is often put forth that in order for followers to follow, leaders must lead. Now in its deepest sense leadership doesn't mean to boss others around, as if directing them from some platform of superiority. True leadership isn't something you *do*; leadership is all about who you *are*. It manifests itself in *why* and *how* we serve others. To the extent that we live as we ought, truly rectifying human life, to that degree we can enlighten others. How? By giving off as it were a beckoning, seductive aroma that at the very least piques others' curiosity, if not envy.

Note, further, that this self-ratification and self-fulfillment does not depend on unequal circumstances or talents or opportunities. Everyone can be a leader, because self-knowing, self-owning and self-giving are operations open to all; they depend only on oneself. If we don't become so, we have only ourselves to blame.

In others' sadness they can't help but compare their messed-up lives with more fulfilling ones. So, the best way of serving others, of helping them remedy their happiness deficit, is to live such a right, good, persuasive life that others can see, eventually, that ours is the way to go. This doesn't happen overnight. It may not happen at all if we're not extremely tactful. If we're to lead, neither can we permit ourselves to seem somehow different, better, eccentric, and the like. It's only over time and through inevitable ups and downs that others can see that our joy is not that of Pollyanna, but rather something deep-seated and authentic.

To do good infectiously, you needn't—shouldn't—become a do-gooder. You needn't join the Peace Corps or feed the homeless to serve others. Every occupation, if done in an exemplary manner, can be an occasion for leadership. Don't let yourself become marginalized. Whatever your profession, you should be shooting for the top, duly earning respect and standing among your peers. And all the while, you're coming up, above all, with creative ways to help both clients and co-workers, at least initially, by how well and hard you work.

But always remember: talk is cheap, and it cheapens. If you truly and perfectly lived in accord with your appetite for bliss, there would be no need for you ever to talk it up. Others couldn't help but realize the true secret, now embodied, of genuine fulfillment. It's paradoxical but true: the best and chief way for you to love others is by truly loving yourself: doing whatever is necessary for you to be (relatively) blissful. At its highest reaches, self-interest melts any prior antagonism between us and others and truly becomes other-interest as well. By thus living your human vocation ever better, you make it possible for others to discover their own, a calling essentially identical to yours. "Example is the school of mankind," wrote Edmund Burke, "and they will learn at no other."

## LEAD BY SERVING

Now do you see how our whole ethical program boils down to the stuff of leadership? If you try to live it all, you'll lead and point the way, even without realizing it. And when you stall (and you will), to get going again, it especially helps to recall repeatedly that you're sitting on the very secret of life that so very few have discovered, yet so desperately need.

In writing this book, I'm trying to lead, to help others. There, finally, you have my motivation. Its contents are necessarily autobiographical: an account of my vital discoveries. I am searching for a few, good, honest persons, to whom I can pass the baton. You really don't realize how lucky you are to be exposed to this program, especially if you try to implement it. Moreover, you've been saved having to devise your own map. These claims may sound less than modest. Yet I haven't invented anything; rather objective discoveries have made me what I am, such as I am. I'm no better than others—just luckier (as you will be too, if you follow suit). So, let's not pat ourselves on the back for doing only what is our duty (although we're being handsomely paid for it besides).

Here are some effective, though hardly exhaustive, ways to blaze a trail for others:

1.   The more you grow morally, the more human you are to become, lest you turn others off. Then they may never discover
that the solution you're living is theirs as well. Don't come
across fatally as a "know-it-all."

2.   Let's do the opposite of what our mothers told us: "Have few
friends, but good ones." Rather, how about: "Have many
friends—and bad ones"?

3.   Be very amenable, approachable, and accommodating.

4.   Avoid in your behavior whatever might trigger others' religious
or ideological phobias or stereotypes.

5.   Be understanding, forgiving, and overlooking. Conversely,
don't be judgmental or moralistic. Be loyal; stick up for others.
Excuse them, even interiorly.

6. Be indiscriminate in your self-giving; don't play favorites. Neither count nor even remember your favors. Don't measure out your generosity with a eye-dropper. Kill others with "excessive" kindnesses; don't be afraid of being "used." And be patient and persevering: we never know when someone's bubble is going to burst, allowing him finally to be able to read correctly the positive signals we may be giving off.

7. Don't volunteer your views, especially your "final" judgments on others. Go through life without holding grudges. When slighted, think: "What's this in comparison with what I deserve?" With respect to religion, morality, or others' foibles, keep a big piece of adhesive tape on your mouth.

8. Come across as someone with a deep reserve; be the strong, quiet type, one whose internal gyroscope is working fine and on its own, a self-directed person.

9. But also come across as someone with a bounce in the step, a twinkle in the eye, something always up the sleeve, usually in the form of favors, good times, services, assistance. Whistle as you work. You will, if you forget about yourself and earnestly try to please and lead others (clients, co-workers, friends, family).

# 16

# TURNING PROSE
# INTO POETRY

> By happy alchemy of mind,
> They turn to pleasure all they find.
> — Matthew Green, *The Spleen*, 1737

NOW HOW AND WHERE are we to enrich ourselves
morally? With ever harder and more heroic feats, as in
any athletic endeavor or acquiring any skill? If so, that
democratic prospect mentioned in the last chapter soon becomes
a very restricted elite. Aren't heroes by definition rare indeed?

You may also object that, if the ultimate purpose in life is
freely to give of oneself in love, why not fully dedicate ourselves to
doing so exclusively? Why bother with ordinary life with its
demands and requirements, with its chain of ever higher, harder
interlocking steps? Why not become a lover *par excellence*? a full-
time guru? Why bother with life's ordinary haunts, wherein so
many get bogged down and run the real risk of forfeiting their
soul?

Obviously many people get totally caught up in life's rat race,
in becoming professional successes, in earning ever more. And of

course that uncommon dedication and specialization does pay off in dollars, power, perks, satisfaction, advancement, records, and prizes. There's also the thrill of the chase, beating off competitors and the like. But all this activism comes at a terrible cost: physical or mental imbalance and maladies, an impoverished family life, meager personal interests, and so on. We might conquer the whole world, but in the process fritter away any soul.

On the other hand, dedicating oneself to self-sacrificing love alone isn't all that feasible either if it involves scorning the world of instrumental means. Were we bodiless spirits, perhaps we wouldn't have to raise the question of *what* we're to love others with, of *how* we're to serve them. But for us humans love can be no mere interior disposition or emotional state that stays cooped up inside. It must manifest and embody itself in concrete deeds of helping others. Otherwise it's an illusion.

If neither all-out activity nor disincarnate loving alone makes sense, isn't there some way of getting around the dilemma of choosing one or the other? Couldn't we unite the two in a higher synthesis, wherein increasing love becomes the spur for doing all secular, natural things ever better for the sake of both parties? Couldn't we try to outdo the workaholics by working harder and better for the sole purpose of doing good to both self and others, while showing onlookers the way to true fulfillment?

## EITHER GROWING OR SHRINKING

We semi-consciously tend to cheat ourselves ethically in at least three ways. First is the tendency to equate morality with "size": we tend to dismiss little misdeeds as harmless, while equating morality with conspicuous feats. Second is the shortsighted, formalistic tendency to equate morality with avoiding evil or harm (especially to third parties), rather than with doing good deeds for good reasons and thereby developing and perfecting one's own existence.

Third is the tendency to disregard purpose: if a particular action isn't "wrong," morally or legally branded as such, we conclude that it must be all right or at least harmless. With that frame of mind we can easily overlook the truth that motivation—the reason why we do this or that—can make neutral and even good deeds bad, while an upright intention can convert neutral deeds into good, virtuous deeds and make good ones even better.

Our current life is pretty much small potatoes, drained therefore of meaning, eliciting minimal responses—just enough to get what we tell ourselves we really aspire to. We're bored and distracted, very self-pitying. We thus set ourselves up for the escapist stuff of blow-outs and binges. Our eating, sleeping, and entertainment, for three unstructured examples, are done with minimal forethought. By going off in so many disparate but halfhearted directions, we make sure we don't really savor, explore any of them. We thus run the real risk of never discovering what can truly make us blissful, if anything can.

Let's face it: so many of our waking hours are one huge ethical wasteland, where, if anything, we shrink through inadvertence. Aren't we currently overlooking and in effect scorning countless daily chances to grow, neglecting so many deeds that seem unimportant or beneath us? So far today I've probably authored some twenty or thirty deeds and, perhaps, almost as many decisions. Did I find them fulfilling? Did they make me blissful? No, probably not; nor, given their nature, were they supposed to make me or others rejoice. Most actions have been routine, tiny, insignificant, only remotely related to the pursuit of ultimate happiness. In fact, I could have mindlessly done them all with at least one hand tied behind my back.

Actually, that's exactly how and what I did, just going through the paces like a dummy, my mind and heart elsewhere. Most of our life in fact is quite schizophrenic, our personality split at least into two, and we're hardly aware of it. We do most deeds because we have to. We're habitually distracted with other things, usually future, apparently more important and promising.

So, what's so bad about mediocre, dispirited deeds or omissions? Probably not very much. At worst such lackluster behavior wrongs others and myself only minimally. But that's not the point. The point is that, with a mere change of intention, the same actions could make a considerable contribution to fulfillment: others' as well as our own.


## PUTTING OTHERS FIRST

Let me tell you about an experiment I conducted yesterday in preparation for this chapter. I set out to answer the question: How many opportunities does a usual day present for putting others first? The results may surprise you, at least they did this relative veteran. There were no chances for huge favors or heroics; at least I didn't spot any, which is about par for the course. What did astound me was how many slight occasions I usually overlook that can easily be converted into tiny tokens of affection, friendship, and civility. I didn't keep count, but there were—are—literally hundreds of ways to help others, to lighten their load, to cheer them up, to listen, to take and show interest, to respect and esteem them. Note: I didn't drop everything and become an exclusive do-gooder for a day. Rather, the idea was to discover occasions for little services and favors in the very thick of my normal workaday routines. I soon realized that the key condition—much easier said than done—was somehow to activate my habitually sluggish mind and heart to make it possible to invest all of myself into what occupied me at each successive moment. I hate to sound original, but the secret seems to boil down to "where there's a will, there's a way."

When I *was* able to engage my "will," what "ways" did I discover?

## 1. SERVICE AS AN ADVERB

Affirming and loving others is much more a matter of attitude than actual deeds; much more an adverb (how and why) than a noun or even verb. It's largely a challenge of bringing a cheerful, endearing spirit to discharging my regular responsibilities. It takes no extra time; it occupies no additional space; it can piggy-back on any occupation or task. It's like juggling: with one hand I do my regular job(s), with the other I try to help others with theirs. It's a smile here, a quip there, an optimistic, unworried air over there; a minute's conversation with Tom, a caring question of Dick, a fond farewell to Harry. A big part of putting others first consists in showing them thoughtful consideration and loyal understanding—neither of which comes naturally or easily. Good manners, politeness, deference, courtesy, modesty, gratitude: all these social graces (and many others) are just awaiting a loving attitude to transform them from knee-jerk reflexes to embodiments of esteem and affirmation.

To pull it off, I must truly relegate my needs, self-pity, whims, and concerns to the back burner. Otherwise, how could I be useful to others? In doing so, I'm also perhaps trusting that they in turn will somehow, sometime, reciprocate, but their response shouldn't affect my initiatives. (Ideally there seems to be a tacit compact inscribed in human nature: I'm to take care of others, while they take care of me—and even when they don't.) This helpful spirit is not some sort of manipulative "winning friends and influencing people" in the cause of gaining customers, clients, or whatever. Nobody's a fool; sooner or later people know when they're being used. This disposition cannot be faked or improvised.

It boils down to sincerely living the golden rule in all its ramifications, no nooks or crannies excluded. Stripped of any feminist dross, "Practice random acts of kindness and senseless acts of beauty" is a call for me to get others, first, to germinate, then to sprout and, eventually, to bloom. "He ain't heavy, he's my brother" is more than a legendary saying and fund-raising appeal from Boys' Town. So far, I've shared some of the friendly, fraternal ways we can manifest our affective and effective concern for others. But what about opportunities when nobody's around?

## 2. Hidden Favors

There are many more opportunities to be useful, where we can truly love others disinterestedly, with no strings attached, expecting no reward or even recognition. Almost all of these are tiny things having to do with order, housekeeping, maintenance. . . that might reduce others' burdens. Returning to an autobiographical mode, here are some inconspicuous good deeds I was tempted to do and even occasionally gave in to: leaving things neat and dry in the bathroom (toilet lid down, towel folded just so, floor dry); straightening a picture on the stairs; fetching a bulb to replace a burnt-out one; straightening out a closet; turning off an unneeded lamp; leaving various paper sections folded the way they came; taking note of an end table in need of some re-gluing; picking up after myself and then a bit more; leaving dishes rinsed and ready for and in the dishwasher; moderating the volume of both TV and radio; putting a CD back in its cover and in its place. This list just covers the first forty minutes of the day. . . . Get the idea? A habitual failure to heed these chances to be useful makes us thoughtless parasites, adding to others' already considerable loads.

## 3. Being Useful on the Job

Then there's the vast area of my ordinary work day: a varied ensemble of tasks, duties, promises, commitments, professionalism, and teamwork. In one way or another all occupations today are

really service professions (or at least ought to be). Instead of unthinkingly, reactively, seeing our job as just a bunch of things we
"have to do," for everyone's sake we should be converting this
seemingly endless landscape into willing expressions of creative
love. But that's just the beginning.

On the heels of professional excellence should follow many
tokens of fraternal helpfulness. Another laundry list: stop complaining; don't interrupt others' conversation or work; be cheerful
and optimistic, a bit of an office clown and recreation director;
motivate subordinates with authentic concern; help others,
especially your associates and underlings, to confront and solve
their problems; defend at least others' good will when they're not
around; be quick to observe and listen, slow to judge and pon-
tificate; unless asked, keep your opinions to yourself, especially on
matters irrelevant to the common undertaking; conciliate, interpret
others' doings positively, translating them to one another; yet be
realistically demanding and challenging of subordinates; help them
to recommit themselves to the big picture and ultimate goals. . . .

## 4. SUCCESS STORIES

Admittedly, practically everything we do in life consists of a cumulus
of trivial, unchallenging tasks. The virtuously challenging thing is
usually not executing any particularly demanding chore, but the
almost staggering, suffocating sum of little things, plus getting and
keeping our priorities straight, while putting others first. Scratch
any famous person's success story, and behind the glowing achievements you find a dogged willingness to meet valiantly a conveyor
belt of near-infinite trifles, details. Thanks, however, to our overactive imagination, we tend to equate such stories with stupendous
feats, daring strokes, in sum, the stuff of Hollywood adventures.

Meanwhile, so long as golden, heroic opportunities come not
our way, we cut corners and slough off, excelling only at mediocrity

and minimizing the worth of the puny challenges that make up our uninteresting days and equally boring weeks. So in our tedious wait we anesthetize ourselves, while claiming that *then*, but no sooner, we'll rise to the occasion, take on all comers, and slay those endless fire-belching dragons.

Whom are we kidding? How can we possibly meet the big challenges, when we've been welshing on the countless, minuscule challenges that endlessly populate our flat, insipid existence? How pitiful to be scorning and killing hours, days, weeks, and months—and ourselves into the bargain! There's nothing wrong with romantic dreams of high adventures; if anything, we probably dream much too little. So, stoke those high hopes and great expectations. What's revolting is our perverse, repeated failures to find soul-consuming enterprises in the ordinary, humdrum haunts and walks of life, wherein, paradoxically, we just might be able to acquit ourselves well. It may be that the whole secret of life consists in pouncing on each of these very viable nothings to make them fully our own and then, most freely and lovingly, to gladden others with them. There's more than enough romance to be discovered and liberated amid the stupid, little nothings of each hour and day. But for that we need perspective; we need to rediscover their value time and again in our quiet time. Otherwise we slack off and defraud both others and ourselves.

## 5. WIN-WIN

I was very far from losing out in this day-long experiment to put others first. Stretched? Yes. Tired? Most definitely. Yet the more I tried to help others, the more I seemed to benefit, too. It also happened that the more chances I unearthed to bring some cheer into others' lives, the more opportunities I spotted waiting to be done. No room for complacency here. However much I might be theoretically persuaded that my deepest happiness is conditional on making others happy, it really helps to experience it in one's blessedly fatigued body. Simply stated: I grow by trying to make others grow; I am rewarded with no little bliss (the deep, lasting kind) to the extent that I sacrifice myself on behalf of those at my side, however unloving, seemingly unlovable, and unresponsive.

In the process, life is turned upside-down (or is it right-side up?). New frontiers and vistas are opened where before there was but monotony, a two-dimensional "prison" bereft of both meaning and challenge. When our workaday, ordinary life is not enlivened, inspirited, with love, is it any wonder that we feel trapped? But it need not be so. The train to fulfillment and joy supreme has not departed once for all, leaving us stranded on the drab, forlorn platform. We needn't think that heroism, adventure, and romance await only those lucky few who can climb Mount Everest or compete in the Olympics or get hitched with Mr. Right or whatever. Each of us can pull off his or her very own Copernican revolution with the least likely raw material. With an effective change of heart, behold, the once-despised prison can be converted into a sumptuous, spacious palace, the trap into deliverance.

There has been much anguished talk as the century has advanced bemoaning the dearth of meaningful, interesting jobs. It's the mindless repetitiveness of the assembly line (not to mention most medical and legal practices) or the bane of specialization (learning more and more about less or less) or the serflike victimhood of slaving for some exploitative, capitalistic machines. Surely less than one in twenty of us is engaged in a stimulating, engrossing occupation. The result is a veritable population explosion of near-zombies. If anything, the future portends even more of the same.

But, again, let's not waste time blaming circumstances outside our reach. Here, too, the best defense is a good, ever better, offense. Let's embrace all that toil and tedium and transform those countless chores into incarnations of other-love. Then not only will our virtue, character, and fulfillment grow thanks to this odyssey, but for others we'll also trigger a chain-reaction of like benefits whose dimensions are unforeseeable. Then *what* I do will be of very relative importance, since all the drama and excitement I crave will be found, in spades, in my labors' renewed *how* and *why*. There will also be a very positive by-product: class distinctions and professional rankings will become well-nigh meaningless. Any job can then become the raw material for becoming a true leader.

## WHERE WEAK STRONG

Now some readers, especially men, may be wondering if most of this chapter's observations and suggestions aren't mainly for women. "I'm too busy to be bothered with all those worthless frills and froth and fizz. Can't we leave all those sentimental nothings to the already predisposed females of the species? It's a jungle out there, man, a slugfest among cutthroat competitors. Besides wasting time and effort, what will the guys think if I turn soft, nice, and sweet?"

At the risk of political incorrectness and even sexism, let me point out that, mentally and morally, men tend to be weak where women are strong—and vice versa. They ought so to complement each other that, if given unhindered expression, these tendencies in married couples constitute a bare minimum for the social matrix that can best raise and educate children. Thus the joined two are better, fuller, more adequate than one. But wouldn't the best set-up be one in which each voluntarily, virtuously adds to his or her natural predispositions and strengths those qualities that don't come naturally, but are acquired by dint of repeated good deeds? If men were to work at acquiring, though with male modes, female qualities—and again vice versa—wouldn't 90 percent of the problems that make up our current wars between the sexes diminish, if not disappear? But there are many more benefits.

## GIANT STEPS

Here are some ways to acquire the Midas touch:

1. *Age quod agis:* "Do what you're about and immerse yourself in it."

2. Stop pining for more suitable circumstances to turn yourself around; it's there at your finger-tips. Ordinary life lived extraordinarily well is all the opportunity we need to acquire, exercise all virtues.

3. Virtue is not doing harder things, but doing them better for better reasons.

4. Thrill to the romance of "here and now" instead of "there and then."

5. Shun applause, stop fishing for compliments. Do and disappear.

6. At quiet time, review all segments of life: see how to do things better, or at least with more love and self-discipline; make successive tiny, concrete resolutions.

7. Keep your room neat; make the bed; put order in your desk, closet, chest of drawers; remember that others must also use the bathroom.

8. Cheerfully do chores, not having to be reminded; never say: "Oh, I forgot."

9. Communicate, communicate, communicate, especially with spouse or parents; don't make them fret when plans go awry. Also, never assume anything; just ask.

10. Pick up after yourself (and even others); take care of things,

furniture, appliances, tools; do a bit more than you're obliged to. Don't leave car messy or "on empty." Avoid loud noises.

11. Serve others at home, surprise them with joys; let them rest in dependable you; help with younger children or siblings. Courtesy, good manners; good grooming, dressing up for meals. "Please" and "Thank you." Tag along when others have errands to run, especially dad or mom. Jump to answer the phone, fill coffee cups or wine glasses, including your own.

12. Compliment, compliment, compliment your wife or mom; make every day "Mother's Day."

13. Have a schedule that covers everything. Don't let free time just happen. Be punctual; lots of so-called "heroic minutes" throughout the day, especially the initial one: getting out of bed.

14. Make yours a habitual state of healthy tension; end each day exhausted, having exercised pretty much to the full all your moral and mental muscles.

So, strive to be ever truer to yourself in your vocation to being a full, complete person. And how to do that? By continuing to take the various, interlocking steps covered in this book. You could do a lot worse than to fire your imagination with a composite of Pied Piper, Johnny Appleseed, and King Midas, with a happy, hilarious, ever expansive ending that may never end. Well, that synthesis is the goal for which we, however weak and inconstant, should resolve to reach, come what may.

# 17

## ARISTOCRATS OF LOVE

Love begets love. This torment is my joy.
— Theodore Roethke, *The Motion*, 1964

AT TIMES THE WORLD seems to be going down in a turbulent, endless sea of conditional love. We all know what conditional love is: I like you so long as I find something likable in you and so long as you, in turn, like me for similar reasons. When, however, we tire of one another, the mutual admiration and affection compact just dissolves.

So long as we like each other, how we treat one another has most of the appearances of love, or at least of niceness and kindness. But what is really going on in this relationship is much more contractual. As the lawyers say, *Do ut des*, which means, "I give, so that you give in return." When what you have to offer no longer pleases or benefits me, my need for you evaporates and with it the veneer of friendship. We both move on in the hopes of finding or putting together a new constellation of "friends" useful and convenient to us in our current needs. Eventually, however, we run out of semi-feigned niceness or of prospects from whom to bribe their nicenesses. Not surprisingly, the rift develops also on the other side: our "associates" begin to resist being used with little payoff for them. Then one's ego can collapse in a cloud of confusion, loneliness, and self-disgust.

All too afraid that allegiance to them is proportional to their good behavior, children tend to rebel and cave in; so do spouses. It's almost as if the object of conditional allegiance perversely misbehaves in order to prove to the other how shallow is his or her commitment. When that happens, pathologies of all kinds— mental, moral, familial, social, even physical—sprout like dandelions in the spring. The reason is simple and obvious: we know only too well that we generate precious few good deeds and thus deserve only scant allegiance from others. We know ourselves to be, for the most part, both unloving and unlovable. If we further peer into others' lives, we soon conclude that we're all in the same boat: all in need of unconditional love, yet both the subjects and objects of all too conditional commitments. A precarious house of cards, if ever there was one.

## WHAT WOULD MAKE US CONTENT

What would we most like to find, but rarely if ever do, in the persons pledged to us? If the golden rule bids us to do for others what we would like them to do for us, we do well to ask first how we'd like to be treated. The sought-after qualities that make up unconditional love are almost too good to be true, but not for that reason less needed. Here are some facets of the unconditional love we need and have yet to encounter:

1. Someone who is always, irrevocably there, in our corner, smiling and encouraging us, righting us when we stumble or give way to real or imagined fatigue; someone who kindly puts a positive spin on our every deed, misdeed, and non-deed, no

matter what, no matter how we misbehave, no matter how badly we mistreat our unconditional friend.

2.  Someone who doesn't need to be asked to understand, condone, forgive us unreservedly; who finds excuses even we had overlooked; who's never scandalized or censorious at our missteps, however frequent, childish, or cheap; whose faithful, perpetual smile is never affected by our scowls; who's eager to adduce reasons why our mountains can justifiably be shrunk to molehills; yet who never compromises with the truth of my self-defeating ways.

3.  Someone who more than merits our fullest trust and confidence, before whom we can discard the mask of our false persona; to whom we can unburden ourselves by confiding all our most embarrassing, self-deflating and even deviant thoughts, addictions, deeds, and urges, the sources of our disappointments, headaches, and heartbreaks, shrunken goals and expectations; on whose capacious and stalwart shoulder we can lean, and even cling, however few or many tears our ducts can still eke out.

4.  Someone, further, who delights in our company; whose pulse is quickened by our mere voice or physical approach; who eagerly awaits our phone calls; whose eyes twinkle even more when we're around; who's quick to listen, observe, ask about, and take a genuine interest in our affairs, however trivial and fleeting; whose laugh, sense of humor, and optimism are rampant and catching; who exquisitely respects and defends our freedom, without trying to remake us into his or her image.

5.  Finally, someone who is not put off by our cynicism, putdowns, recidivism, and downright wretchedness, but who, on the contrary, entertains in our regard the highest hopes, the greatest expectations, the most unlimited dreams; who's keenly

interested in, while fanning, our growth and betterment in every dimension; who ever invites us to soar like eagles in our healthy ambitions and aspirations in lieu of floundering around like barnyard hens; who's ever sketching new, unexpected vistas for our ideals, lest we settle for making mud-pies in squalid gutters; who, like a coach, patiently teaches us the steps to achieving full personhood for both ourselves and others; who resells us time and again on how desperately others need to perceive the fruits of fully ratifying human existence as aristocrats of love.

## GENERATING UNCONDITIONAL LOVE

A tall order, you say? Indeed. But would anything less do justice to the agonies and ecstasies that make up the human condition? Moreover, if that's the genuine love each of us would like to be the object of, isn't that what our very own being calls us to do for others? The unconditional commitment and love that others need of us is what will actually make both the subject and objects of this boundless, unreserved self-giving as fulfilled and blissful as both parties can possibly be in this life. Whether or not we're the object of others' unconditional allegiance (something that would doubtless make it easier for us to maintain this heroic tenor), we owe it both to ourselves and to others to love them so, for that is the best way for us authentically to love ourselves (super-enlightened self-interest). If volunteers are needed to get the ball rolling and thereby trigger a chain-reaction of reciprocating but unconditional commitments, how about you and I? However much others may benefit, we can't help but be the chief beneficiaries. Surely some of the others at least will begin to respond in kind and will shore us up and spur us on, when our efforts flag, as doubtless they will.

What will assuredly keep us plodding along is to see, first in hope and dream, and then in actuality, the heights of creativity, development, truth, and virtue to which human beings will scale, when they know themselves to be loved unconditionally and begin so to love others. If this total, reciprocal commitment were to catch on and spread contagiously, what a new world and society would soon arise, phoenix-like, from the ashes of our barren, blind, self-defeating selfishness! It would make the combined utopias the world has dared to dream seem like mere ineffectual wills-o'-the-wisp in comparison.

## To Guard against Reneging

Now for this good infection to spread far and wide and thus wreak such transformations of persons, families, and societies, more than enthusiasm and good intentions are requisite. Otherwise, the pessimists will deservedly have the last cynical laugh. What, more realistically and practically, can weak, volatile, vindictive and cunning persons do to redeem their pledge to love others unconditionally? Besides trying our best to live the program in felicity and wisdom outlined in the preceding chapters, what further steps could we take to defy the all too usual atrophy that, termite-like, infects all things human? Here are some suggestions, based on the first impulse of real love to eternalize itself and to hedge itself round with all kinds of self-imposed but public protestations, restraints, vows, witnesses, and the like:

1. To see ourselves through the sloughs of despond, dark nights, inevitable doubts, confusions, and temptations to weasel out of this exacting pledge, it would be wise at least to commit ourselves in writing, a mission statement, if you will. This "testament" will naturally highlight the end pursued, the steps and means thereto, the obstacles and the benefits. Having it

in writing will permit us to revisit this declaration periodically to inspire serial re-commitments.

2.  We won't go very far or last very long, unless we find an ethical coach-confidant-friend. To such a mentor we must submit our perverse tendency to deceive ourselves and revert to unenlightened ways. We all need someone, who, with objectivity and disinterestedness, can guide, counsel, encourage, challenge, and (why not say it?) love us. Such an adviser must know us inside out; we can hold back no secrets, especially the most embarrassing and shameful infidelities to our life's project and to others. These huddles give us an opportunity to look bad, to "gossip" about ourselves. We should elicit from our confidant the commitment to tell us the truth, especially when we're backing away from it, lest in our worse moments we forget that, while hurting, the truth also heals. Ideally, our guide will have both the strength and vision to fan our desire for the goal—bliss, ecstasy—while showing us that we keep seeking it in the wrong places or ways. Topics? Hits and misses; desires, hopes, disappointments; deeds, misdeeds, and omissions; review of the jointly tailored plan to make the project a reality; particular targets of struggle. Frequency? Initially, at least once a month.

Does this second step seem excessive? Such an assessment is but the natural voice of the defensive, inexperienced outsider. A person who has no or very reduced standards, which are effortlessly kept (at least some of the time), can probably dispense with a guide. But persons who recognize that, in so many ways, they are their own worst enemies will understand that they need help to raise their level of performance towards their lofty goals. For precedents, one need go no further than the toils and travails of the athlete determined to go for the gold, who would never think of going it alone without the best of coaches.

3.  As mentioned earlier, Peanuts' Lucy got it only too right: "I love humanity, it's people [smelly, pushy, disagreeable, flesh-and blood individuals encroaching on me] I can't stand." While one may want to love and serve everybody, at least in theory, true love is a matter, not of sweet words, but of gratuitous deeds and favors to very concrete and usually unappreciative people. However universal my aspirations, these must be proved and forged in my daily interchanges with those closest to me. In other words, each of us needs to have a handful of persons, be it one's natural family or a chosen group of friends, whom we commit ourselves, in our heart of hearts, to love and serve. For their sake, to be sure, but no less for ours.

Across the human spectrum, there's no doubt that the deepest, most lasting joys we observe are those associated with maternity and even paternity; such is human nature. How mothers and fathers of infants beam and bloom, unthinkingly glad to sacrifice themselves, quite uncharacteristically, for their utterly dependent loved ones! Well, if biological generation almost invariably brings out the best in us, what deeper joys might not spiritual paternity—discipleship, apprenticeship in life—bring in its wake? To coax forth, amid however much more blood, sweat, and tears, children of the spirit is surely the adventure we're all called to, but so few hit upon.

## HANDLING UNREQUITED LOVE

True love is born and further matures in the face of unrequitedness. It's so easy to love those who respond in kind. But is that really other-love or, rather, camouflaged and relatively unenlightened self-love? Most of us, to be sure, can fairly easily go out of our way to generate three or four unbidden favors, but when these go unrecognized and we find ourselves being taken for granted, and even despised, well, that's another matter. Yet only then does it become possible for us to bestow an absolutely *free* gift of self.

Whatever our age, it may very well be that we have so far generated few, if any, tokens of truly unselfish other-love. Parents should be forewarned that they really don't and can't start loving their spouses or children with utter disinterest, until they've stopped liking them (this dislike need not be precipitated intentionally, it will soon enough arise on its own). It's ironic but only too true: most marriages today break up just when they were about to get under way, just when the partners need to slough off the confining skin of positive feelings and inclinations that make up "liking." This painful step necessarily presages the advent of genuine other-love. Only then are we psychologically and morally free to surprise others stealthily by joy.

The following two chapters suggest in considerable detail how newfound "aristocrats of love" might embody their disinterested self-giving as spouses and parents, in what are undoubtedly the most common relationships calling for selfless commitment.

# 18

# REINVENTING MARRIAGE

> If love is blind, marriage is a good eye-opener.
> —Anonymous, 1940s

MARRIAGE TODAY looks almost as if it were down for the count. In fact, the only unions likely to survive the ever-growing moral undertow in the third millennium may be those pairing two virtue-strengthened aristocrats of love. The chickens born of inadequate and improvised "love" are coming home to roost.

This we soon learn in spades if we happen upon any country-Western radio station. How can there be anything other than broken hearts and vows when morally unprepared people un-thinkingly commit themselves to a potentially lifelong venture light-years beyond any acquired capacity for self-giving? The wonder isn't that one out of every two unions comes unstuck, but rather that half the marriages somehow stick it out, amid however much despair. Exaggerated? According to Ann Landers' readership, some six mothers out of ten regret having brought their very own children into the world. We can do much better than that. Have we any other option?

If today's family is bankrupt, it's because too many couples have been welshing on their marriage vows. When the chips are down, spouses prove to be Indian givers (if you'll permit me just this one politically very incorrect expression). Or as a grade school teacher recently told me, "Parents' love gives out when their kids start sassing back."

What's wrong with so many marriages today? As the teacher says, there's too much conditional, revocable love. No good behavior, no continued parental (or spousal) love and allegiance. And today, when there are so many chances for misbehavior and consequently much more misbehavior, children (and spouses) are correspondingly loved less, if at all. Yet that's when they need to be loved much more, given their befuddled, sorry state.

Back in the hand-to-mouth days, people used to get married and sire children for lots of reasons other than, or perhaps short of, love: needed skills, cheap labor, old-age assistance, security. But today's children, if anything, are the opposite of financial assets. Neither are most contemporary women, highly educated, liberated and self-sufficient, their hubbies' needed, though dependent, helpmates of old. Consequently, marriage and its issue are all too often viewed as very open-ended experiments in private fulfillment, durable only so long as one's personal investment is exceeded by its yield.

## CHOOSING A MATE

Apropos of spouses, if the option is still open to you, choose a *good* one. Now that doesn't necessarily mean somebody attractive who appeals to you, who's moreover fun to be with, who, besides, provides a good target for the IRS. All those are bonuses, but not essential qualities. Above all, seek someone who generally shares your philosophy on life (agreement on principles) and whose virtues complement your own, such as they are, and any strong points.

In terms of innate qualities, men tend to be weak where women are strong and vice versa. They're to pool their strengths and thus compensate for each other's shortcomings. Then the pair make up a minimally adequate seedbed for rearing children. Before seriously engaging in the matrimonial sweepstakes, both men and women should, with brutal honesty, take an inventory of their respective moral (if not financial) assets and liabilities. How otherwise can they know which complementary qualities to look for in prospective mates? Always keep in mind that with marriage you're forming a permanent partnership to build something bigger and better than the two of you. You're more than mutual recreation directors.

Somewhere or other Antoine de Saint-Exupéry says that the best image of marital love is not the usual one of the moonstruck couple gazing fondly, even hypnotically, into the eyes of one another. Rather, the composition should feature them side by side with their loving gazes intersecting in the future and riveted on the fruits begotten of their loving partnership. Surely the idea is that, while the other-pledged couple should delight and love one another, they have, no less and maybe even more, promised to help one another to build a joint venture: children, family, home, extended family friendships. Let them luxuriate in the initial gratifications arising from their intimacy and union. But if their primary end is still to create, by reinventing, the home through the complementary contributions of both, then the inevitable shortcomings of one's mate do not loom so large or so tragic. It's easier to rise above the disappearance of the honeymoon once the fruits of that honeymoon begin to make their wailing appearance.

Another suggestion to keep the pair focused on their partnership is the idea of jointly drawing up a blueprint (or charter) for their very own unique marriage during the months after the engagement. Ends and means, family dreams and policies, anticipated problems and trials, how the couple are to complement each other, even rewards and penalties for the children—these are but a sampler of what the affianced couple may wish to commit to paper. Drawing it up will help them reach fundamental unity at the level of principles. This document could then be revisited each year on their anniversary, subject to further additions, subtractions, and amendment.

Even if you're wholly committed to becoming an aristocrat of love, keep in mind that it's nearly impossible to keep up such a heroic tempo and pitch on the sole basis of personal efforts and any rewards. You'll accumulate failures and discouragements aplenty. Would that your spouse were also an aborning aristocrat of love; then you can sustain one another. When you're up, for example, she may be down—and, let's hope, vice versa. When the going gets tough, the odds against chucking the whole "impossible" venture would be greatly lessened if one's eventual bed-mate were also one's soul-mate and virtue-mate. Ideally, one should try to turn inside out the venerable saying: "Marry in haste, repent in leisure."

## MONSTER OR MASTERPIECE?

Then we come to the fruit of that creative partnership. Today there's a near-universal fear of seeing one's children become, not masterpieces, but monsters. How to deal with such rebels? It may very well be the case—since the proposition is relatively untested—that raising children amid all kinds of unconditional love is the only possible way to spare parents innumerable headaches and heartbreaks. But more than reducing troubles, won't making unconditional love the medium in which children grow up convert them into moral, intellectual, and creative giants?

It's hard to imagine the outer limits of human growth, both personal and collective. Doubtless we've seen only rare and more or less distant approximations, brought forth by usually obsessed and one-sided trail-blazers. But what might not ensue from fully integrated and disinterested youths who avail themselves as freely as responsible of all the past achievements and current opportunities open to them? As they culturally cross-fertilize each other, surely they'll ratchet their way to unsuspected heights that will make the Renaissance pale in both extent and quality. Won't we all benefit from the flowering of humanity brought about by first one and then another generation of new men and women? It's about time.

## Good not Good Enough

It used to be the case that good parents raised good children: "Like father, like son; like mother, like daughter" is, alas, far from being the contemporary case—no, not even in the so-called "best" families. Things were more settled and predictable back in the days when "father knew best." But today's corrosive circumstances have raised the ante severely. Gone forever—and good riddance—are the days when ordinary parents could just coast, improvising all the way, and relying overmuch on apparently sound institutions, such as church, school, and community. A bit of common sense here, a veneer of virtue there; a shot of folk wisdom here, a tad of discipline there ("there" being out behind the wood shed). Our parents or their parents assumed they knew how to raise kids, since they themselves had been raised more or less well.

Until fairly recently, thanks to more benign circumstances, those less committed to their families could navigate the familial shoals with, usually, minimal harm. But no longer. Merely good parents today, if lucky, tend to have kids that leave a trail of disappointments. By the way, that's why so many contemporary couples are afraid to have children. Having seen how others' kids turn out, the last thing they want or need is to be penned up for twenty or thirty years with a monster or two. Isn't the solution self-evident? Parents need to be two or three notches better than how they want their children to turn out. Very good isn't good enough today. Ultra-good might even fall short. We may seriously doubt whether anything less than a personal commitment to full-fledged dedication and uncommon virtue will do the trick. Sorry, everything less has been tried and found wanting.

But that demanding formula, you might object, is the quickest way to misery compounded. Yet the paradoxical truth is that such self-sacrificing parents stand to gain everything and to lose nothing; nothing, that is, but a bumper crop of headaches and heartbreaks with each backfiring kid.

Nothing new is being invented in the call for unlimited dedication and love from spouses. Rather this pledge only echoes, while particularizing, the call inscribed in human nature, not to mention the marital vows themselves. What's good for me (loving unconditionally) is exactly what's good for both my spouse and children (being loved unconditionally). There's nothing wrong with marriage and kids today that can't be cured by the couples' personal decision and all-out plan to right themselves.

There you have a new theory wherewith to reform and reinvent parenthood today. Down with band-aids and superficial savvy. Nothing less than such pure, self-forgetting love can adequately address the home front today. Nothing less will get kids to interiorize indispensable truth and morality. Nothing less will weather the kids' refusal to do so. But couples need to understand what they're getting into—something most, alas, never fully realize or commit themselves to, either before the nuptials or after.

What an excellent, concrete field for all that free self-giving has been given you in your misbehaving, ungrateful, unloving children! You'll never be supremely happy as you're supposed to until you overcome your fretting and self-pity and truly become a willing servant of others, starting with your family, with no expectation of rewards. But what truly spoils family life is to wear a martyr's mask or to display a victim's complex: "Nobody loves me; nobody listens; nobody does what I say; nobody appreciates all the troubles and travails your mom (or dad) and I have been put through. . . ."

## TAKING LOVE BACK

Love is fine and dandy in theory, but terribly hard in practice, especially when initial positive feelings are replaced by negative ones. We go out of our way to be nice, to do favors for others, to please them, to sacrifice our interests and likes for their benefit—and when they don't respond? When they don't even acknowledge our efforts and unthinkingly take us for granted? How do we react then? Well, for one thing, we never forget. Then, we start rationing our little favors and services. We also harbor grudges and resentments; we soon formulate some pretty final negative judgments of them. Then come the snide comments, the put-downs, the barbs, the outbursts, the quarrels, and so on. Yet love never reaches maturity unless we keep on loving, no matter what, even when all liking—whether of spouse or kids—has disappeared. We can never say we love until we're ready to put up with everything from everybody with infinite patience and understanding. That's what unconditional, unrequited love entails.

You see, children who don't experience totally gratuitous, unconditional love at home can't help but disappoint. Is there any other reason for all the self-defeating behavior and immorality that soon develops into so much mental illness and other psychic hells? When children don't catch glimpses and echoes of such absolute love in those around them, they can't help but despair, and that none too quietly.

The ultimate goal is for the children to become responsible self-directing persons who, let's hope, wisely choose to do the right things for the right reasons. We must help them, through good example and counsel, to interiorize the right motivation. Parents who treat their children as if they were putty in their hands usually spend the next forty to fifty years regretting the mistake of their meddling interference. Behind all those contrary appearances lies a young mind learning to reason and a will yearning to be free and a heart craving true love.

As early as possible good parents must recognize and respect their kids' "vital space," their innate freedom, and their ability to learn from their mistakes. If they never freely commit mistakes, how will they ever experience that your love for them is unconditional, irrevocable, merciful? The more parents trust their children to manage their lives well, the sooner they'll right themselves and do so. If parents must err in any direction, let it be in the direction of overtrusting permissiveness. A misdeed freely chosen and as freely regretted is so much more valuable than a reluctant good deed bribed out of a child by pushy parents. Experience, both good and bad, can be a terrific teacher so long as parents don't continually badger their children to draw the right conclusions. Have a lot more faith in them and in human nature, and a lot less in your own preaching.

## JUST STEWARDS

If parents want to die a thousand deaths, here's a surefire way: see children as totally malleable extensions of yourself whose every shortcoming reveals another failing in you as a parent. Yes, blame yourself for their every blunder and very conspicuously pay the emotional price. It also helps to smother and pamper them, especially sparing them the pain and sufferings stemming from their mistakes. On the other hand, if you don't want parenthood to be an unending burden, try this rule of thumb: Treat your kids the way you'd treat an exchange student who's moved in for a year. Since that child doesn't belong to you and you are only standing in for others, you'd be more inclined to see him as an independent agent with his own mind and will. You'd more likely appeal conscientiously to his reasonableness, its better nature. You'd be more thoughtful, deliberate, considerate, courteous, and so forth.

Aren't children also supposed to be their own men or women—and that as soon as possible? Here's the good news—and the bad: Parents are only stewards. Now this rightful perspective and deliberate distancing doesn't come easily or automatically. It's especially hard for parents who are trying to do the best thing or for those weakling parents who emotionally depend on their kids' approval. The problem is always, how can you treat kids as free and responsible persons when they're so obviously not? Isn't doing so a cruel disservice? Aren't dad and mom with their superior wisdom and experience obliged in justice and charity to call their children's shots? Really, it's a chicken-or-egg quandary. But the only way out may be for parents as early and often as possible to treat their kids *as if* they were reasonable, free, and responsible, providing them with criteria whereby they can decide for themselves. And then for both parties to suffer the consequences and reap the rewards. The more you treat them, not the way they are, but the way you want them to become, the faster they'll grow into maturity. Especially if they're left to answer for their deeds and omissions. That's the way they'll learn how to direct and redirect themselves. Trust them: it's a manifestation of your unconditional love. And then trust them again and again, however often they take advantage of you. What misbehaving children need above all is to know that dad and mom are lovingly in their corner always, regardless.

So, let's love them out of all proportion to their merits; let's treat them like potential adults. Let's confide to them whatever their mind and heart need to think and act aright. Let's acquaint them with themselves and the human condition. And then, let's step back so they can learn to maneuver on their own and thereby grow into fully free and fully responsible human beings.

To stop from being the eternal kibitzer, it might be good to keep handy a roll of two-inch adhesive tape to be applied liberally to the mouth. Sit back; you've done what you can; you rightly raised them to be autonomous; they must now answer for their beliefs, choices, and deeds, since they are their very own. Sure: with all that rope and vital space, your children will make lots of mistakes, some of them even major; likely as not, they'll break your heart not a few times. But what is the thing that will most readily get them to recognize their self-deceiving ways and help them recover their senses? Positive and repeated proofs of your undying and disinterested love and hopes for them. The truth is, broken hearts, with each mending, become bigger and more resilient than ever. Fear not.

## SALVATION BY SUBURBS?

But, you might object, if negative circumstances are to blame, can't I with my family get away from them or at least blunt them? A safe environment, a safe school, safe entertainment, safe books, a safe church, safe companions—won't all these safeguards protect them? The problem with this suburban greenhouse outlook is that the kids aren't stupid, they realize they're being manipulated, kept away from all those "forbidden fruits." Such shielded kids from the 'burbs tend to be the biggest rebels—or at least appear so to their parents. Moreover, parents tend to exaggerate external threats and to minimize the internal seeds of disorder that come with belonging to the human race. Yes, even their darling child.

There *is* a way to immunize your children against all the sex, beer, drugs, and all other kinds of self-destructive ideas and behavior that are so prevalent out there. But that way has nothing to do with blaming nasty circumstances or trying futilely to turn the clock back or keeping them away from such wayward occasions as long as possible. The only way to immunize them in the face of today's cornucopia of temptations is to raise kids in such a way that they themselves see what's wrong, what boomerangs, and personally, freely choose not to cheat themselves. And they won't do that very much or for very long unless they're really sold on doing the right thing with their lives for all the right reasons.

With all this insistence on unreserved parental love for children, some readers may wonder if they've fallen into the clutches of a hawker of permissiveness. Aren't parents supposed to be the primary educators of their children, to teach them right from wrong, to correct, discipline, and punish them, when they get out of hand? Yes, they are, very much so. Parents as authority figures should and need to intervene, to practice "tough love" and all the rest. In all their educating and forming, parents, however, must make sure that it is love they are manifesting and acting on—not frustration, not disappointment, not spite, not resentment, not deep-seated anger. Now, as you well know, that's much easier said than done. Consequently parents can never assume that theirs is the best of good wills. They must go back time and again to scrutinizing both their deeds and motives.

## WHAT HE CAN DO

Do I believe that a woman's place is in the house? Most certainly. But I also believe that a man's place is—or at least ought to be, and increasingly must be—no less in the home, for his wife's sake, for his children's sake, but above all for his own sake. That said, let's turn to nervous male readers and try to sell them on the urgent need to upgrade their preparation for, and contribution to, their family role. These days, unlike the two prior millenia, it is the newly virtuous man who, in the joint undertaking of marriage, must blaze the trail.

You're probably not much of a fan of how-to-do-it kits, especially those catalogs bulging with the 49,731 tips that contemporary dads should be heeding. What's needed today is not more practical suggestions; today's dads are drowning in myriad sins of fatherly omission—and they're well aware of it. They don't need their consciousness raised—they need their hopes and spirits raised.

But why pick on husbands? First, you're supposed to be the head of the family and that means to lead, to set, and implement the strategy—and that largely by infectious example. Second, to bring about a much higher level of maturity in your children as soon as possible, there's going to have to be a lot more real educating and forming going on at home, most of it private and personal. And that's a job for which you dads are uniquely qualified and yet a job you've been shirking all too long. There you have the gist of what you're to do. Even good fathers have good excuses: too little time and energy; not enough encouragement or role models, and so on. But all those excuses really prove your need to get extra time, energy, and motivation; and where will you get them except by increased virtue? What you dads really need is lots more heart and a bit more head. Your fatherly role demands today nothing less than honest-to-goodness love.

The prudential challenge of parenting consists in applying unchanging, perennial principles to ever changing circumstances, when not to ever moving behinds. In this regard dads today seem to be at a big disadvantage as opposed to moms, whose role is more biologically and instinctively laid out. Mothers' role hasn't changed all that much. Most contemporary fathers, however, recognize the unsuitability of their old model. But what's to take its place? The bungling, superfluous, misguided dad of TV's sitcoms? Hardly.


## WHEN LUST ISN'T THROTTLED

As I see it, the new husband and father will arise in part from a long overdue embrace of chastity and even virginity. Now it's no secret that man, the sexual predator, has traditionally been brought, if at all, to the altar with no little defensive kicking and screaming.

If male chastity were a big challenge before the sexual revolution, it's an overwhelming, almost impossible, one today, leaving many lives and marriages in tatters, if not destroyed. Moreover, with the disappearance of the "double standard," many contemporary women have given up on the naked nomad. But, then, who will civilize and domesticate him to be a fit spouse and father?

There are only two possible answers. We can return to the previous status quo, as recommended by George Gilder in his masterful *Men and Marriage*, or we can go in search of a more radical solution. From time immemorial women, acting out of a combination of conventions, fears, and virtue, used to withhold or ration their sexual favors. They thus got men to shape up and to abandon the chase after sexual thrills. But hasn't this compromise deserved the good riddance pronounced over it by contemporary history? Didn't the failure to kill lust, not merely cramp it, bring in its wake the following disadvantages?

1. This stop-gap approach evokes at best semi-virtue from women and reluctant, if sporadic, conformity from still largely lustful men.

2. Chastity thus comes across as a killjoy. Chastity's theoretical and practical tie-in with self-giving has rarely been explained, nor have therapeutic tips to living chastely been articulated and broadcast.

3. Then, as usual, men merely tolerate romance in order to get sex.

4. Men tend to being just bread-winners, leaving mom to rear the children.

5. As kids have gone from financial assets to liabilities, births have dwindled.

6. Unchaste men willy-nilly exploit: the spirit may be willing, but the flesh is weak and rapacious.

7. The decline of secondary reasons for wedlock (security, hedge against old age, free, specialized labor, and the like) has left wives less distracted from their mates' sexual exploitation.

8. Unchaste husbands continue to roam: infidelity, masturbation.

9. As we have seen, sexual addiction breeds all others; this dependency, coupled with ever-present salacious stimuli, leaves many men in a perpetual state of semi-arousal.

10. Once fixated on orgasm and discovering that heterosexual concourse must be painstakingly negotiated and thus rarely occasioned, men have increasingly turned to their own sex to satisfy their dreams for unending kicks. Indeed, a veritable homosexual epidemic may be sweeping through college ranks.

Exaggerated? Why then at countless colleges is the gay, lesbian, bisexual student group the most active and popular? Another case in point: at a high school in northern Virginia—which currently generates more National Merit Scholars than any institution, public or private—a reporter was recently hard pressed to find a single student who would claim to be heterosexual. Surely there were some, but cowed into the closet of silence by the prevailing ethos.

11. The divorce rate continues to soar, and in many marriages that last, depression abounds.

12. No wonder men today are haunted by the fear of, and inability to make, lasting commitments.

In the final analysis, the half-answer of women braking male lust was based on the dirty little pessimistic lie that in matters sexual men just can't help themselves. Now true it is that the male sexual drive can be triggered in a nanosecond and, once aroused, for all practical purposes cannot be denied. But instead of looking the other way and hoping men will grow out of it, why not teach them how and when to avoid sexual stimuli? Given the moral worsening of society, Gilder's recommendation to turn back the clock offers little hope.

## HIS NEW JOB DESCRIPTION

Following Edmund Burke's tip, mightn't we catch glimpses, amid the gathering decline, of how things should have been from the outset? Behold the radical solution: the new chaste, virtuous man committed to disinterested self-giving, capable of converting sex into glad embodiment of other-love. Yes, a little secret: men, even adolescents, can be chaste. Led by ever more enlightened self-interest, this new aristocrat of love will truly lead both wife and children to the promised land. But his must be a full-blown, all-out commitment of head and heart to kill the lustful desire to use and to replace it with loving self-giving, however weak in practice he may still be. No more improvisation and temporizing. Here are some of the advantages likely to ensue:

1. Such a virtue-strengthened man will be able to weather the demise of emotional attraction to both wife and kids; the almost necessary death of liking will give way to loving.

2. He will duly lead by serving, exercising a discreet and endearing headship; no more will he go AWOL with respect to the kids.

3. He will find the whys and wherefores of becoming the primary educator of his offspring; he'll turn the home into a school of virtue; he'll become his children's best guide and friend.

4. This new dad and hubby will have the moral resources to become a font of indispensable unreserved love and reasonableness, for both his wife and children.

5. He'll resemble celibates in that he's given up all the women the world over but one.

6. He'll also judiciously keep sexual stimuli at bay; mistrusting himself he'll work toward the courage that empowers him to flee before passion turns unstoppable; he'll conclude that there are no innocent looks or harmless nibbles with respect to sex.

7. This same mistrust will probably lead to asking his wife to become the sexual initiator; at least his decision to bestow on his wife the gift of sexual union will precede arousal.

8. He'll be able besides ever to court and woo his wife in a crescendo of romance.

9. He'll find ways to teach his kids all their mom has done for them and thus to revere her.

## THE PROMISES OF SUBLIMATION

Now, where is this new man to find the energy to carry out even a part of the above program? For starters, he's to find it in sublimating, *à la* Freud again, his sexual drive, harnessing his sexual power to higher endeavors. The best portrayal of the powerful transformation wrought by sublimating lust is found in the "lustful lizard" scene from C. S. Lewis' *Great Divorce*. The scene takes place in some sort of anteroom to heaven, wherein angels ply errant humans with temptations to goodness.

A visitor from earth, bearing a lizard on his shoulder with access to his ear, is taking his leave of a large, man-like creature giving off both light and heat. He apologizes for the lizard's inappropriate shenanigans. The angel offers to quiet him, evoking a tentative agreement from the earthling. When, however, it becomes clear that "quieting" means "killing," the lizard's host objects. He'll think about this too-drastic proposal back home. Maybe a gradual process would be better? In any case today he's not feeling well: some other time perhaps. "How can I tell you to kill it? You'd kill *me* if you did." The angel claims it will hurt the earthling but kill only the lizard. Back and forth, back and forth goes the dialogue, until the man reluctantly gives his permission. The reptile is throttled and has its back broken, as its host screams in agony. Then both bodies begin to undergo transformations. A new, complete man materializes. But from the dead lizard arises a great stallion, "silvery white but with mane and tail of gold." The man and horse nuzzle one another, as all nature voices its approval. The new man with tears of joy falls at the angel's feet. Then he leaps onto the horse and scales the mountainous peaks, as if to hasten to a rendezvous with the "rose-brightness of that eternal morning." Then earth and waters and woods begin to pulsate with a primal noise whereby the nature of that land rejoiced "to have been once more ridden, and therefore consummated, in the person of the horse."

An observer then asks the angel about the scene just witnessed. The angel replies: "Lust is a poor, weak, whimpering whispering thing compared with that richness and energy of desire which will arise when lust has been killed."

What a transformation of man takes place when lust is throttled! The mole-like, probing, ubiquitous sexual itch that stealthily incarnates itself as flattery, cajolery, sweet-talk, flirting, wheedling and whatnot is turned inside out. Only then does man become capable of freely bestowing his unconditional love. (Could this be the Prince Charming women have ever hoped and prayed for?) But how his metamorphosis fades in comparison with that wrought in women as a result of that nearly despaired-of bestowal! See how the loving couple are to ratchet their respective ways ever upward? His heart unleashes hers, and hers fecundates his. And thus, back and forth, they each contribute everything that marriage was meant to be, even enough unconditional love for them to be able to transform their children (or at least to weather whatever storms the latter engineer).

## WHAT SHE CAN DO

"What a beautiful, powerful, wonderful, faithful thing is a woman when she's loved unconditionally. And when she isn't. . . ." So observed a friend of mine years ago. William Congreve (1670-1729) beat him to the punch with his claim: "Hell [has] not a fury, like a woman scorn'd." Many female shortcomings stem from men not duly loving women for the spouses and mothers they're called to be. That's why, if marriage is to be reinvented, the major and certainly first overhaul has to be that of men. But that's only the opening movement. Because, when as a result, pumps all primed, women in turn start loving unconditionally both husband and children, all heaven will break out.

Even when not loved quite so absolutely, it's no secret that women are by nature and instinct kinder, gentler, stronger, more personal and intuitive, more loyal, generous, and resourceful. Without such a woman, with her characteristically melting smile, in their corner, dad and kids can't help but malfunction. But when she is there, what won't her mate and offspring do, lest they defraud such implacable and undeserved warmth, understanding, and affection?

Need more be said? Eminently applicable to women so loved and so loving is Augustine's apparently reckless cry, "Love, and do what you will." Such women neither need nor are likely to heed a particularized program; each will create her very own as she goes along. Still and all, some women, pleading fairness, may want a few pointers to tide them over, when love runs low. While I may, very tentatively, put forth a few suggestions, let it be noted (and notarized) that I do so solely under duress, with no little fear and trembling.

For everyone's sake, not least yours, be an enterprising, inventive gourmet cook, one who liberally condiments her fare with lots of love and spirits. Wine, brandy, and rum cover a multitude of culinary sins, not unlike charity. Even more so today, the way to a man's heart (plus that of children) is still through his stomach. If you want your husband to be better, don't harp; rather, heap him with varied, delectable food. This fact was driven home to the me very eloquently several years back when I made the acquaintance of a man who'd been married five years but gave every impression of still being on the honeymoon. To the inquiry, he replied: "In all these years I don't think my wife's ever served the same dinner menu twice." Little did he know how artful (and lovingly understanding) his wife was in repackaging leftovers and old stand-bys.

Then, don't hound your hubby. You don't know how biting and enervating your acid-like tongue can be. Nor do you fully appreciate how much talking, good and bad, you generate. Linguists in their research have documented that in any given day women talk roughly twice as much as do men. (As Gary Smalley wryly points out, by the time men reach home in the evening, they've roughly exhausted the day's verbal quota, while wives are just getting started.) One of the reasons for this talkativeness is the female's ability to split her attention relatively well among four or five competing interests (an absolute necessity in raising children), one of which is often a semi-conscious flow of conversation. With such verbal output, some of it is bound to be less than mind-filtered or tactful. Is it any wonder, then, that the English language has at least eleven printable terms for the sharp-tongued and plaintive woman: vixen, virago, termagant, shrew, harridan, hag, scold, harpy, ogress, nag, she-devil? So, women, curb, restrain, delay, domesticate that flapping tongue.

Finally, wives: continue to woo and win your lesser part every day, more so as your marriage matures. But keep your conspiracy to yourselves. Meanwhile, bribe and surprise him with tantalizing meals; home improvements; your attractive appearance, however much cosmetically upgraded; and so many other tokens of affection and understanding. If you take exquisite care of the board and its environs, the bed (and so much else) will take care of itself.

If marriage is first to survive and then ultimately thrive, it needs to be reinvented as the joint embodiment of the pair's unlimited love. Nothing less than a dedication that echoes what Mother Teresa (honored by Congress in 1996 as only the third "honorary citizen" of the United States) expected of her sari-clad followers will do. So, start beating the drums for a much better millennium than the two previous, one that arises from their jetsam but youthfully committed to bringing forth "a new civilization of love." It will be a habitat finally fit for humanity, something much better and greater than anything the world has ever witnessed. And therein will the pioneering "aristocrats of love" work their magic through osmosis, spreading democratically their good infection to Everyman. Then, before too long won't the Irish dream finally come true: that of every man a King and every woman a Queen?

# 19

# REINVENTING DAD

Good dads should be seen and not heard.
—Author (see below)

THERE ARE NINE ways to rejuvenate and reinvent father-
hood as this turbulent century draws to a close.

Before doing so, however, let's anticipate a warranted
objection from any readers who have peeked to see if there is a
chapter corresponding to the reinvention of mom. None exists,
for two simple reasons. I am not alone in opining that there's
little to reinvent on that front. And even if there were, most wives
and mothers, be they current or future, are not about to cede any
redesign to a mere male of the species. Mom merely has to be
motivated via her husband's unconditional love to discharge her
customarily self-sacrificing role to make both hubby and children
shine.

And what have women been doing for centuries with little or
no recognition? What haven't they done? They've cooked meals,
done washing, ironing, and mending, cleaned house, mowed the
lawn, painted bathrooms, sewed curtains and clothes, helped with

homework, spent an incalculable amount of time shopping, helped at school functions, arranged the kids' parties, shopped for Christmas, birthday, and other gifts, done the banking and paid the bills, decorated several houses, weeded the garden, taken care of the family pets, handled repairs, nursed the sick, soothed hurt feelings, chauffeured the kids to sports, dance classes, and music lessons, provided all or part of the family income—and also changed diapers. All this after carrying however many babies for nine months and then giving birth—not exactly a picnic.

**1. Lavish love on your wife.** One of the best and highest gifts you can give your children is for them to see how much and how persistently you love and serve your spouse. You must keep very much alive by dint of virtue and will power all those things—gifts, considerations, services, surprises, displays of affection—that came so easily during courtship, on the honeymoon, and in the early days of marriage. Now that most of the emotional facilities and incentives to woo her have diminished and even disappeared, much more deliberate and voluntary virtue must take over to generate the same pitch of romance, if not greater. Don't be surprised that the bubbly feelings are gone; that's the way things happen. Don't even be surprised if negative feelings have replaced positive. In fact, if you're wise, you should be learning to rise virtuously above your instinctive likes and dislikes.

Give your wife your undivided attention. Anticipate her needs and even whims. Linger over that second and even third cup of coffee. Sympathize, sympathize, sympathize: women need understanding more than expert male problem-solving. Lighten her burdens, preferably behind her back. Surprise her with little notes, phone calls, a bouquet of the first dandelions of the season. . . . Compliment her on her appearance, that new perfume or hairdo, that new furniture arrangement, that extra-good meal. Be very courteous and refined, especially in your speech, but also in your dress and grooming. Waste time alone together. Meet her more than halfway in doing those things women so much prize and that we men couldn't care less about.

If your children see how much you respect and revere your wife, how grateful you are for all her many thankless household and child-rearing chores, how attentive and accommodating you are to all her moods and tiredness, how you value her opinion, how graciously you overlook her defects and digs, how considerately you back her up, then nine-tenths of the problems involved in raising kids will take care of themselves. They'll not only learn how to esteem their mom, but will also get unmistakable whiffs of what unconditional love is all about. And that's an invaluable lesson, for now and later.

**2. Benignly neglect your children.** If you're wrapped up in your wife, this recommendation should come easy. Insecure Americans tend to smother their too-few children. As someone once said, America is the only country where parents implicitly obey their kids. There's way too much parental emotional attachment and dependence on their kids' approval. Dads especially must keep their balance and perspective and deliberate detachment. All fathers should fervently pray for the gift of unflappability. If dads are to be the voice of reason (thereby letting their wives be the voice of heart), somehow they must stay above the fray. They must at least come across as disengaged and uninvolved. Otherwise it will be very difficult for them to remain objective and fair, to see and understand what's really going on beneath the surface. Dads should be quick to observe and slow to act, react, and intervene. Theirs is the job to reflect and to see what steps, if any, should be taken. If anybody, dad should have a congenital preference for delay, for letting time pass and prove its curative powers.

Never forget that children compulsively conspire at all hours and in all situations to get dad (and other authority figures, such as teachers) to blow his stack, to lose his cool and control. They're always probing for chinks in the armor, for the hot buttons. But once they discover that their ploys don't and won't work, that dad isn't about to get all riled up, then they're freed up to engage in more positive pursuits. And none too soon.

**3. Good dads should be seen and not heard.** This piece of advice is obviously linked to the preceding one. It represents a considerable departure from the olden view of father as authoritative patriarch. By it is meant, positively, that dads should be very busy and quite vocal—but behind the scenes, not throwing their weight around in public. Only half in jest, I've been known to suggest that the best service to the family (and the nation) that Congress could enact would be to offer a tax break to those families who add a den for dad onto their homes. If our reinvented dad is to do a better job on the home front, it would really help for him to have a room of his own, with a door and a minimum of privacy (even if little more than a closet with two chairs). In any case, our new father should have many more reasons and occasions for talking alone with each of his children. That's just another way of saying that much of what dad usually does in public—correcting, directing traffic, laying down the law and order—should best be handled a bit later and more calmly behind closed doors.

But these huddles should be much more than punishment summits. Dad should use them, for example, to suggest to his children positive things they might do to enliven family life, to celebrate a birthday, to please their mom, to apologize, to show appreciation to grandma. . . .They also come in handy to spark and review performance in chores, studies, hobbies; to recount dad's own youth, especially his escapades and peccadilloes; to share a newly heard joke or two, even slightly off-color ones with his boys; to offer feedback, compliments, and encouragement; to dissolve tensions by helping individual family members better understand each other.

It would be ideal if these huddles—sometimes in the car or over a soda—were a regular fixture of family life, perhaps weekly—

something the kids were to see as the most natural thing in the world and something to look forward to. If in the kids' eyes the pluses of these chats are to exceed the necessary minuses, if dad is to endear himself to his offspring and win thereby their affection, obviously he can't leave their content to chance or improvisation and, least of all, to pique. These tête-à-têtes can't come across as manipulative ways to minimize family damage or parental hassles or the kids' fun. The good father will reflect on each of the kids several times during the week; he'll jot down observations, including his wife's; he'll pray for and dream about each of them, winnowing out the negative, accentuating the positive; he'll formulate realistic and positive goals wherewith to challenge them.

There is, however, one occasion when dad can—and positively ought to—erupt in no uncertain terms, and that is when children disrespect their mother or take her for granted. Let this prohibition be the single, unarguable, non-negotiable, untouchable, even irrational principle of family life that justifies almost every paternal disciplinary excess, even those the neighbors can hear. "Listen, you ungrateful twerp, never, ever do I want to hear you treat your mom like that again, as if she were your slave. . . ."

**4. Act—don't react.** In a nutshell the problem with most dads is that in this parenting game they feel so inferior to their wives, who operate much more naturally on the basis of intuition and instinct. That liability, coupled with a shortage of time and updated role models, makes for interior complications and exterior hesitations, when and if dad gets around to asking himself what he's supposed to be doing back at the ranch anyway. The worst thing to do is what's the most frequent: waiting behind the newspaper for trouble to break out. Here as most everywhere, the best defense is a good offense. Have your own agenda and priorities—and act on them. Plan and plot your evenings and weekends, even your personal hobbies and recreations, lest they just happen. If every day you were to generate at least one specific pro-family deed (helping Sue with math homework, working on the washer with Steve, running an errand with Butch, having a personal chat with Maribeth, discussing the kids with your wife, and so on), your conscience would be much clearer and the family would largely take care of itself. "Divide and conquer" was the Romans' prescription for winning wars; it's dad's for keeping peace. Because if you don't act deliberately, with generous forethought, with each of your children, one on one, you'll find yourself reacting in ways that undermine the family, as you well know and soon enough regret.

**5. Good reasons—not good behavior.** Dad especially should be attuned to the danger of kids doing right things for wrong reasons. Such inadequate reasons as: "Because I said so" or "that's the way we do things around here, kiddo" or "tough, that's life" or "what will the neighbors think?" and hundreds more of the same ilk. External compliance, especially in non-essentials, is not the goal, especially as the children grow older and admit of reasonable appeals to their "better angels." So, explain, explain, explain, going as deep as you both can, again as privately as possible. It may seem a lot simpler and easier to just bark, but here too a stitch in time saves nine headaches and heartaches.

Help them to see that their unthinking actions and omissions have consequences that impinge on others no less than on themselves, not to mention family finances. Help them to see how easily we all can be ambushed and deflected by pleasures, fears, selfishness, and thoughtlessness. Consequently curbing these self-defeating tendencies is the task of the basic cardinal virtues. Striving to acquire these good habits is therefore in their own best interests: something they above all owe themselves. Virtuous behavior should never be authoritatively imposed from without nor seem merely the onerous price for domestic tranquillity.

**6. Help them face debts.** As you've probably noticed by now, selfishness has been known to infect children too. Consequently, much of the parents' educational challenge is to convert the sow's ear of self-centeredness into the silk purse of recognizing, justly, realistically what one has received from others. In this instance, children should be fair and truthful to their parents. Again, dad has a special role to play in helping children overcome the tendency to take others for granted, to convert gifts and privileges into entitlements, to bend all of reality to shortsighted whims and wishes. Kids who don't straighten out this most basic and obvious relationship become practically incapable of any healthy relationships, with whomever. (A fuller account of this topic is found in chapter 13.)

Now of course it isn't easy for dad to point out to his kids what all their father's done for them without apparently angling for praise or compliments. The same goes for mom. But dad can point out to kids the countless services their mother has generously done for them, while still being and seeming disinterested. So can mom, each for the other and for their kids' sake. What is so painfully obvious to the parents themselves can be almost hidden from the kids.

Parents can bare their souls to their children in the intimacy of non-directed confidences or perhaps in an annual birthday letter. In such a missive they can less inhibitedly express the dreams, hopes, loves, and sentiments they're too shy or embarrassed to say face-to-face. What a keepsake! Once acquainted with the full truth of what they mean to their parents, kids can then better see what makes their parents tick and can better appreciate the highly voluntary and loving nature of parental services and allegiance. Then they can more easily and readily correspond to all the debts they've contracted with their parents. Then too they can better understand and forgive their parents' shortcomings in such an arduous and one-sided undertaking, especially their good-willed if misguided possessiveness, meddling, and even occasional anger.

Parents owe their children the full truth of their relationship with and dependence on dad and mom. This will boost their understanding and shrink their self-centeredness, which tends to disfigure and distort the truth of both parents and siblings, not to mention beyond the family. Another good reason why dad should remain above the family fray is that he is thus free to play a very needed role as mediator, conciliator, and translator. He can thus busy himself in promoting mutual understanding—the truth that will make both parents and children free. When, for example, there are squabbles, he can and should explain separately each party to the other, helping both to see no bad will was involved. When, for instance, mom "unexpectedly" blows her stack, dad can explain her tiredness, and frustrations and expose the child's unacknowledged provocations. And so forth. Dad's job is to find and even fabricate excuses for apparent slights. On the other hand, he's to help the offended parties to see how they unwittingly come across with plenty of slights of their own. Dad's is a painstaking but so worthwhile job of translating family members to one another. Now do you see how busy dad will keep that den of his?

**7. Transmit the legacy.** Children are to understand what makes their parents run and to interiorize the truths and principles that should make them run too as free and responsible individuals. For that, some more educating and explaining is called for. How about conveying any religious truths, moral principles, and family policies and customs that good parents want to bequeath to their children (though, let's hope, much before the former die)? Granted: all these treasures are best seen in practice and picked up through osmosis. But even the best of examples isn't completely self-explanatory, and therefore parents can't excuse themselves from verbally sharing with their kids the way things should be, how to get there and, above all, why. Again, dad would seem to be better suited for this somewhat less informal instruction.

Before too many more decades slip by, the I hope to bring out a book entitled *The 200 Things Your Children Should Know*, though it wouldn't contain all the factual, cultural, and scientific things that should properly be learned in school or elsewhere. Rather, this book would feature all the theoretical and practical elements necessary for a going philosophy of life, starting as early as possible. Are there two hundred, or just fifty such items? The idea is for dad to huddle once a week for ten to fifteeen minutes with each of his children while in grades five through eight, and fifty times four totals two hundred. The book would furnish the outline and background for each topic to be covered. Dad would consult the entries beforehand and then explain and discuss them spontaneously, without working out of the manual.

Some topics would be dealt with at different levels over the four years, but the whole package should end before the child enters, say, high school. And that for several reasons: Knowing that these talks are not perpetual will help both dad and child to take them more seriously. Knowing besides that, come high school, parents are going to step aside and let the child learn to run his life amid hits and misses and to shoulder the consequences is a scary summons to early maturity. The high schooler is to be told of course that mom or dad can still be consulted, though except for major infractions of a necessary minimum of "house rules," the initiative will usually be the child's. Finally, high school is too short a time for parents and children to be anything other than friends who trust and respect one another. And for friendship to gel, the subordination of pupil to teacher must give way to something resembling equality.

A rare dad with a rare child might be able to pull a structured plan off, but in most cases "a session every Wednesday at 7:15 in the den" might not work and might even backfire. It can't come across as too artificial, one-sided, stilted, and awkward, smelling besides of indoctrination, brainwashing, manipulation, and partypooping. If dad and son or daughter are truly good and close friends, an obvious program might work. Where that condition doesn't necessarily hold, however, something more oblique, casual, spontaneous, Socratic, and unstructured would be best. In any case, busy, distracted dads doubtless need a list and resource materials, plus lots of initiative and creativity. For example, selected videos and books might spark discussions; then too dad's reflecting on incidents at home or school might uncover possible ice-breakers and conversation-starters.

Meanwhile, let's all experiment. For starters, until that book gets written, dad might find a quiet hour or two to jot down all the things he'd like to pass on to his kids, a list which his wife would undoubtedly add to or subtract from. Dad would want to descend to a lot of practical home economies and personal frugalities, for instance, plus the rationale behind them, something not likely to be picked up elsewhere. In explaining and selling all these virtues, dad should relate them as much as possible to enlightened self-interest: "do yourself a favor: you'll be the major beneficiary."

Then there's the matter of explaining family traditions and policies. Since the former are strictly up to you, let's concentrate on the policies. First, to minimize parental improvisation, inconsistencies, and apparent vindictiveness, there should be policies governing such matters as TV, homework, dating, chores, allowances, use of car, curfew, jobs, paying for college and beyond, alcohol and drugs, common meals, any joint religious practices, including "compulsory" services. These policies, with their carrots and sticks, should be formulated, announced, and explained well ahead of time. Here are two policies I favor. If parents were to splurge on high school education, but contribute nothing towards college or grad school, a lot more responsibility and diligence would descend a lot earlier on a lot more high schoolers. And how about making kids take public transportation for almost everything, while they're still at home and can't provide their own means? Also lavish love, trust, understanding, kindness on them, but few needless gifts and even less money. . . .

**8. Be a reader.** This will be a short recommendation, although another one for which that den will prove useful. So many of your parental worries would disappear if your kids were to get hooked on books. And for that to happen, parents should be hooked on them, especially dad (otherwise boys at least get the distinct impression that books and schooling and suchlike are for sissies). C. S. Lewis and Tolkien have explained why good books are not only an antidote but a treasure besides. We most suffer, they tell us, from an impoverished moral imagination that makes it almost impossible for us to catch glimpses of and to desire to commune with any superior, intangible, spiritual world. How rich and attractive and illuminating is the image of Aslan in the *Chronicles of Narnia*. Well, see good literature as so many little windows whereby goodness and beauty and truth and romance attractively appear on the stage beckoning us on to our true homeland.

About the only way that kids get addicted to books is when they see their parents benefiting therefrom. For parents, moreover, reading is enlightening and relaxing; it shows the kids that mom and dad have other interests; it helps parents keep their sanity; it justifies proper distance and detachment from the kids. . . . But make sure yours and theirs are truly good books giving off whiffs of a higher, better world—not just exciting escape entertainment. And try your best to make sure your kids don't see reading as a chore or punishment; if anything, as a privilege and reward. Because they so much enjoyed it when you read to them early on?

**9. Share those dreams.** I've been encouraging dad to spend more time alone with the kids to hear them out, to let them hear him out; so each can tell the other how to do better (yes, dad should also invite constructive criticism). Now we come to the summit of these heart-to-heart huddles. These confidential encounters are an excellent time for dad to voice his highest hopes, his greatest expectations, his secret dreams for each.

O to be growing up in the next millennium under the wing of a great dad who tells me, while showing me, life's deepest truths! Only then will a child find motive enough to be chaste and studious and fair and courageous and enterprising in both leadership and friendship. The only thing wrong with today's kids is that they hunger and thirst for a reason for living and a reason for even dying to themselves. Don't waste precious time and moral capital bemoaning today's pop culture and its sick purveyors. Help them to want to be aristocrats of love themselves. Without that, parent-imposed codes of behavior too often become today a straitjacket that harbors the greatest rebels this side of Sing-Sing.

If the above nine-point program seems somewhat overwhelming, perhaps dad can get started with the following bare-bones plan. Its weekly execution is spread over a twenty-two-hour period. Brown-bag Friday lunch (or skip); park in some quiet place; there re-commit yourself to being unappreciated; forgive and forget; recharge your hopes; resell yourself on marital self-sacrifice. Then have Friday dinner out (or alone) with your wife: a splendid chance to hear her out and sympathize to the nth degree. Finally, on Saturday mornings, make it breakfast out with each kid on a rotating basis, with no ulterior objectives other than getting to know, appreciate and befriend them, with no gripes or "lessons"; just relax and ask questions; listen; recount your youthful peccadilloes. Your job may not be over by ten a.m. on Saturday, but, finally, no longer need you wonder where and how to begin with such non-stop, refractory "monsters." At the end of the last chapter we spoke of building a new civilization of love. And do you know how we'll build it? We'll build it on the backs of a multitude of once prodigal sons and daughters, who, try as they might, couldn't forget how much and how unrequitedly and how wisely their parents loved and raised them. Even their dads. Especially their dads.

# EPILOGUE:
## NOW WHAT?

By the time men are finally delivered
from disease and decay—all pasteurized,
their genes counted and rearranged,
fitted with new, replaceable, plastic organs,
able to eat, copulate
and perform other physical functions
innocuously and hygienically as and when desired—
they will all be mad,
and the world one huge psychiatric ward.
— Malcolm Muggeridge, *The Observer*, 1969

NOW I MAY OPENLY DISCUSS what I didn't dare raise
with readers at the start. Had I then claimed to be offering
a do-it-yourself happiness kit, you doubtless would have
scoffed and branded me as "one more charlatan." Perhaps after
nineteen chapters (unless you're one of those who unfairly peek
first at the last chapter) you are somewhat more receptive to that
claim.

"For once," you may be wondering, "has there fallen into my
hands the real article? Will this program, finally, deliver where

others have merely teased? Is it in fact an authentic owner's manual for human nature? And if it does effectively address *the* question assailing every man, woman, and child that ever trod the earth, won't it become the best-selling book of all times?"

Let's hope those questions all merit a Yes answer (especially the last). Whether or not they do, however, has less to do with the book, the I suspect, than what its readers do with its contents. After all, isn't it a *do*-it kit? For myself, I didn't create or invent anything. I just studied and plied the contours of the human condition, as mapped initially by Socrates, Plato, and Aristotle, and filled in some completing blanks.

What really surprises me is that no one had ever penned this book before. The objective reality has been out there, just waiting for someone to walk it and thereby to chart it. As noted earlier, some people, especially among the ancients, did honestly try but didn't go far enough and consequently never won general acceptance. To avoid their pitfalls, I tried to analyze what went wrong or at least was left unfinished. Will my map meet with greater welcome? That partly depends on how far historical circumstances have changed and, as a result, have made potential takers more receptive. For everyone's sake, let's hope more people do decide to follow the map and thereby find out for themselves where it leads, with all its rewards.

For myself, however, I'm not holding my breath. While certainly not averse to seeing this product of two years' labors climb to the top of the charts and stay there, somehow I suspect that it's not likely to happen—at least not in the short term. Chalk up part of that shortfall to the book's (or is it the author's?) short-comings, inevitable as they are. Chalk up another part to the public's (or is it the reviewers'?) pervasive skepticism. That said, however, those two reasons still do not account for what is likely to be the work's initially limited appeal. And that, largely for the same reasons why no one so far has bothered fully to chart the moral territory lying out there awaiting validation and description.

Here's the main reason: There's a rampant and very deep-seated prejudice (fear, more likely) that the cure may be worse than the disease. People are simply afraid that all this self-knowing, self-owning, and self-giving business will, if anything, top their current misery and desperation. And that baseless fear comes from just reading about, instead of incrementally living and rewardingly experiencing, this ethical program. Yet that deficiency dogs even the best of merely bookish theories, which fall victim to irrational and quite involuntary fears.

Remember the "lustful lizard" scene from *The Great Divorce* summarized two chapters ago? The lizard's host, awash in all kinds of hesitation and fear, was nearly paralyzed by anxiety. Fear and suffering there are bound to be, arising in part from the cumulus of attachments from which we're insufficiently weaned and also from unfamiliarity with any new step, seemingly a leap in the dark. But these can only be overcome by throttling the "lizard." To see us through, we must keep before our eyes the result of this sublimation: the new man astride the silvery-white stallion, symbolizing the richness and energy of desire that arise when the scheme of bogus happiness is "broken" and finally tamed.

There's only one way to get around those fears. We only unmask them by confronting them. And we do so by living the moral program prescribed above, which is only the blueprint of our objective but still rudimentary human nature. The whole ethical project will sell and prove itself with all kinds of confirming rewards, but only to the extent that it is tried. So, don't be an armchair scoffer. Get out there and play the game. There's no other way for you to perceive its guaranteed benefits. Further, there's no better way for you to persuade others than to let them see vicariously the positive, enviable results in your life. That will trigger a stampede to bookstores in search for the same map.

Then, don't give up—or if you do, start all over again, sadder perhaps but also wiser. The haul is long, the going arduous. No therapy is painless. The gradual but cumulative dividends, however, will not be long in coming. I'd guarantee that the book will work or your money back, if only my publisher would agree. But, promises or not, let your own experience be the best teacher.

Moreover, with largely just a change in attitude, all your current occupations and duties, instead of being distractions and impositions, can make for a better you and yours, beginning this very hour, if you so desire. Since you already have to work (or study, or both), get on with others, make a home, plan ahead, plus honor debts and agreements, why not do all that with an ever more enlightened purpose? Doing so will make you a stronger more fulfilled, caring, commanding, virtuous, judicious, principled, considerate, happy, generous, inspiring person. What more could you ask for? What a bargain! But keep in mind your ethical transformation won't get very far or last very long if you proceed solely on the basis of mere grit. Sooner or later you must escalate to the loving gift of self that alone can energize and motivate you and make the whole project more than worthwhile. Only then will you have discovered *the* virtue that is indeed its own reward.

The key to the whole program is chapter six: "Indispensable Quiet Time." Now might be a good time to read it again (and again). Without regular time for reflection and meditation, we can't stop being our own worst enemies. That reserved quarter-hour is an absolutely essential minimum, if we're to play it straight with ourselves. Truthfulness doesn't come easily; self-deception and wishful thinking do. And isn't it about time we called a halt to all the frustrating and childish untruthfulness in our lives?

Again, as recommended earlier, we shouldn't modify at will the time dedicated to this active silence. Let it always be a fixed time. That quarter-hour may grow on us, in the sense that we need more: maybe a half-hour. But even that increase may not be enough or may be thrown overboard, as we read in a perceptive and prescriptive warning from Samuel Johnson, written in 1751:

> As we all know our own faults, and know them commonly
> with many aggravations which human perspicacity cannot

discover, there is, perhaps, no man, however hardened by impudence or dissipated by levity, sheltered by hypocrisy, or blasted by disgrace, who does not intend some time to review his conduct, and to regulate the remainder of his life by the laws of virtue. New temptations indeed attack him, new invitations are offered by pleasure and interest, and the hour of reformation is always delayed; every delay gives vice another opportunity of fortifying itself by habit; and the change of manners, through sincerely intended and rationally planned, is referred to the time when some craving passion shall be fully gratified, or some powerful allurement cease its importunity. Thus procrastination is accumulated on procrastination, and one impediment succeeds another, till age shatters our resolution, or death intercepts the project of amendment. Such is often the end of salutary purposes, after they have long delighted the imagination, and appeased that disquiet which every mind feels from known misconduct, when the attention is not diverted by business or by pleasure.

Nothing surely can be more unworthy of a reasonable nature, than to continue in a state so opposite to real happiness, as that all the peace of solitude and felicity of meditation, must arise from resolutions for forsaking it. Yet the world will often afford examples of men, who pass months and years in a continual war with their own convictions, and are daily dragged by habit or betrayed by passion into practices, which they closed and opened their eyes with purposes to avoid; purposes which, though settled on conviction, the first impulse of momentary desire totally overthrows.

The influence of custom is indeed such that to conquer it will require the utmost efforts of fortitude and virtue, nor can I think any man more worthy of veneration and renown, than those who have burst the shackles of habitual vice. This victory however has different degrees of glory as of difficulty; it is more heroic as the objects of guilty gratification are more familiar, and the recurrence of solicitation more frequent. He that from experience of the folly of ambition resigns his offices, may set himself free at once from temptation to squander his life in courts, because he cannot regain his former station. He who is enslaved by an amorous passion, may quit his tyrant in disgust, and absence will without the help of reason overcome by degrees the desire of returning. But those appetites to which every place affords their proper object, and which require no preparatory measures or gradual advances, are more tenaciously adhesive; the wish is so near the enjoyment, that compliance often precedes consideration, and before the powers of reason can be summoned, the time for employing them is past.

Indolence is therefore one of the vices from which those whom it once infects are seldom reformed. Every other species of luxury operates upon some appetite that is quickly satiated, and requires some concurrence of art or accident which every place will not supply; but the desire of ease acts equally at all hours, and the longer it is indulged in, the more increased. *To do nothing is in every man's power* [emphasis added]; we can never want an opportunity of omitting duties. The lapse to indolence is soft and imperceptible, because it is only a mere cessation of activity; but the return to diligence is difficult, because it implies a change from rest to motion, from privation to reality. . . .

Of this vice, as of all others, every man who indulges it is conscious; we all know our own state, if we could be induced to consider it; and it might perhaps be useful to the conquest of all these ensnarers of the mind, if *at certain stated days life was reviewed* [emphasis added]. Many things necessary are omitted, because we vainly imagine that they may be performed, and what cannot be done without pain will for ever be delayed if the time of doing it be left unsettled. No corruption is great but by long negligence, which can scarcely prevail in a mind regularly and frequently awakened by periodical remorse. He that thus breaks his life into parts, will find in himself a desire to distinguish himself with the approach of the *day of recollection* [emphasis added], as of the time which is to begin a new series of virtue and felicity.

We all want to shed habits contrary to happiness, but we give in to the twins of indolence and delay. To escape that spell, Johnson recommends an occasional "day of recollection," monthly or quarterly. But be sure to set the date ahead of time. Therein we are to review our life and thereby "begin a new series of virtue and felicity."

Those who commit themselves to live in this fashion, however much they might fail or fall short, come to the realization that this good, virtuous, philosophical life is something they owe to themselves—not to anybody else. This way of living is no imposition from without; if anything, it's a self-imposed liberation of what we bear within. In other words: we need to kill in ourselves, through self-denial and self-sacrifice, the things that are killing us, if we're to accede to our heritage of full bliss. The resulting euphoria (though muted and unsensational) will be more than its own recompense.

So, welcome aboard, all you wannabe aristocrats of love! You've signed on for the only program that can assure you the joy that till now has eluded you.


Utopian? Unrealistic? Peyote-primed pipe dreams? Well, almost. There *may be* something missing from this book's scheme and invitation (though that conclusion must follow upon your having lived it out). Without it at least we're more likely to falter and even perhaps toss in the towel, as did our classical predecessors over two millennia ago. What can possibly convert the conditional lovers all humans are into unconditional self-givers? Then, even if we could muster enough moral capital to embark on such generous dedication, will these stabs at self-forgetfulness and -transcendence actually satisfy our insatiable hunger for bliss unbounded and unending? Or has our ethical program just succeeded in post-poning the human condition 's deepest craving?

We began our inquiry asking how far we could go in charting an objective, reliable map to human fulfillment, a complete ethical system for all comers. We've tried to show that virtuously escalating to the third moral stage (the super-enlightened self-interest of disinterested self-giving) is not only the deepest completion of our nature, but also the surest path to the highest and most authentic joy we can reach. In doing so, haven't we successfully completed the ethical project launched by Socrates, Plato, and Aristotle and thereby reached the outer limits of what ethics or morality can deliver? To live accordingly is to ratify as fully as possible our definition as free, reasonable, bliss-hungry animals.

By exercising the cardinal virtues, we can free both mind and will from pesky bodily tugs and pulls born of our animal instincts and fanned by our overactive imagination. Doing so allows these two liberated powers to be about their proper business without external hindrance. We can also try to reconcile intellect and will, so that the latter can submit itself to the truth-finding prowess of the former. We can further discover that our virtuous self-ownership only makes sense (and whatever higher joy) when harnessed to serving others.

If there are still further needs and questions to explore, at least we can now approach them with an open, undeceived mind and with a chastened, expectant will. Just such a question may be the religious case for and against a Supreme Being. The stakes are indeed high. Therein might we not find a more than adequate object to silence for good our roving, restless heart? And also perhaps the Unconditional Lover *par excellence*, who can spur us to echo, however fitfully, his prodigal self-giving? It may just be worth an initially dispassionate try.

# APPENDICES

# Appendix 1
## Supplmentary Readings

Mortimer Adler, *Aristotle for Everybody*

William Bennett, *The Book of Virtues*

Allan Bloom, *The Closing of the American Mind*

George Gilder, *Men and Marriage*

William Kilpatrick, *Why Johnny Can't Tell Right from Wrong*

C. S. Lewis, *The Abolition of Man*

David McCullough, *Brave Companions*

Michael Novak, *Business as Calling*

Josef Pieper, *The Four Cardinal Virtues*

E. F. Schumacher, *Good Work* and *A Guide for the Perplexed*

Karl Stern, *Flight from Woman*

Gerald Vann, *Morals Makyth Man*
(American title: *Morals and Man*)

# APPENDIX 2
## ANCIENT SAGE SAYINGS

FOLLOWING ARE SOME APHORISMS, culled from a host of ancient Greek and Roman thinkers and writers. They represent the peak of the ethical system born and developed in the Mediterranean world some 2,500 to 1,700 years ago. Having to do with the way we should live, they are a summons to reflection and action, more than something just to be read through. The headings are arranged according to the order of the book's fifteen practical chapters, as shown below.

## SELF-KNOWLEDGE

1. Any man can make a mistake, but none but a fool will continue it.
— *Cicero*

2. Nothing is more disgraceful than insincerity.          — *Cicero*

3. A good conscience fears no witness, but a guilty conscience is solicitous even in solitude. If we do nothing but what is honest, let all the world know it. But if otherwise, what does it signify to have nobody else to know it, so long as I know it myself? Miserable is he who slights that witness.          — *Seneca*

4. The greatest incitement to wrongdoing is the hope of doing so with impunity.          — *Cicero*

5. Whenever I wish to enjoy the quips of a clown, I am not compelled to hunt far; I can laugh at myself.          — *Seneca*

6. Everyone is least known to himself, and it is very difficult for a man to know himself.          — *Cicero*

7. There is wickedness in the intention of wickedness, even though it be not perpetrated in the act.          — *Cicero*

8. There is nothing good or evil save in the will.          — *Epictetus*

9. Let not sleep fall upon your eyes till you have thrice reviewed the transactions of the past day. Where have I turned aside from rectitude? What have I been doing? What have I left undone, which I ought to have done? Begin thus from the first act, and proceed; and, in conclusion, at the ill which you have done, be troubled, and rejoice for the good.
— *Pythagoras*

10. The precept "Know yourself" was not solely intended to obviate the pride of mankind; but likewise that we might understand our own worth.
— *Cicero*

11. We should every night call ourselves to an account: What infirmity have I mastered today? what passions opposed? what temptation resisted? what virtue acquired? Our vices will abate of themselves if they be brought every day to light.          — *Seneca*

12. Other men's sins are before our eyes; our own are behind our back.
— Seneca

13. Such as your words are, such will your affections be esteemed; and such will your deeds as your affections, and such your life as your deeds.
— Socrates

14. I regard that man as lost, who has lost his sense of shame.   — Plautus

15. Shame may restrain what law does not prohibit.   — Seneca

16. When a man is beset by some trouble, it is then that he remembers there is a god, and that he is only a man.   — Pliny the Elder

17. If you would be good, first believe that you are bad.   —Epictetus

18. Nothing is so easy as to deceive one's self, for what we wish we readily believe; but such expectations are often inconsistent with the reality of things.   — Demosthenes

19. I follow nature as the surest guide, and resign myself, with implicit obedience, to her sacred ordinances.   — Cicero

20. When Thales was asked what was difficult, he said, "To know one's self." And what was easy, "To advise another."   — Diogenes

21. What is the first business of one who studies philosophy? To part with self-conceit. For it is impossible for anyone to begin to learn what he thinks that he already knows.   — Epictetus

22. Eyes will not see when the heart wishes them to be blind. Desire conceals truth, as darkness does the earth.   — Seneca

23. Observe your enemies, for they first find out your faults.   —Antisthenes

24. We cannot live better than in seeking to become better, nor more agreeably than in having a clear conscience.   — Socrates

25. There is no witness so terrible, no accuser so powerful, as conscience which dwells within us.   — Sophocles

26. You believe easily that which you hope for earnestly.   — Terence

27. Let death be daily before your eyes, and you will never entertain any abject thought, nor too eagerly covet anything.   — Epictetus

28. We are all wretched; and whatever one of us blames in another, each will find in himself. — *Seneca*

## KNOWLEDGE & WISDOM

29. We in vain summon the mind to intense application, when the body is in a languid state. — *Gaius Cornelius Gallus*

30. Memory is the receptacle and sheath of all knowledge. — *Cicero*

31. Memory tempers prosperity, mitigates adversity, controls youth, and delights old age. — *Cicero*

32. The wise are instructed by reason; ordinary minds, by experience; the stupid, by necessity; and brutes by instincts. — *Cicero*

33. Atheism is a disease of the soul, before it becomes an error of the understanding. — *Plato*

34. We are slow to believe that which if believed would hurt us. — *Ovid*

35. When once a man is determined to believe, the very absurdity of the doctrine does but confirm him in his faith. — *Junius*

36. All wish to possess knowledge, but few, comparatively speaking, are willing to pay the price. — *Juvenal*

37. That learning is most requisite which unlearns evil. — *Antisthenes*

38. Acquire new knowledge while thinking over the old, and you may become a teacher of others. — *Cicero*

39. The learning and knowledge that we have is, at the most, but little compared with that of which we are ignorant. — *Plato*

40. Men learn while they teach. — *Seneca*

41. The aim of education is the wise use of leisure. — *Aristotle*

42. It is better to be a beggar than ignorant; for a beggar only wants money, but an ignorant person wants humanity. — *Aristippus*

43. Better be unborn than untaught, for ignorance is the root of misfortune. — *Plato*

**44.** Thinking is the soul talking with itself. — *Plato*

**45.** Seven years of silent inquiry are needful for a man to learn the truth, but fourteen in order to learn how to make it known to his fellowmen.

— *Plato*

**46.** Truth is established by investigation and delay; falsehood prospers by precipitancy. — *Tacitus*

**47.** Really to inform the mind is to correct and enlarge the heart.

— *Junius*

**48.** Perfect wisdom has four parts, viz., prudence, the principle of doing things aright; justice, the principle of doing things equally in public and in private; fortitude, the principle of not flying danger, but meeting it; and temperance, the principle of subduing desires and living moderately.

— *Plato*

**49.** It was through the feeling of wonder that men now and at first began to philosophize. — *Aristotle*

**50.** Philosophy is the art of living. — *Plutarch*

**51.** Nature and wisdom always say the same. — *Juvenal*

**52.** He only employs his passion who can make no use of his reason.

— *Cicero*

**53.** To study philosophy is nothing but to prepare oneself to die.

— *Cicero*

**54.** All wisdom lies in two words: sustain and abstain. — *Epictetus*

**55.** Beware lest you lose the substance by grasping at the shadow. —*Aesop*

**56.** Our understandings are always liable to error. Nature and certainty are very hard to come at, and infallibility is mere vanity and pretense.

—*Marcus Aurelius*

**57.** I am satisfied that we are less convinced by what we hear than by what we see. — *Seneca*

**58.** Men trust rather to their eyes than to their ears. The effect of precepts is, therefore, slow and tedious, while that of example is summary and effectual. — *Seneca*

59. Know how to listen, and you will profit even from those who talk badly. — *Plutarch*

60. Wind puffs up empty sails; opinion, fools. — *Socrates*

61. Under the veil of aphorisms are hid those germs of morals which the masters of philosophy have afterwards developed into so many volumes. — *Plutarch*

62. We should not be so taken up in the search for truth, as to neglect the needful duties of active life; for it is only action that gives a true value and commendation to virtue. — *Cicero*

## PRUDENCE

63. Nature has given us two ears, two eyes, and but one tongue, to the end that we should hear and see more than we speak. — *Socrates*

64. No fool can be silent at a feast. — *Solon*

65. The origin of all mankind was the same: it is only a clear and good conscience that makes a man noble, for that is derived from heaven itself. — *Seneca*

66. Human affairs are not so happily arranged that the best things please the most men. It is the proof of a bad cause when it is applauded by the multitude. — *Seneca*

67. The wavering mind is but a base possession. — *Pythagoras*

68. Among mortals second thoughts are wisest. — *Euripides*

69. The good and wise lead quiet lives. — *Euripides*

70. If we do not watch, we lose our opportunities; if we do not make haste, we are left behind; our best hours escape us, the worst are to come. The purest part of our life runs first, and leaves only the dregs at the bottom; and that time which is good for nothing else we dedicate to virtue, and only propose to begin to live at an age that very few people arrive at. — *Seneca*

71. To arrive at perfection, a man should have very sincere friends or inveterate enemies; because he would be made sensible of his good or ill

conduct, either by the censures of the one or the admonitions of the other. — *Diogenes*

72. There is a mean in everything. Even virtue itself has its stated limits, which, not being strictly observed, it ceases to be a virtue. — *Horace*

73. The greatest flood has soonest ebb; the sorest tempest, the most sudden calm; the hottest love, the coldest end; and from the deepest desire often ensues the deadliest hate. — *Socrates*

74. Few things are brought to a successful issue by impetuous desire, but most by calm and prudent forethought. — *Thucydides*

75. Consult your friend on all things, especially on those which respect yourself. His counsel may then be useful where your own self-love might impair your judgment. — *Seneca*

76. Tomorrow I will live, the fool does say: today itself's too late; the wise lived yesterday. — *Martial*

77. Levity of behavior is the bane of all that is good and virtuous. — *Seneca*

78. Command large fields, but cultivate small ones. — *Virgil*

79. When we live habitually with the wicked, we become necessarily their victims or their disciples; on the contrary, when we associate with the virtuous we form ourselves in imitation of their virtues, or at least lose, every day, something of their faults. — *Agapetus I*

80. It is easy when we are in prosperity to give advice to the afflicted. — *Aeschylus*

## Health

81. The mind ought sometimes to be diverted that it may return to better thinking. — *Phaedrus*

82. Sleep: repose of all things; gentlest of the duties; peace of mind, from which care flies; who does soothe the hearts of men wearied with the toils of the day, and refits them for labor. — *Ovid*

83. Rest is the sweet sauce of labor. — *Pliny the Elder*

84. The best of healers is good cheer. — *Pindar*

85. Now learn what and how great benefits a temperate diet will bring along with it. In the first place you will enjoy good health.          — Hesiod

## HAPPINESS

86. Call no man happy till you know the end of his life. Till then, at most, he can only be counted fortunate.          — Herodotus

87. The foundation of true joy is in the conscience.          — Seneca

88. If sensuality were happiness, beasts were happier than men; but human felicity is lodged in the soul, not in the flesh.          — Seneca

89. A wise man will always be contented with his condition, and will live rather according to the precepts of virtue, than according to the customs of his country.          — Antisthenes

90. You traverse the world in search of happiness, which is within the reach of every man: a contented mind confers it all.          — Horace

91. Contentment is natural wealth; luxury is artificial poverty.  — Socrates

92. The mind that is cheerful at present will have no solicitude for the future, and will meet the bitter occurrences of life with a smile.  — Horace

93. Health, beauty, vigor, riches, and all the other things called goods, operate equally as evils to the vicious and the unjust, as they do as benefits to the upright.          — Plato

94. There are no greater wretches in the world than many of those whom people in general take to be happy.          — Seneca

95. Good cheer is no hindrance to a good life.          — Aristippus

## SELF-DISCIPLINE

96. Great is he who enjoys his earthenware as if it were silver, and not less great is the man to whom all his silver is no more than earthenware.
          — Seneca

97. Since the incontinent [weak] man is apt to pursue, not on conviction, bodily pleasures that are excessive and contrary to the right rule [reason], while the self-indulgent man is convinced that he is entitled to pursue

them, it is the former that is easily persuaded to change his mind, while the latter is not. — *Aristotle*

98. No man ever arrived suddenly at the summit of vice. — *Juvenal*

99. Be not affronted at a jest; if one throws ever so much salt at you, you will receive no harm, unless you are raw and ulcerous. — *Junius*

100. Vices are contagious, and there is no trusting the well and sick together. — *Seneca*

101. All who know well how to obey will know also how to rule. — *Flavius*

102. Most powerful is he who has himself in his own power. — *Seneca*

103. The more a man denies himself, the more he shall obtain from god. — *Horace*

104. No man is free who cannot command himself. — *Pythagoras*

105. The passionate are like men standing on their heads; they see all things the wrong way. — *Plato*

106. Example is the best precept. — *Aesop*

107. Asked what he gained from philosophy, Aristotle answered, "to do without being commanded what others do from fear of the laws."— *Diogenes*

108. Conversion is not implanting eyes, for they exist already; but giving them a right direction, which they have not. — *Plato*

109. Choose always the way that seems the best, however rough it may be; custom [habit] will soon render it easy and agreeable. — *Pythagoras*

110. Reason should direct and appetite obey. — *Cicero*

111. A well-governed appetite is a great part of liberty. — *Seneca*

112. Without the assistance of natural habits, rules and precepts are of no efficacy. — *Quintilian*

## INTEGRITY

113. The shortest and surest way to live with honor in the world, is to be in reality what we would appear to be; all human virtues increase and strengthen themselves by the practice and experience of them. — *Socrates*

**114.** It is the admirer of himself, and not the admirer of virtue, that thinks himself superior to others.    — *Plutarch*

**115.** Why does no man confess his vices? Because he is yet in them. It is for a waking man to tell his dream.    — *Seneca*

**116.** It is impossible to live pleasurably without living prudently, and honorably, and justly; or to live prudently, and honorably, and justly, without living pleasurably.    — *Epicurus*

**117.** Man perfected by society is the best of all animals; he is the most terrible of all when he lives without law, and without justice.    — *Aristotle*

**118.** He is armed without who is innocent within; be this your screen, and this your wall of brass.    — *Horace*

**119.** Every guilty person is his own hangman.    — *Seneca*

**120.** We are always complaining that our days are few, and acting as though there would be no end of them.    — *Seneca*

**121.** Let all your views in life be directed to a solid, however moderate, freedom; without it no man can be happy nor even honest.    — *Junius*

**122.** Let him who would move the world, first move himself    — *Socrates*

**123.** To be doing good is man's most glorious task.    — *Sophocles*

**124.** The most virtuous of all men is he that contents himself with being virtuous without seeking to appear so.    — *Plato*

**125.** Where you are is of no moment, but only what you are doing there. It is not the place that ennobles you, but you the place; and this only by doing that which is great and noble.    — *Plutarch*

**126.** To foolish men belongs a love for things afar.    — *Pindar*

**127.** Outside show is a poor substitute for inner worth.    — *Aesop*

**128.** It is not enough to know about virtue, but we must endeavor to possess it, and to use it, or to take any other steps that may make us good.    — *Aristotle*

**129.** If you should lay up even a little upon a little, and should do this often, soon even this would become great.    — *Hesiod*

130. Seize now and here the hour that is, nor trust some later day!

— *Homer*

131. He who acts wickedly in private life, can never be expected to show himself noble in public conduct. He that is base at home, will not acquit himself with honor abroad; for it is not the man, but only the place that is changed.    — *Aeschines*

132. The integrity of men is to be measured by their conduct, not by their professions.    — *Junius*

133. The perfection of virtue is to conceal virtue.    — *Quintilian*

## TEMPERANCE

134. Lust is an enemy to the purse, a foe to the person, a canker to the mind, a corrosive to the conscience, a weakness of the wit, a besotter of the senses, and, finally, a mortal bane to all the body.    — *Pliny the Elder*

135. Modesty is the color of virtue.    — *Diogenes*

136. We must prune bashfulness with care, so as only to remove the redundant branches and not injure the stem, which has its root in a generous sensitiveness to shame.    — *Plutarch*

137. Consider pleasures as they depart, not as they come.    — *Aristotle*

138. With parsimony a little is sufficient; without it nothing is sufficient; but frugality makes a poor man rich.    — *Seneca*

139. It is the constant fault and inseparable evil quality of ambition, that it never looks behind itself.    — *Seneca*

140. All houses well stocked with provisions are likely to be full of mice, so the bodies of those who eat much are full of diseases.    — *Diogenes*

141. As in a man's life, so in his studies, it is the most beautiful and humane thing in the world so to mingle gravity with pleasure, that the one may not sink into melancholy, nor the other rise up into wantonness.

— *Pliny the Elder*

142. Those wretches who never have experienced the sweets of wisdom and virtue, but spend all their time in revels and debauches, sink downward day after day, and make their whole life one continued series of errors.

They taste no real or substantial pleasure; but, resembling so many brutes, with eyes always fixed on the earth, and intent upon their loaded tables, they pamper themselves in luxury and excess. — *Plato*

143. Prosperity is the touchstone of virtue; for it is less difficult to bear misfortunes, than to remain uncorrupted by pleasures. — *Socrates*

144. Since some pleasures are necessary while others are not, and are necessary up to a point while the excesses of them are not, nor the deficiencies, and this is equally true of appetites and pains, the man who pursues to excess necessary objects, and does so by choice, for their own sake and not at all for the sake of any result distinct from them, is self-indulgent; for such a man is of necessity unlikely to repent, and therefore incurable, since a man who cannot repent cannot be cured. — *Aristotle*

145. The self-indulgent man is not apt to repent; for he stands by his choice. But any incontinent [weak] man is likely to repent. Wickedness is like a disease such as dropsy or consumption, while incontinence is like epilepsy; the former is a permanent badness while the latter is intermittent. — *Aristotle*

146. Chastise your passions, that they may not chastise you. Deliver yourself from appetite, and you will be free. — *Epictetus*

147. One that has wine as a chain about his wits, lives no life at all. — *Alcaeus*

148. The first draft serves for health, the second for pleasure, the third for shame, and the fourth for madness. — *Anacharsis*

149. Not to be covetous, is money; not to be a purchaser, is revenue. — *Cicero*

150. There is no gain so certain as that which arises from sparing what you have. — *Publilius Syrus*

151. Temperate anger well becomes the wise. — *Philemon*

152. Anger begins in folly, and ends in repentance. — *Pythagoras*

153. The greatest remedy for anger is delay. — *Seneca*

154. It is not he who gives abuse that affronts, but the view that we take of it as insulting; so that when one provokes you it is your own opinion which is provoking. — *Epictetus*

## FORTITUDE

**155.** God helps them that help themselves.    — *Traditional proverb*

**156.** I call him braver who overcomes his desires than him who conquers his enemies; for the hardest victory is the victory over self.    — *Aristotle*

**157.** Look at a man in the midst of doubt and danger, and you will learn in his hour of adversity what he really is. It is then that true utterances are wrung from the recesses of his breast. The mask is torn off; the reality remains.    — *Lucretius*

**158.** Prosperity is no just scale; adversity is the only balance to weigh friends.    — *Plutarch*

**159.** Nothing is harder to direct than a man in prosperity; nothing more easily managed than one in adversity.    — *Plutarch*

**160.** Every man has his chain and clog, only it is looser and lighter to one than to another; and he is more at ease who takes it up and carries it than he who drags it.    — *Seneca*

**161.** I see the right, and I approve it too; condemn the wrong and yet the wrong pursue.    — *Ovid*

**162.** It is easy to be brave from a safe distance.    — *Aesop*

**163.** Difficulties are things that show what men are.    — *Epictetus*

**164.** Badness—beware—you may choose easily in a heap: level is the path, and right near it dwells. But before virtue the immortal gods have put the sweat of man's brow; and long and steep is the way to it, and rugged at the first.    — *Hesiod*

**165.** He has half the deed done, who has made a beginning.    — *Homer*

**166.** Fame is the perfume of heroic deeds.    — *Socrates*

**167.** We are sure to get the better of fortune if we do but grapple with her.    — *Seneca*

**168.** Difficulties strengthen the mind, as labor does the body.    — *Seneca*

**169.** He conquers who endures.    — *Perseus*

170. Courage in battle is half the battle.          — *Plautus*

171. Courage consists not in hazarding without fear, but being resolutely minded in a just cause.          — *Plutarch*

172. The gods conceal from men the happiness of death, that they may endure life.          — *Lucan*

173. The best way out of a difficulty is through it.          — *Traditional proverb*

174. No man can be brave who considers pain the greatest evil of life; or temperate who regards pleasure as the highest good.          — *Cicero*

175. Burdens become light when cheerfully borne.          — *Ovid*

176. Begin; to begin is half the work. Let half still remain; again begin this, and you will have finished.          — *Ausonius*

177. No evil is without its compensation. The less money, the less trouble. The less favor, the less envy. Even in those cases which put us out of wits, it is not the loss itself, but the estimate of the loss that troubles us.
          — *Seneca*

178. Consider how much more you often suffer from your anger and grief, than from those very things for which you are angry and grieved.
          — *Marcus Aurelius*

179. Suffering itself does less afflict the senses than the anticipation of suffering.          — *Quintilian*

180. Every noble acquisition is attended with its risks; he who fears to encounter the one must not expect to obtain the other.          — *Metastasio*

181. It is part of a good man to do great and noble deeds, though he risks everything in doing them.          — *Plutarch*

182. Heaven never helps the man who will not act.          — *Sophocles*

183. Adversity has the effect of eliciting talents which in prosperous circumstances would have lain dormant.          — *Horace*

## INDUSTRIOUSNESS

184. Toil and pleasure, in their nature opposites, are yet linked together in a kind of necessary connection.          — *Livy*

**185.** Work conquers all. — *Traditional Latin proverb*

**186.** The end of labor is to gain leisure. — *Aristotle*

**187.** He does not seem to me to be a free man who does not sometimes do nothing. — *Cicero*

**189.** I look upon indolence as a sort of suicide; for the man is efficiently destroyed, though the appetite of the brute may survive. — *Cicero*

**190.** Nothing is more unworthy of a wise man, or ought to trouble him more, than to have allowed more time for trifling, and useless things, than they deserved. — *Plato*

**191.** Flee sloth, for the indolence of the soul is the decay of the body.
— *Cato the Elder*

**192.** Too much rest itself becomes a pain. — *Homer*

**193.** Waste of time is the most extravagant and costly of all expenses.
— *Theophrastus*

**194.** He who labors diligently need never despair; for all things are accomplished by diligence and labor. — *Menander of Athens*

**195.** There is not a moment without some duty. — *Cicero*

**196.** Employment is nature's physician, and is essential to human happiness. — *Livy*

## Generosity

**197.** I would so live as if I knew that I received my being only for the benefit of others. — *Seneca*

**198.** It is possible that a man can be so changed by love as hardly to be recognized as the same person. — *Terence*

**199.** Who can all sense of others' ills escape, is but a brute, at best, in human shape. — *Juvenal*

**200.** He who confers a favor should at once forget it, if he is not to show a sordid, ungenerous spirit. To remind a man of a kindness conferred on him, and to talk of it, is little different from reproach. — *Demosthenes*

201. Ask yourself daily, to how many ill-minded persons you have shown a kind disposition.                           — *Marcus Aurelius*

202. I had rather never receive a kindness, than never bestow one. Not to return a benefit is the greater sin, but not to confer it, is the earlier.
                                                              — *Seneca*

203. If you hate your enemies, you will contract such a vicious habit of mind as by degrees will break out upon those who are your friends, or those who are indifferent to you.                  — *Plutarch*

204. A rational nature admits of nothing which is not serviceable to the rest of mankind.                          — *Marcus Aurelius*

205. Nothing more detestable does the earth produce than an ungrateful man.                                           — *Ausonius*

206. What I gave, I have; what I spent, I had; what I kept, I lost.
                                                    — *Old Latin epitaph*

207. In nothing do men approach so nearly to the gods as in doing good to men.                                         — *Cicero*

208. There is as much greatness of mind in acknowledging a good turn, as in doing it.                                   — *Seneca*

209. In order that you may please, you ought to be forgetful of self.
                                                              — *Ovid*

210. Self-interest is the enemy of all true affection.       — *Tacitus*

211. The cause of all the blunders committed by man arises from excessive self-love. He who intends to be a great man ought to love neither himself nor his own things, but only what is right, whether it happens to be done by himself or by another.                              — *Plato*

## FRIENDSHIP

212. It is a true saying that we must eat many measures of salt together to be able to discharge the functions of friendship.        — *Cicero*

213. True friendship's laws are by this rule expressed: welcome the coming, speed the parting guest.                            — *Homer*

214. Friendship is one mind in two bodies.                 — *Mencius*

**215.** Be slow to fall into friendship; but when you are in, continue firm and constant.  — *Socrates*

**216.** Get not your friends by bare compliments but by giving them sensible tokens of your love. It is well worth while to learn how to win the heart of a man the right way. Force is of no use to make or preserve a friend, who is an animal that is never caught nor tamed but by kindness and pleasure. Excite them by your civilities, and show them that you desire nothing more than their satisfaction; oblige with all your soul that friend who has made you a present of his own.  — *Socrates*

**217.** Every man, however wise, needs the advice of some sagacious friend in the affairs of his life.  — *Plautus*

**218.** I would have a man generous to his country, his neighbors, his kindred, his friends, and most of all his poor friends. Not like some who are most lavish with those who are able to give most to them.
 — *Pliny the Elder*

**219.** Every gift, though it be small, is in reality great if given with affection.
 — *Pindar*

**220.** We should give as we would receive, cheerfully, quickly, and without hesitation; for there is no grace in a benefit that sticks to the fingers.
 — *Seneca*

**221.** Prosperity makes friends, adversity tries them.  — *Publilius Syrus*

**222.** Reprove your friend privately; commend him publicly.  — *Solon*

**223.** Honest men esteem and value nothing so much in this world as a real friend. Such a one is as it were another self, to whom we impart our most secret thoughts, who partakes of our joy, and comforts us in our affliction; add to this, that his company is an everlasting pleasure to us.
 — *Pilpay*

**224.** Nothing is more noble, nothing more venerable than fidelity. Faithfulness and truth are the most sacred excellences and endowments of the human mind.  — *Cicero*

**225.** Forgive many things in others; nothing in yourself.  — *Ausonius*

**226.** In poverty and other misfortunes of life, true friends are a sure refuge. The young they keep out of mischief; to the old they are a comfort and aid in their weakness, and those in the prime of life they incite to noble deeds. — *Aristotle*

227. All men have their frailties; and whoever looks for a friend without imperfections, will never find what he seeks. We love ourselves notwithstanding our faults, and we ought to love our friends in like manner. — *Cyrus*

228. Dignity and love do not blend well, nor do they continue long together. — *Ovid*

229. The company of just and upright men is better than wealth and a rich estate. — *Euripides*

230. This is the law of benefits between men: the one ought to forget at once what he has given, and the other ought never to forget what he has received. — *Seneca*

## JUSTICE

231. He that does good to another, does good also to himself, not only in the consequences, but in the very act. — *Seneca*

232. Heaven's eternal wisdom has decreed, that man should ever stand in need of man. — *Euripides*

233. No one will dare maintain that it is better to do injustice than to bear it. — *Aristotle*

234. Justice is to give every man his own. — *Aristotle*

235. Justice consists in doing no injury to men; decency in giving them no offense. — *Cicero*

236. How much easier it is to be generous than just! Men are sometimes bountiful who are not honest. — *Junius*

237. Only the just man enjoys peace of mind. — *Epictetus*

238. To find fault is easy; to do better may be difficult. — *Plutarch*

239. Fidelity is the sister of justice. — *Horace*

240. Envy always implies conscious inferiority wherever it resides. — *Pliny the Elder*

241. Refrain from covetousness, and your estate will prosper. — *Plato*

## A Note on the Author

DENNIS HELMING attended Harvard College and the University of Navarre in Spain, where he taught philosophy. He has worked widely as a journalist, educator, writer, translator, editor, lecturer, and public relations consultant and served in the Reagan administration.

He has written for such publications as *First Things*, *National Review*, and the *Harvard Educational Review* and is the author of *Footprints in the Snow* (Scepter Press, 1986). He lives in Washington, D.C., where he teaches privately the course from which this book was developed.

This book was designed and set into type

by Mitchell S. Muncy,

with cover art by Stephen J. Ott,

and printed and bound

by Thomson-Shore, Inc., Dexter, Michigan

The text face is Goudy Old Style,

and the titling is Copperplate Gothic.

The paper is acid-free and is of archival quality.

4